CAMBRIDGE LANGUAGE TEACHING SURVEYS

The surveys in this series were originally commissioned for and published in the journal *Language Teaching* (formerly *Language Teaching and Linguistics: Abstracts*). Together they provide a valuable overview of work and developments in a number of subjects and disciplines which contribute to the field of applied linguistics and language teaching.

Surveys 1

Surveys 1

Eight state-of-the-art articles
on key areas in language teaching

Edited by
VALERIE KINSELLA
for
The Centre for Information on Language Teaching and
Research (CILT)
and The British Council

Cambridge University Press
Cambridge
London   New York   New Rochelle
Melbourne   Sydney

Published by the Press Syndicate of the University of Cambridge
The Pitt Building, Trumpington Street, Cambridge CB2 1RP
32 East 57th Street, New York, NY 10022, USA
296 Beaconsfield Parade, Middle Park, Melbourne 3206, Australia

First published 1982

Printed in Great Britain by
Spottiswoode Ballantyne Ltd., Colchester and London

Library of Congress catalogue card number: 82-4332

British Library Cataloguing in Publication Data

Surveys I: eight state-of-the-art articles on key
areas in language teaching. –
(Cambridge language teaching surveys)
1. Language and languages – Study and teaching
I. Kinsella, Valerie
407   P51

ISBN 0 521 24886 8
ISBN 0 521 27046 4 Pbk

AS

CONTENTS

INTRODUCTION

This is a collection, the first in a series, of eight survey articles which were originally published in the journal *Language Teaching* (formerly *Language Teaching and Linguistics: Abstracts*). They were specially commissioned for the journal by the editorial board, who aim to pinpoint areas in the language learning and teaching process where developments have been complex, and commission survey articles to trace these developments and clarify problem areas. A full bibliography is an essential part of such surveys, which provide an authoritative guide to students beginning studies in the various subjects, as well as a critical review of recent work for specialists working in the same fields. The authors are acknowledged specialists in their field.

Collectively, the surveys provide a valuable overview of work in a number of subjects and disciplines which all contribute to the field of applied linguistics and language teaching. As with the journal, we hope that this bringing together of different aspects of the same broad subject will generate a cross-fertilisation of ideas between those concerned with the teaching of different foreign languages (e.g. German, French, English, Russian) as well as between practising teachers, applied linguists and educational researchers. We hope that teachers will find the articles particularly valuable for bringing themselves up to date both rapidly and cheaply with recent research.

The articles appear in their original form apart from minor corrections to the text and references, where necessary. Authors have been invited to add short postscripts covering work since the original date of publication shown for each survey.

A companion volume called *Language Teaching & Linguistics: Surveys* (CUP, 1978) which predates this series, contains the surveys which *Language Teaching* commissioned between 1975 and 1977.

The surveys in Volume 1 cover how languages are actually learned (*Cook*), the cognitive aspects of bilingualism (*Swain & Cummins*), how meaning systems are described in the systemic model of linguistics (*Butler*), the importance of situational context in the study of natural languages (*Enkvist*), bilingual education for migrants in Europe (*Tosi*), current work on the acquisition of vocabulary (*Meara*), and a double article on testing (*Davies*). Brief summaries appear below.

V. J. Cook   *Second-language learning: a psycholinguistic perspective*
The learner's development in a second language is discussed under (1) methodological issues: the relationship of the learner's language to time, and what counts as evidence of the learner's language; (2) grammatical morpheme studies (order

1

in which grammatical points are acquired); (3) studies of syntactic development in English and other languages. The learner's contribution to second-language learning is dealt with under (i) learning and production strategies; (ii) attitudes and motivation; (iii) speech and memory processes; (iv) the learner's age. The learner's situation consists of (a) the language he hears, (b) his social interactions, and (c) the language-teaching classroom. The application for teachers of such research is the importance of recognising the learner's contribution and encouraging him to communicate meaningfully.

Merrill Swain & James Cummins *Bilingualism, cognitive functioning and education*
Studies are discussed which report either a negative or a positive association between bilingualism and cognitive functioning (i.e. measures involving general intellectual and linguistic skills). Studies reporting negative associations indicate that bilinguals suffer from a language handicap. Studies reporting positive associations indicate improved linguistic skills, a more analytic orientation to linguistic and perceptual structures, greater sensitivity to feedback cues, a higher level of general intellectual development, and better performance in measures of divergent thinking. Factors accounting for the contradictory reśults of the various studies are reviewed: positive findings tend to be associated with children from majority-language groups and negative findings with children from minor-ity-language groups. Other factors are the perceived value and prestige of L1 and L2, the socioeconomic status of the learner, and school programme variables (positive results with immersion and negative with submersion programmes). Educational implications are that school programmes must aim to promote an additive form of bilingualism if optimal development of minority-language children's academic and cognitive potential is their goal.

C. S. Butler *Recent developments in systemic linguistics*
Work carried out within the framework of systemic linguistics, developed largely by Halliday in the last 20 years, is reviewed. The model evolved in the late fifties and sixties; this article is mainly concerned with developments in the seventies and with recent proposals by others. The background is sketched in by tracing Halliday's work back to Firth and Malinowski. After 1970, the two main trends are the increased importance of semantic choice within the model and a renewed emphasis on the social functioning of language. Halliday's views on language acquisition or 'learning how to mean' and its functional basis are discussed. The functional organisation of the adult linguistic system is then related to the child's model of language: the change from the child to the adult system is one of 'functional reduction'. Halliday is concerned with language as social behaviour: the semantics, or 'meaning potential', is related both to social factors and to syntax and lexis. Halliday later set this notion within the

framework of an overall sociolinguistic theory. Later developments include Fawcett's 'systemic functional generative grammar', work by Hudson on systemic syntax, the influence of such work on discourse analysis, and applications of systemic theory to the description of varieties and styles of English.

Nils Erik Enkvist *Categories of situational context from the perspective of stylistics*
Attitudes to language varieties and context (of situation) range from a desire to study ideal speakers in ideal speech communities to an insistence on studying the whole complexity of natural languages. Context analysis is necessary in linguistics: anyone analysing linguistic data must take into account the context of his or her corpus. The latter has long been of interest to students of style. Various principles are suggested for the description and classification of contexts and particularly for the extraction of their linguistically relevant features. Sociolinguists offer useful concepts such as role-relationships, congruence of behaviour, domain, speech events and speech acts. Different lists of context features are cited as examples, from Enkvist, Crystal and Davy, and Gläser. Functional stylistics (characteristic of the Prague School) works from a small set of predetermined social functions of language and then describes the language used for each function. Riffaterre, however, appeals to intratextual context rather than situation.

Arturo Tosi *Mother-tongue teaching for the children of migrants*
The aim is to survey recent studies on the philosophy, objectives and implications of bilingual education, and to outline their relevance in the context of the migration workers in Europe. Migrants generally have bilingualism foisted on them—when their children go to school they are obliged to speak the language of the majority. As a result, they may be considered handicapped. 'Semibilingualism' describes someone who can function in two languages without being proficient in either. Minority children seem backward in cognitive development and literacy skills in the school language, while the home language fails to develop from an informal, repetitive jargon. The arguments for mother-tongue teaching concern (1) the new status of minority languages and (2) the therapeutic effects of teaching in the mother tongue on linguistic/cognitive development. The policies of most European countries towards the schooling of migrants' children contradict their avowed aims of accepting such children on their own terms. Groups of migrants receive what help they do get from their country of origin only, although their linguistic rights in Europe began to be recognised in the mid-1970s. An EEC directive recommends that the language and culture of the country of origin should be taught in school hours. Different categories of bilingual and bicultural programmes are: (1) compensatory/transitional, (2) language maintenance, (3) enrichment orientated.

3

Introduction

Paul Meara *Vocabulary acquisition: a neglected aspect of language learning*
Current work on vocabulary acquisition is summarised. Bibliographies suggest that the research is largely atheoretical and unsystematic. Areas which are being investigated are (a) vocabulary control (frequency counts, statistical analyses by computers), and (b) mnemonics ('key word' method). These areas share a common defect, however, in that they are more concerned with vocabulary teaching than with vocabulary learning. Work on how bilingual speakers store words in their mental dictionaries may be useful as a model against which to assess the more limited abilities of less fluent learners. Experiments reviewed here are concerned with (i) the general question of whether the bilingual's lexicons are separate or interdependent, and (ii) the semantic relationships between words in the bilingual's lexicons. [Tables summarise the findings of both types of study.]

Alan Davies *Language testing*
The article is in two parts. The first discusses discrete point tests with particular reference to the major textbooks on language testing. Testing changed radically between the mid-1960s and mid-1970s, from the behaviourist/structuralist view to an emphasis on meaning and communication (exemplified by a comparison of Valette, 1967 and Valette, 1977); or from the analytic to the integrative. The most useful language test combines these two approaches. Lado is the spokesman of the structural testing school, of analytical, discrete point tests. Textbooks owe much to his *Language testing* (1961, 1964). His framework has been extended and developed by others for the testing of achievement. Yet other writers have taken a psycholinguistic/sociolinguistic view, supporting integrative as against discrete point tests. Various achievement and proficiency tests are briefly described for several languages. Tests of reading comprehension are discussed, followed by a note on criterion referenced tests.

Part II begins by discussing the arguments for integrative tests. Cloze procedure was introduced to measure the readability of texts: the main issues concern choice of text, seen or unseen text, rate and type of deletion, scoring procedure, reliability and validity. Views on dictation became more positive in the 1970s, when Oller brought it back into popularity as a global test of overall proficiency. Findings are, however, contradictory, so caution is needed. Productive tests (spoken and written) are the most integrative type of test. Testing the communicative skills requires putting more emphasis on meaning than grammaticality. Examples are discussed.

SECOND-LANGUAGE LEARNING:
A PSYCHOLINGUISTIC PERSPECTIVE

V. J. Cook
University of Essex

In the early 1960s we were satisfied that we knew all about how people learnt a second language. Then the impact of Chomsky's ideas exposed the extent of our ignorance. Some people's reactions were that we should stop interfering with the learner, since nature knew best (Newmark & Reibel, 1968). Others admitted the error of their ways in principle but in practice continued to use the same teaching techniques; by and large the changes in the content of language teaching from 'structures' to 'functions' were not accompanied by any changes in teaching methods. However, in the past few years the question of second-language learning has been reopened; this review attempts to give a critical account of some directions that research in this field is taking. Our ignorance is not quite as boundless as it once was; before long we may be able to base language teaching at last on a solid foundation of knowledge about second-language learning itself.

1. The learner's development in a second language

1.1 *Methodological issues*

One starting point is the language that the learner produces and understands. Inevitably this involves several methodological problems. One is the relationship of the learner's language to time; to show how learning takes place we need to see development in time: we need pictures of 'before' and 'after'. One way of achieving this is to describe the longitudinal language development of a group of learners or a single learner, as in Hakuta (1975). Another is to relate different points of time in different learners, as in Padilla and Lindholm (1976). Yet another is to relate the learner's language to the final point in time, the language of the native speaker, the approach often used in 'error analysis'. A second methodological problem is deciding what we count as evidence of the learner's language. The most common approach is to gather more or less natural samples of the learner's language; this has the disadvantage common to corpus-based descriptions of making it hard to know when generalisations can be made to the learner's language system as a whole. Kellerman (1974) has suggested supplementing it with 'lateralisation', that is to say, eliciting further information from the learner about specific points. There are also dangers in relying solely on the analysis of errors since this provides partial information about the learner's language; to describe it adequately we need to know more about it than its differences from the target language (Corder, 1971). An alternative approach consists of designing particular techniques that tap only the part of the learner's language that we are interested in. Also, compared to first-language acquisition, the second-language learner is more aware of learning a language and can be asked direct questions about what he knows.

Already in the previous paragraph it was accepted implicitly that the learner has a language system of his own; though this system is related to both his first and second languages, it has its own distinctive characteristics. This implicit assumption has been called, with slightly different emphases, 'interlanguage' (Selinker, 1972), 'transitional competence' (Corder, 1967), 'approximative system' (Nemser, 1971), and 'language learner's system' (Sampson & Richards, 1973). It parallels the common assumption that a child acquiring a first language has a systematic language that is not simply a defective version of the adult's. In itself the assumption tells one nothing about the system or how it develops except that it *is* a system. For the description of learning, an important characteristic of the learner's language system is that it is changing rather than static: Corder (1977) calls it a 'dynamic goal-oriented language system of increasing complexity'. However, one should not forget the effect of 'fossilisation', in which some aspects of the learner's language system remain fixed and do not develop (Selinker, 1972).

1.2 Grammatical morpheme studies

An aspect of the learner's development that has interested many people is the order in which particular grammatical points are acquired. A common approach starts from part of Roger Brown's work on first-language acquisition. Brown (1973) discovered that the chronological order in which children start to use grammatical morphemes such as *the* and *on* is fairly constant: the child first uses *-ing*, then *in* and *on*, then the plural *-s* and so on. Dulay and Burt (1973) first tried this approach on second-language learning, using the Bilingual Syntax Measure (BSM) to elicit samples of language from children at one moment of time: they scored the accuracy for grammatical morphemes and established an order of difficulty; though they found a common order among the children, this order had certain differences from Brown's order. This method was extended to show that children with different native languages share the same order (Dulay & Burt, 1974); that adults have a similar order to children (Bailey, Madden & Krashen, 1974; Krashen, Sferlazza, Feldman & Fathman, 1976); that the order varies according to the task involved (Larsen-Freeman, 1975); and that the order is not much affected by one month's classroom teaching (Perkins & Larsen-Freeman, 1975). At first glance, then, this research suggests that second-language learners share a common order of acquisition for grammatical morphemes in English. At closer inspection, the connections between the learner's language and time seem slightly dubious. The criteria used in Brown (1973), in which points of acquisition are arranged into a chronological order, are replaced by criteria of relative success at one point of time: Brown is talking about a 'codebreaking' order, the second-language research about a 'decoding' order, to borrow two terms from cryptography. Rosansky (1976) argues that it is necessary to show that order of difficulty is the same as order of acquisition, if these results are to mean anything in terms of development. Furthermore, comparison with Brown's results is obscured by the different methods of collecting data, on the one hand elicitation techniques such as the BSM, on the other natural recordings; indeed, native children tested with the BSM do not show Brown's order (Porter, 1977). A naturalistic study has in fact shown similarity between chronological order of acquisition in young bilingual children and Brown's order, but less similarity in older children (Padilla, to appear). So order of difficulty for grammatical morphemes is at present hard to interpret; it certainly does not in itself justify any statements about chronological order of acquisition or about differences from first-language acquisition.

1.3 Studies of syntactic development

Other aspects of syntactic development have been investigated in less controversial ways. Much of the research has dealt with English and has been concerned with children. Many results show a fair amount of variation between learners (Cancino, Rosansky & Schumann, 1975; Bertkua, 1974). Even within the speech of one learner there is great variation; Dickerson (1975) has suggested employing variable rules such as those in sociolinguistics to account for the variation from one situation to another. Out of the plethora of studies one can mention a representative handful concerned with different points of English syntax: negation (Milon, 1974); pluralisation (Natalico & Natalico, 1971); auxiliaries (Cancino et al., 1975); pronouns (Katz, 1976); possessives (Padilla & Lindholm, 1976); eager/easy to please (Cook, 1973; d'Anglejean & Tucker, 1975). Other languages have been studied to a lesser degree: French relative clauses and indirect objects (Chun, 1976); Spanish verb and noun phrases (Dato, 1975); Swedish negation (Hyltenstem, 1977). Mostly the writers have concluded that there are general similarities between the order of acquisition in foreign learners and native children, though there are some differences; for example a stage has been described in the learning of English negation by

7

Germans in which a negative element occurs immediately after the verb, unlike any stage in first language acquisition (Wode, 1976 *b*).

This wealth of information about the learning of English syntax should not blind us to the paucity of research in other areas of development; semantic development has hardly been touched upon, apart from Young (1973); phonological development is equally under-researched, with some exceptions (Dickerson, 1975; Tarone, 1976; Wode, 1976 *a*). This bias towards syntax leaves the study of learner's language in a curiously isolated position. On the one hand, it is cut off from recent ideas in first-language acquisition which are more concerned with semantic, cognitive and social development than with syntax. On the other hand, it is cut off from recent work in applied linguistics which stresses communicative functions rather than grammatical form. While the grammatical data that have been unearthed are interesting in themselves, one may question where they lead. Ultimately, so far as learning is concerned, the learner's language and the order in which he acquires various items are only interesting as evidence for underlying processes at work: the question to be answered is why his language takes the form that it does. So, rather than attempt to summarise the vast mass of descriptive studies of learner's language that are now available, a task resembling Hercules' in the Augean stables, the rest of this survey looks at some of the underlying causes of the learner's language system.

2. The learner's contribution to second-language learning

2.1 *Learning and production strategies*

Confronted with a new language the learner applies certain strategies both conscious and unconscious to what he hears, which partly determine his language system (Selinker, 1972; Richards, 1971). The positive effects of the learner's conscious awareness that he is learning a new language have been described in terms of the strategies that the good language learner adopts (Rubin, 1975; Stern,1975; Naiman, Fröhlich & Stern, 1975). Broadly speaking, the profile of the good learner shows that he is actively involved in the learning process: he listens carefully and checks what he says himself; he is eager to participate and to communicate with others; he practices the language of his own accord. Though these strategies necessarily appear 'obvious', any model of second-language learning has to take them into account; if, for instance, adult learners feel that second-language learning is chiefly a matter of vocabulary (Hatch, 1976), this clearly has an effect on their learning, regardless of whether they are right or wrong. At the opposite pole from these conscious strategies are those revealed in an experiment, where, after 27 minutes of exposure to an unknown language, people were able to distinguish pauses located at grammatical boundaries from those that were not: somehow they had employed a strategy that yielded quite accurate information about the grammatical structure of the language (Wakefield, Doughtie & Yom, 1974). The learner then, consciously or unconsciously, absorbs or extracts information from what he hears. One strategy is to impose the structure of his first language: he transfers rules or items to his learner-language system from his first language and shows signs of 'interference' (Selinker, 1972). Another strategy is to attempt to guess the system of the target language, resulting in 'overgeneralisation'; his use of this strategy increases as he learns more of the language (Taylor, 1975). The learner also pays great attention to word order (Chun, 1976; Lattey, 1975). He may appear to 'simplify' the second language; his sentences have a simpler grammar and use reduced forms, similar in many ways to a pidgin language (Schumann, 1975 a). Indeed Schumann claims this similarity is no coincidence: pidgins and learner languages are both produced under the pressure of a need to communicate with people from another culture. There are nevertheless difficulties in accepting either that the pressures on an individual and on a community are the same, or that the similarities between pidgins are necessarily due to a general communication strategy rather than common source languages. A slightly different explanation for simplification is that it represents an attempt to return to an earlier, more basic form of the language (Corder, 1977), resembling the view that early language is closest to deep structure (McNeill, 1965). There are, however, dangers in the over-literal use of the term 'simplification' since this suggests that in some way the learner is aware of the whole grammar of the language rather than extracting a 'simple' system from what he hears. Finally there are the production strategies that the learner uses in a speech situation. One of these is 'avoidance'; Schachter (1974) pointed out that learners often do not make the predicted mistakes because they can avoid producing a form that they are likely to get wrong. The idea of avoidance has been extended to include various types of lexical avoidance (Blum & Levenston, 1977). In general, the conscious and unconscious strategies that the learner employs are of vital importance and we need to know more about them, not only in linguistic terms but also in the cognitive and social terms that are starting to be studied (Chun, 1975; Fillmore, 1976).

2.2 Attitudes and motivation

The ways in which a learner learns a second language are also affected by his attitudes and psychological motivations. The two main types of motivation that have been described are the 'integrative', in which the learner wants to communicate actively with the speakers of the other language, and the 'instrumental', in which he wants to use the language for some utilitarian purpose; of these two the integrative now seems more important (Gardner, Smythe,

Clement & Glicksman, 1976). A way in to the large body of literature on this subject can be found in the annotated bibliography compiled by Desrochers, Smythe & Gardner (1975). The causes of motivation are attitudes; success in second-language learning depends on the attitudes towards the foreign culture, towards learning a foreign language, and towards the classroom situation (Gardner *et al.*, 1976). One's native language is an important factor in one's sense of identity as an individual and as a member of a group: learning a new language means adopting a new identity. Lambert (1974) distinguishes 'additive' bilingualism, in which the learner loses nothing by learning a second language, from 'subtractive' bilingualism, in which he is forced to give something up; Clarke (1976) talks of a clash between the level of 'modernity' in the two cultures; Schumann (1976) draws attention to the 'social distance' separating the learner from the target culture. While these concepts have obvious relevance to contact or immigrant situations, they are less important to language teaching in schools. However, one idea of equal importance to both is the loss of personal identity in learning a second language: culture-shock is like the alienated state of a schizophrenic unable to make sense of his surroundings (Clarke, 1976) and this is supported by similarities between the language of schizophrenics and second-language learners (Meara, 1977). Guiora, Brannon & Dull (1972) postulate a 'language ego' that is threatened by the new language; Green (1977) claims that students regress to an earlier Freudian stage in a foreign language and express ideas that are more childish than their level of thinking in their native language.

2.3 Speech and memory processes

Understanding and producing speech involves psychological processes that are only now starting to be understood. In second-language learning their nature is even more obscure. One issue is whether these processes are substantially the same in all languages; some semantic processes involved in verifying the truth of sentences have in fact been found to be similar in different languages (Just & Carpenter, 1975). Another issue is whether these processes can be transferred to a second language; in terms of syntax it has been shown that foreign adults do not benefit from knowing embedding in a first language but fall back on the same processes as the young native child (Cook, 1975). The work on grammatical morphemes can also be interpreted as showing some of the processing limitations common to learners. At least some speech processes then have to be relearnt in a second language. Indeed some of them may never be so efficient in a second language: even skilled bilinguals are worse at a cloze test in their second language (d'Anglejean & Tucker, 1973); advanced learners cannot summarise texts as well as natives (Long & Harding-Esch, 1977).

Turning now to memory processes, it is convenient to distinguish short-term from long-term memory. The characteristics of short-term memory are that information is stored for only a few seconds, capacity for information is small, and the information is stored in the form of sounds. Nothing is known about the duration of short-term memory in a second language but some research has looked at capacity. Glicksberg (1963) found adult learners of English remembered 6·4 digits at a time compared with 7·1 in their first language, improving to 6·7 during five weeks of an intensive course; Cook (1977) found a capacity of 5·9 in beginners and 6·7 in advanced learners. So far as the form of storage is concerned, capacity has been related to syntactic complexity (Harris, 1970) and to phonological encoding (Cook, 1977); Henning (1973) traced a development from phonological to semantic storage. So short-term memory seems to work in a similar fashion in a second language; we can store slightly less information than in our first language but we store it in similar ways. Long-term memory has also been studied. Lambert (1956) tested word associations and concluded that, while advanced learners were more like native speakers in such aspects as number and range of associations, they were still unlike them in type of associations; the clustering effect in which adults normally remember words from the same semantic category together was not found to any great extent with advanced foreign learners nor was there much difference between advanced learners and beginners (Cook, 1977). Ultimately this line of research leads to the issue of how the two language systems are related in the mind of the bilingual: is there a distinct memory system for each language or are they linked in some way? The evidence is inconclusive: in the same kind of task where bilinguals had to switch languages, Taylor (1971) found the languages were stored separately, while Neufeld (1976) found they were stored together; a task involving naming colours, on the other hand, produced evidence for close links between the languages (Lambert & Preston, 1967).

   The answer to the question about transfer to a second language is then complex. The conclusion arrived at in Cook (1977) was that memory processes are transferred more easily the less they depend on language. This has affinities with the claim that 'capacity increases with processing depth since we can make greater use of learned rules at deeper levels of analysis' (Craik, 1973), if language is equated with learned rules. Indeed some recent experiments can be taken to support this claim by showing little difference between beginners, advanced learners, and bilinguals in a deductive reasoning task in their second language (d'Anglejean, Gagnon, Tucker & Winsberg, 1977). A related issue is the extent to which these memory processes can be employed in learning a second language, as opposed to using it, in codebreaking rather than decoding. Some attempts have been made to apply conscious mnemonic techniques to the learning of vocabulary: Atkinson (1975) describes a 'keyword' technique and Paivio (1976) a 'pegword' technique, both of which involve forming mental images. However, as Rivers and Melvin (1977) point out, 'a word learnt out of context is for the most part a useless bauble': mnemonic techniques are only useful if the vocabulary learnt with them is available to the speaker for normal language use. A general application of memory research is discussed in Melvin and Rivers (1976), who describe an information processing model which emphasises that procedures for speaking and learning are learnt through meaningful use of language rather than memorisation. A two-stage model of memory has also been proposed in which an initial memory fills up with formulas, and a second-stage memory creates rules to account for the overflow (Gallagher, 1976); this connects with the discovery of 'prefabricated utterances' in a young Japanese learner of English (Hakuta, 1974).

2.4 The learner's age

Many people take it for granted that an important factor in second-language learning is the learner's age; most discussions assume that children are better than adults and then go on to suggest explanations for this. It is useful to consider the evidence that might support this assumption. Some Canadian research indeed showed that children who arrived there under the age of seven fared better at learning English than those who arrived at an older age (Ramsay & Wright, 1974). But on the other hand there is a mass of evidence that adults are either superior to, or the same as, children: adults are better than children at understanding spoken Russian by the total physical response method (Asher & Price, 1967); teenagers are better at learning grammar than younger children whether in English (Fathman, 1975) or Dutch (Snow & Hoefnagel-Höhle, 1975); nine-year-olds learn French morphology and syntax faster than four-year-olds (Ervin-Tripp,1974); Israeli census returns show that the age of immigration makes no difference to the pattern of acquisition, in terms of reported use, and that, while there is decline with age, the main watershed is at the age of 30 (Smith & Braine, n.d.). Nevertheless, some people might say, the superiority of children is at learning pronunciation rather than grammar. Again some evidence confirms this belief: older learners either retain more foreign accent (Oyama, 1976; Asher & Garcia, 1969) or report they retain it (Seliger, Krashen & Ladefoged, 1975); the younger children tested in Fathman (1975) were better at pronunciation than the teenagers. But, on the other hand, adults learn German sounds better than children in the same teaching situation (Olson & Samuels, 1973); adults have an initial advantage at pronouncing and imitating Dutch (Snow & Hoefnagel-Höhle, n.d.); older children up to ten make fewer mistakes with unfamiliar phonological structure (Kuusinen & Salin, 1971). So far from showing the superiority of children, most of the hard evidence warrants the opposite conclusion: adults are better than children at learning a second language when the tests are conducted under controlled conditions.

This lack of evidence has not prevented many ingenious explanations being offered for children's alleged superiority at second-language learning. The most general is that there is a critical period for language learning; after we have left this period we can learn language only with difficulty. The reasons for this critical period may be 'lateralisation', that is to say, the tendency for brain functions to become specialised to one side or the other in the early teens (Scovel, 1969). The evidence for locating lateralisation in the early teens is, however, debatable (Krashen, 1975), and the causal connection between lateralisation and language learning necessarily rests on evidence from pathological cases. A second explanation distinguishes 'acquisition', the normal process through which children learn a first language, from 'learning', an alternative process that can be used by adults because of their greater maturity (Krashen, 1976). This distinction has been enlarged into the 'monitor model' (Krashen, 1977), which claims that the distinctive feature of adult 'learning' is that adults can monitor what they are producing; thus tasks which show similarities between adults and children test 'acquisition' and do not provide sufficient time for the adult to monitor what he is doing. Obviously independent evidence of this monitor needs to be supplied; advanced learners, for example, have not been found to be better at correcting their own mistakes than beginners, as might have been expected (White, 1977). A third type of explanation is cognitive development: Rosansky (1975) suggests that the crucial point is the transition to the Piagetian stage of formal operations in the early teens; Tremaine (1975) correlates the transition to the earlier Piagetian stage of concrete operations at about seven with the syntactic development of bilingual children.

Interesting as these explanations are, it is not clear they are needed. What differences there are between children and adults can be explained without recourse to some unique feature of language learning that changes with age. One simple cause is differences in situation: Macnamara (1973) distinguishes succinctly between the demands of the street and of the classroom; often the adult meets the classroom, the child the street. The types of social interaction also vary; the language play described in Peck (to appear) is rarely allowed to adults; children talk about different topics from adults (Hatch, to appear); the peer-group pressures on children are considerably different from those on adults (Macnamara, 1976) and the motivations and attitudes of the learner vary according to age (Schumann, 1975 b). The common factor to the research cited above that found no disadvantage to adults was precisely that the situation of children and adults was kept the same (Asher & Price, 1967; Olson & Samuels, 1973). Another factor that the research on accents does not take into account is historical changes in the status of immigrants: age of arrival confounds moment of arrival. While it is certainly possible to explain some of the differences in terms of cognitive maturity, this does not necessarily involve linking them to the acquisition of formal operations or to some special process such as

13

V. J. Cook: Second-language learning

monitoring without further evidence. Given all the factors that distinguish adults from children, it would be strange if we found no differences between them but it is not necessary to invoke some peculiar property of language learning to explain them. While one does not wish to deny the strong impression that many people have that some adult immigrants speak their new language poorly, this may be ascribed not so much to an intrinsic defect in the adult's mind as to differences in situation, in motivation, in willingness to surrender part of one's identity, and so on, that separate children from adults.

3. The learner's situation

3.1 The language the learner hears

One important element in the learner's situation is the language he hears. Ferguson (1975) described 'foreigner talk', that is to say, the language variety addressed to foreigners, typified by its 'simpler' grammar and by certain vocabulary items. In a natural setting the learner may well encounter this variety; indeed it is not entirely unknown in the classroom (Hatch, 1978). While there are resemblances between 'simple' foreigner talk addressed to learners and 'simple' pidgin-like language produced by learners, there is no evidence that foreigner talk assists second-language learning any more than there is proof that babytalk helps the native child. Both these simple varieties reflect partly the adult's intuition about what learners find easy to understand, partly the language used by learners themselves, partly the sociolinguistic convention of what is appropriate for learners. Aside from foreigner talk, some work has linked the learner's language to what he hears and the types of interaction in which he takes part (Larsen-Freeman, 1976; Hatch, 1976). This link between input and learning is vital to language teaching. A feature of most teaching methods is that they control the language the learner hears in several dimensions – situationally, functionally, grammatically, notionally, and in other ways. Yet evidence for the effects of input hardly exists. Only Valdman (1975) has shown the possibility of basing the sequence of presentation of grammatical items on learner's errors. Though a central feature of most classrooms is the structuring and sequencing of input, we still have no solid evidence to challenge the assertion that a natural unstructured input is as effective (Newmark & Reibel, 1968).

3.2 The learner's social interactions

In second-language learning, Evelyn Hatch has pioneered the study of conversational interactions between learners and native speakers (Hatch, to appear; Hatch, 1976). The central feature of interaction she sees as the need to find something to talk about: adults interpret children's utterances as naming a topic for discussion; foreign adults struggle hard to establish a topic of conversation. Adults in particular need 'repairs' to be able to check that they and the native are talking about the same thing (Hatch, 1976). The order of natural second-language acquisition is derived primarily from the learner's communicative needs rather than from grammatical complexity or frequency: the learner's language is a consequence of his interactions (Hatch, 1978). Some of the strategies for interaction among children have also been described in Fillmore (1976). As yet these interaction studies offer interesting insights into the learner's behaviour rather than a coherent theory; nevertheless they complement the ideas of integrative motivation and production strategies.

3.3 The language-teaching classroom

Many language learners, however, do not engage in social interactions with native speakers; they sit in a classroom facing a teacher. This contrast is often put in terms of 'informal' learning which takes place in a natural setting and 'formal' learning which takes place inside a classroom. Macnamara (1976), however, denies that language teaching is strictly speaking formal, since the teacher cannot provide formal rules that are linguistically and psychologically valid. Krashen (1976) sees aspects of both formal and informal learning in the classroom, defining 'formal' as teaching one rule at a time and having feedback; he suggests that an adult may benefit from formal teaching since this exploits his adult capacity to 'learn' rather than 'acquire' language. But we still have little idea of what goes on in a classroom in terms of interaction; certainly it is very different from the conversation strategies that Hatch describes. We do have some ideas about correction of errors (Cohen, 1975; Holley & King, 1971) but more information is needed about all the other aspects of classroom behaviour by students and teachers.

4. General remarks

One obvious conclusion from this research is the complexity of second-language learning; any model has to account not just for grammatical development but also for the contributions made by the learner and by the learner's environment, not to mention the individual differences between learners, and the effects of learning a second language on the learner, a field too vast to include here. If nothing more, we can rule out simple accounts of second-language learning. A further general issue is whether a second language can be learnt in the same way as a first. An adequate discussion of this can only take place if we settle in advance which model of first-language acquisition we are comparing to second-language learning: it is hardly satisfactory to try to prove or disprove the similarity between the processes by choosing select examples from either field. At present this issue can only be discussed in fairly limited terms because the research in second-language learning is restricted in scope. Nevertheless there have been several discussions of this issue (Cook, 1969; Ervin-Tripp, 1975; Macnamara, 1976; McLaughlin, 1977; Spolsky, 1977). The general tenor of these emphasises the broad similarities between first- and second-language learning but draws attention to some specific differences. Much of the grammatical evidence has already been mentioned in section 1.3 above. In addition, one can mention an analysis of learner's errors that found most could be explained in terms of first-language acquisition rather than interference (Dulay & Burt, 1972) and the results of an experiment in which foreign adults and native children repeat sentences in similar ways (Cook, 1973).

One firm conclusion, as in any research survey, is that more research is needed; in some areas we have barely started to scratch the surface. Nevertheless, since the interest of this research for many people lies in its potential application to language teaching, it seems fair to risk some tentative conclusions. Obviously any teaching syllabus or materials will be more effective if they pay attention to what is known about the developmental sequence the learner goes through, the comprehension and production strategies he uses, his attitudes and motivations, the interactions he wants to take part in, and so on. But what can the teacher do who is unable to change the syllabus or course that he uses? Above all, the teacher has to recognise the active contribution made by the learner; regardless of what the teacher wants him to do, the learner adopts certain learning and production strategies; success in learning is a product of many different factors in the learner, most of them out of the teacher's control. In particular, the successful learner wants to communicate actively through the language. The teacher's recognition of the learner's contribution, in particular of the integrative motivation, will lead him not only to stress the ultimate aim of interacting with native speakers but also to encourage the students to interact with each other and with him in meaningful ways in the classroom; this probably means providing a variety of interaction patterns, not just the one in which all communication is channelled through the teacher. The teacher's awareness of the learner's contribution will also make him more conscious of the extent to which he can call upon the maturer cognitive processes of the second-language learner in activities where language is less involved. In terms of teaching techniques, it leads to activities that encourage the students to communicate and interact through the new language about things that vitally concern them, here and now in the classroom, rather than with a native speaker on some far-off occasion in the future; thus the teacher will rely heavily on role-play, communication games, and the like. This new emphasis brings us to a point where the goals of language teaching are no longer defined simply by the language syllabus the student is expected to know, or by the usefulness

V. J. Cook: Second-language learning

of the language to some conjectured function in the student's later life, but by their contribution to the social and psychological development of the individual; it may restore a central educational role to language teaching in addition to its academic and utilitarian roles.   *April 1978*

Addendum, December 1981

Since the original publication of this article, a large amount has been published, too much to summarise here as a postscript. The following, however, represent the essential reading in book form that has become available.

Eckman, F. & Hastings, A. J. (eds.) (1977). *Studies in first and second language acquisition.* Rowley, Mass.: Newbury House, 1979.
Hornby, P. A. (ed.) (1977). *Bilingualism.* New York: Academic Press.
Felix, S. W. (ed.) (1980). *Second language development.* Tubingen: Gunter Narr.
Gingras, R. C. (ed.) (1978). *Second language acquisition and foreign language teaching.* Arlington, Va.: Center for Applied Linguistics.
Krashen, S. D. (1981). *Second language acquisition and second language learning.* Oxford: Pergamon Press.
Larsen-Freeman, D. (ed.) (1980). *Discourse analysis in second language research.* Rowley, Mass.: Newbury House.
McDonough, S. H. (1981). *Psychology in foreign language teaching.* London: Allen & Unwin.
McLaughlin, B. (1978). *Second-language acquisition in childhood.* Hillsdale, N.J.: Lawrence Erlbaum Associates.
Nehls, D. (ed.) (1980). *Studies in language acquisition.* Heidelberg: Julius Groos.
New York Academy of Sciences (to appear). *Proceedings of the Conference on First and Second Language Learning; January 1981.*
Paivio, A. & Begg, I. (1981). *Psychology of language.* Englewood Cliffs, N.J.: Prentice-Hall.
Ritchie, W. G. (ed.) (1978). *Second language acquisition research.* New York: Academic Press.

References

Abbreviations to journals titles: *LL*, Language Learning; *MLJ*, Modern Language Journal.
d'Anglejean, A., Gagnon, N., Tucker, G. R. & Winsberg, S. (1977). Solving problems in deductive reasoning: the performance of adult second language learners. Paper presented to the 8th Conference on Applied Linguistics, University of Michigan.
d'Anglejean, A. & Tucker, G. R. (1973). Communicating across cultures: an empirical investigation. *Journal of Cross Cultural Psychology,* **4**, 1, 121–30.
d'Anglejean, A. & Tucker, G. R. (1975). The acquisition of complex English structures by adult learners. *LL,* **25**, 2, 281–93.
Asher, J. J. & Garcia, R. (1969). The optimal age to learn a foreign language. *MLJ,* **53**, 334–41.
Asher, J. J. & Price, B. S. (1967). The learning strategy of the total physical response: some age differences. *Child Development,* **38**, 1219–27.
Atkinson, R. C. (1975). Mnemotechnics in second-language learning. *American Psychologist,* **30**, 821–8.
Bailey, N., Madden, C. & Krashen, S. (1974). Is there a 'natural sequence' in adult second language learning? *LL,* **24**, 2, 235–43.

V. J. Cook: Second-language learning

Bertkua, J. S. (1974). An analysis of English learner speech. *LL*, **24**, 2, 279–86.

Blum, S. & Levenston, E. (1977). Strategies of communications, through lexical avoidance in the speech and writing of second-language teachers and learners and in translation. Mimeo.

Brown, R. W. (1973). *A first language: the early stages*. Harvard University Press.

Cancino, H., Rosansky, E. J. & Schumann, J. H. (1975). The acquisition of the English auxiliary by native Spanish speakers. *TESOL Quarterly*, **9**, 4, 421–30.

Chun, J. (1975). Selected processes in second language acquisition. Paper presented to the Fourth AILA Congress, Stuttgart.

Chun, J. (1976). Word order in second language acquisition. In G. Drachman (ed.), *Proceedings of the First Salzburg Colloquium on Children's Language*. Tubingen: Verlag Gunter Narr.

Clarke, M. A. (1976). Second language acquisition as a clash of consciousness. *LL*, **26**, 2, 377–90.

Cook, V. J. (1969). The analogy between first and second language learning. *IRAL*, **7**, 3, 207–16.

Cook, V. J. (1973). The comparison of language development in native children and foreign adults. *IRAL*, **11**, 1, 13–28.

Cook, V. J. (1975). Strategies in the comprehension of relative clauses. *Language and Speech*, **18**, 3, 204–12.

Cook, V. J. (1977). Cognitive processes in second language learning. *IRAL*, **15**, 1, 1–20.

Cohen, A. C. (1975). Error correction and the training of language teachers. *MLJ*, **59**, 414–22.

Corder, S. P. (1967). The significance of learners' errors. *IRAL*, **5**, 2/3, 161–70. Reprinted in Richards (1974).

Corder, S. P. (1971). Idiosyncratic dialects and error analysis. *IRAL*, **9**, 2, 147–60. Reprinted in Richards (1974).

Corder, S. P. (1977). Language continua and the interlanguage hypothesis. In S. P. Corder & E. Roulet (eds.), *The notions of simplification, interlanguages and pidgins and their relation to second language pedagogy*. Geneva: Droz; Neuchâtel: Université de Neuchâtel.

Craik, F. I. M. (1973). A 'levels of analysis' view of memory. In P. Pliner, L. Kramer & T. Alloway (eds.), *Communication and affect*. New York: Academic Press.

Dato, D. P. (1975). On psycholinguistic universals in children's learning of Spanish. In D. P. Dato (ed.), *Developmental psycholinguistics: theory and application*. Georgetown University Press. (Georgetown University Round Table.)

Desrochers, A. M., Smythe, P. M. & Gardner, R. C. (1975). *The social psychology of second language acquisition and bilinguality: an annotated bibliography*. Research Bulletin No. 340, University of Western Ontario.

Dickerson, L. (1975). The learner's language as a system of variable rules. *TESOL Quarterly*, **9**, 4, 401–7.

Dulay, H. C. & Burt, M. K. (1972). Goofing: an indicator of children's second language learning strategies. *LL*, **22**, 2, 235–52.

Dulay, H. C. & Burt, M. K. (1973). Should we teach children syntax? *LL*, **23**, 2, 245–58.

Dulay, H. C. & Burt, M. K. (1974). Natural sequences in child second language acquisition. *LL*, **24**, 1, 37–53.

Ervin-Tripp, S. E. (1974). Is second language learning like the first? *TESOL Quarterly*, **8**, 2, 111–29.

Fathman, A. (1975). The relationship between age and second language productive ability. *LL*, **25**, 2, 245–53.

Ferguson, C. A. (1975). Toward a characterization of English foreigner talk. *Anthropological Linguistics*, **17**, 1, 1–14.

18

V. J. Cook: Second-language learning

Fillmore, L. W. (1976). Individual differences in second language acquisition. Asilomar Conference on Individual Differences in Language Ability and Language Behaviour.

Gallagher, W. E. (1976). Investigation of the relationship between memorisation and rule acquisition. In. J. E. Fanselow & R. H. Crymes (eds.), *On TESOL 1976*. Washington DC: TESOL.

Gardner, R. C., Smythe, P. C., Clement, R. & Gliksman, L. (1976). Second language learning: a social psychological perspective. *Canadian Modern Language Review*, 32, 3, 198–213.

Glicksberg, D. H. (1963). A study of the span of immediate memory among adult students of English as a foreign language. University of Michigan, PhD thesis.

Green, M. F. (1977). Regression in adult learning of a second language. *Foreign Language Annals*, 10, 2, 173–83.

Guiora, A. Z., Brannan, R. C. L. & Dull, C. Y. (1972). Empathy and second language learning. *LL*, 22, 2, 111–30.

Hakuta, K. (1974). Prefabricated patterns and the emergence of structure in second language acquisition. *LL*, 24, 2, 287–97.

Hakuta, K. (1975). Learning how to speak a second language: what exactly does the child learn? In D. P. Dato (ed.), *Developmental psycholinguistics: theory and application*. Georgetown University Press (Georgetown University Round Table.)

Harris, D. P. (1970). Report on an experimental group-administered memory span test. *TESOL Quarterly*, 4, 203–13.

Hatch, E. (1976). Conversational analysis: an alternative methodology for second language acquisition research. Proceedings of the NWAVE-V Conference, Georgetown.

Hatch, E. (1978). Discourse analysis and second language acquisition. In E. Hatch (ed.), *Second language acquisition*. Rowley, Mass.: Newbury House.

Henning, G. H. (1973). Remembering foreign language vocabulary: acoustic and semantic parameters. *LL*, 23, 2, 185–96.

Holley, F. M. & King, J. K. (1971). Imitation and correction in foreign language learning. *MLJ*, 55, 494–8.

Hyltenstem, K. (1977). Implicational patterns in interlanguage syntax variation. *Work in Progress*, 10, 1–20. Department of Linguistics, Edinburgh University.

Just, M. A. & Carpenter, P. A. (1975). Comparative studies of comprehension: an investigation of Chinese, Norwegian and English. *Memory and Cognition*, 3, 465–73.

Katz, J. T. (1976). Case, gender, and pronominal diamorphy in child second language acquisition. Paper delivered at First Annual Boston Conference on Language Development.

Kellerman, E. (1974). Elicitation, lateralisation and error analysis. *York Papers in Linguistics*, 4. Reprinted in *Interlanguage Studies Bulletin*, 1, 1 (1976), 79–114.

Krashen, S. (1975). The development of cerebral dominance and language learning: more evidence. In D. P. Dato (ed.), *Developmental psycholinguistics: theory and application*. Georgetown University Press (Georgetown University Round Table).

Krashen, S. D. (1976). Formal and informal linguistic environments in language acquisition and language learning, *TESOL Quarterly*, 10, 2, 157–68.

Krashen, S. D. (1977). The monitor model for adult second language performance. In M. Burt, H. Dulay & M. Finocchario (eds.), *Viewpoints on English as a second language*. New York: Regents.

Krashen, S. D., Sferlazza, V., Feldman, L. & Fathman, A. K. (1976). Adult performance on the SLOPE test: more evidence for a natural sequence in adult second language acquisition. *LL*, 26, 1, 145–51.

Kuusinen, J. & Salin, E. (1971). Children's learning of unfamiliar phonological sequences. *Perceptual Motor Skills*, 33, 559–62.

Lambert, W. E. (1956). Developmental aspects of second language acquisition: I. Associational fluency, stimulus provocativeness and word order influence. *Journal of Social Psychology*, **43**, 83–9.

Lambert, W. E. (1974). Cultural and language factors in learning and education. In F. Aboud & R. Meade, *The Fifth Western Symposium on Learning*. Washington: Western Washington State College.

Lambert, W. E. & Preston, M. S. (1967). The interdependences of the bilingual's two languages. In K. Salzinger & S. Salzinger (eds.), *Research in verbal behaviour and some neurophysiological implications*, 115–21. New York: Academic Press.

Larsen-Freeman, D. E. (1975). The acquisition of grammatical morphemes by adult ESL students. *TESOL Quarterly*, **9**, 4, 409–19.

Larsen-Freeman, D. E. (1976). An explanation for the morpheme acquisition order of second language learners. *LL*, **26**, 1, 125–34.

Lattey, E. (1975). Second-language acquisition: environments and strategies. In C. Molony, H. Zobl & W. Stolting (eds.), *German in contact with other languages*. Monographs in Linguistics and Communication Sciences. Kronberg: Skriptor Verlag.

Lightbown, P. M. (1977). French L2 learners: what they're talking about. Paper presented at the first annual Second Language Acquisition Research Forum, University of California, Los Angeles.

Long, J. & Harding-Esch, E. (1977). Summary and recall of text in first and second languages; some factors contributing to performance differences. In H. W. Sinaiko and D. Gerver (eds.), *Proceedings of NATO Symposium on Language, Interpretation and Communication*. New York; London: Plenum Press.

McLaughlin, B. (1977). Second language learning in children. *Psychological Bulletin*, **84**, 3, 438–59.

Macnamara, J. (1973). Nurseries, streets and classrooms: some comparisons and deductions. *MLJ*, **57**, 250–4.

Macnamara, J. (1976). Comparison between first and second language learning. *Die Neuren Sprachen*, **75**, 175–88.

McNeill, D. (1965). Some thoughts on first and second language acquisition. Mimeo, Harvard University.

Meara, P. (1977). Schizophrenic symptoms in foreign-language learners. Paper presented to BAAL Annual Conference, Colchester.

Melvin, B. S. & Rivers, W. M. (1976). In one ear and out the other: implications of memory studies for language learning. In J. E. Fanselow & R. Crymes (eds.), *On TESOL*. Washington DC: TESOL.

Milon, J. P. (1974). The development of negation in English by a second-language learner. *TESOL Quarterly*, **8**, 2, 137–43.

Naiman, N., Fröhlich, M. & Stern, H. H. (1975). *The good language learner*. Toronto: Ontario Institute for Studies in Education.

Natalico, D. S. & Natalico, L. F. S. (1971). A comparative study of English pluralization by native and non-native English speakers. *Child Development*. **42**, 1302–6.

Nemser, W. (1971). Approximative systems of foreign-language learners. *IRAL*, **9**, 2, 115–23. Reprinted in Richards (1974).

Neufeld, G. G. (1976). The bilingual's lexical store. *IRAL*, **14**, 1, 15–31.

Newmark, L. & Reibel, D. A. (1968). Necessity and sufficiency in language learning. *IRAL*, **6**, 3, 145–64.

Olson, L. L. & Samuels, S. J. (1973). The relationship between age and accuracy of foreign-language pronunciation. *Journal of Educational Research*, **66**, 6, 263–8.

V. J. Cook: Second-language learning

Oyama, S. (1976). A sensitive period for the acquisition of a nonnative phonological system. *Journal of Psycholinguistic Research*, **5**, 3, 261–83.

Padilla, A. M. (to appear). Acquisition of 14 grammatical morphemes in the speech of bilingual children.

Padilla, A. M. & Lindholm, K. J. (1976). Development of interrogative, negative and possessive forms in the speech of young Spanish/English bilinguals. *Bilingual Review*, **3**, 2, 122–52.

Paivio, A. (1976). On exploring visual knowledge. Paper presented at the Iowa Invitational Conference on Visual Learning, Thinking and Communication. University of Iowa.

Peck, S. (to appear). Language play in second language acquisition. In C. Henning (ed.), *Proceedings of the First Annual Los Angeles Second Language Research Forum*.

Perkins, K. & Larsen-Freeman, D. (1975). The effect of formal language instruction on the order of morpheme acquisition. *LL*, **25**, 2, 237–43.

Porter, J. H. (1977). A cross-sectional study of morpheme acquisition in first language learning. *LL*, **27**, 1, 47–61.

Ramsey, C. A. & Wright, E. N. (1974). Age and second language learning. *Journal of Social Psychology*, **94**, 51–121.

Richards, J. C. (1971). Error analysis and second language strategies. *Language Sciences*, **17**, 12–22.

Richards, J. C. (ed.) (1974). *Error analysis*. London: Longman.

Rivers, W. M. & Melvin, B. S. (1977). Memory and memorization in comprehension and production: contributions of I P theory. *Canadian Modern Language Review*, **33**, 4, 497–502.

Rosansky, E. J. (1975). The critical period for the acquisition of language; some cognitive developmental considerations. *Working Papers in Bilingualism*, **6**, 92–102.

Rosansky, E. J. (1976). Methods and morphemes in second language acquisition research. *LL*, **26**, 2, 409–25.

Rubin, J. (1975). What the 'good language learner' can teach us. *TESOL Quarterly*, **9**, 1, 41–51.

Sampson, G. P. & Richards, J. C. (1973). Learner language systems. *Language Sciences*, **26**, 18–25. Reprinted in Richards (1974).

Schachter, J. (1974). An error in error analysis. *LL*, **24**, 2, 205–14.

Schumann, J. H. (1975a). Implications of pidginization and creolization for the study of adult second language acquisition. In J. H. Schumann & N. Stenson (eds.), *New frontiers in second language learning*. Rowley, Mass.: Newbury House.

Schumann, J. H. (1975b). Affective factors and the problem of age in second language acquisition. *LL*, **25**, 2, 209–35.

Schumann, J. H. (1976). Social distance as a factor in second language acquisition. *LL*, **26**, 1, 135–43.

Scovel, T. (1969). Foreign accents, language acquisition, and cerebral dominance. *LL*, **19**, 2/4, 245–53.

Seliger, H. W., Krashen, S. D. & Ladefoged, P. (1975). Maturational constraints in the acquisition of second language accent. *Language Sciences*, **36**, 20–2.

Selinker, L. (1972). Interlanguage. *IRAL*, **10**, 3, 209–31. Reprinted in Richards (1974).

Smith, K. H. & Braine, M. D. S. (no date). Miniature languages and the problem of language acquisition. Mimeo.

Snow, C. E. & Hoefnagel-Höhle, M. (1975). Age differences in second language acquisition. Paper read to Fourth AILA Congress, Stuttgart.

Snow, C. E. & Hoefnagel-Höhle, M. (no date). Age differences in the pronunciation of foreign sounds. Mimeo, University of Amsterdam.

Spolsky, B. (1977). The comparative study of first and second language acquisition. Paper read at Sixth Annual University of Wisconsin–Milwaukee Linguistics Symposium on Language Acquisition.
Stern, H. H. (1975). What can we learn from the good language learner? *Canadian Modern Language Review*, **31**, 4, 304–18.
Tarone, E. (1976). Some influences on interlanguage phonology. *Working Papers in Bilingualism*, **8**, 87–111.
Taylor, B. P. (1975). The use of overgeneralization and transfer learning strategies by elementary and intermediate students of ESL. *LL*, **25**, 1, 73–107.
Taylor, I. (1971). How are words from two languages organized in a bilingual's memory? *Canadian Journal of Psychology*, **23**, 3, 228–40.
Tremaine, R. V. (1975). Piagetian equilibration processes in syntax learning. In D. P. Dato (ed.), *Developmental psycholinguistics: theory and application*. Georgetown University Press. (Georgetown University Round Table.)
Valdman, A. (1975). Error analysis and pedagogical ordering and the determination of pedagogically motivated sequences. In S. P. Corder & E. Roulet (eds.), *Some implications of linguistic theory for applied linguistics*. Brussels: AIMAV.
Wakefield, J. A., Doughtie, E. G. & Lee Yom, B. H. (1974). The identification of structural components of an unknown language. *Journal of Psycholinguistic Research*, **3**, 3, 261–9.
White, L. (1977). Error analysis and error correction in adult learners of English as a Second Language, *Working Papers in Bilingualism*, **13**, 42–58.
Wode, H. (1976a). Redding→[wedin]: the acquisition of L2 /r/. *Arbeitspapiere zum Spracherwerb*, **11**. English Department, University of Kiel.
Wode, H. (1976b). Developmental sequences in naturalistic L2 acquisition. *Working Papers in Bilingualism*, **11**, 1–31.
Young, R. W. (1973). The development of semantic categories in Spanish–English and Navajo–English bilingual children. In P. T. Turner (ed.), *Bilingualism in the South West*. Tucson: University of Arizona Press.

BILINGUALISM, COGNITIVE FUNCTIONING AND EDUCATION

Merrill Swain and James Cummins

Modern Language Centre, The Ontario Institute for Studies in Education

The purposes of this paper are to review recent studies which have investigated the relationships between bilingualism and cognitive functioning, and to outline the implications of these research findings for educational settings.

Terminology

The term 'bilingualism' has not been used in a consistent way among researchers and theoreticians. Definitions vary considerably. Macnamara (1967), for example, defines bilinguals as those who possess at least one of the language skills (listening, speaking, reading and writing) even to a minimal degree in their second language. At the other end of the scale, bilinguals have been defined as those who demonstrate complete mastery of two different languages without interference between the two linguistic processes (Oestreicher, 1974) or who have native-like control of two or more languages (Bloomfield, 1933). The tendency has been to focus on speaking and listening skills (e.g. Haugen, 1953; Pohl, 1965; Weinreich, 1953).

Other definitions of bilingualism have considered the age at which the second language is learned (simultaneous v. sequential; early v. late); the contexts in which the two languages have been learned (compound v. coordinate (Osgood & Sebeok, 1965), artificial v. natural (Stern, 1973)); or the domains in which each language is used (e.g. Fishman, 1968; Oksaar, 1971).

It is clear, then, that there is little consensus as to the exact meaning of the term 'bilingualism', and that it has been used to refer to a wide variety of phenomena. Research associated with bilingualism reflects this semantic confusion. It is essential, therefore, in reconciling contradictory results associated with bilingualism, to be aware of the levels of bilingualism attained by the experimental Ss, and the social and psychological factors which lie behind the particular 'bilingualism' attained.

This review is specifically concerned with the association between bilingualism and cognitive functioning. Cognitive functioning is used in this paper to refer to measures involving general intellectual and linguistic skills such as verbal and non-verbal IQ, divergent thinking, academic performance, and metalinguistic awareness.

23

For the purposes of this review it is also important to introduce two terms associated with educational programmes. Both terms – 'immersion' and 'submersion' – relate to situations where the child is required to use in school a language that is different from that used in the home. Immersion refers to a situation in which children from the same linguistic and cultural background who have had no prior contact with the school language are put together in a classroom setting in which the second language is used as the medium of instruction. Submersion, on the other hand, refers to the situation encountered by some children wherein they must make a home–school language switch, while others can already function in the school language. Within the same classroom, then, one might find children who have no knowledge of the school language, varying degrees of facility in the school language through contact with the wider community, and native speakers of the school language (Swain, in press).

In the next two sections, studies which report a negative association between bilingualism and cognitive functioning and studies which report a positive association between bilingualism and cognitive functioning will be reviewed. Following that, several of the factors which appear to differentiate the positive and negative studies will be reviewed, and the resultant implications for educational programmes will be summarised.

Studies reporting negative associations

Several comprehensive reviews exist of studies conducted prior to 1960 (see Darcy, 1953; Macnamara, 1966; Peal & Lambert, 1962) and consequently these studies will not be considered here. Although the majority of these early studies had serious methodological defects, taken together they seemed to indicate that bilinguals suffered from a language handicap when measured by verbal tests of intelligence or academic achievement.

The general findings of earlier studies are supported by those of Skutnabb-Kangas & Toukomaa (1976) who reported that children of Finnish migrant workers in Sweden tended to be characterised by 'semilingualism', i.e. their skills in both Finnish and Swedish (as measured by standardised tests) were considerably below Finnish and Swedish norms. The extent to which the mother tongue had been developed prior to contact with Swedish was strongly related to how well Swedish was learned. Chidren who migrated at age ten maintained a level of Finnish close to Finnish students in Finland and achieved Swedish language skills comparable to those of Swedes. However, children who were seven to eight years of age when they moved to Sweden or who moved before starting school were most likely to achieve low levels of literacy skills in both languages. Skutnabb-Kangas and Toukomaa argue on the basis of these results that the minority child's first language (L1) has functional significance in the developmental process and should be reinforced by the school.

Vernacular education is also supported by Macnamara's (1966) study of bilingualism in Irish primary education. Macnamara reported that Irish primary school children, whose home language was English but who were instructed through the medium of Irish, were eleven months behind in problem arithmetic relative to other Irish children taught through the medium of English. No differences were found between the Irish immersion group and comparison groups in either mechanical arithmetic or English achievement. Macnamara's study has been criticised (Cummins, 1977 *b*, *c*) on the grounds that the Irish immersion group was administered the problem arithmetic test through their weaker language (Irish) whereas comparison groups took the test in their stronger language (English). Thus, according to Cummins, Macnamara's study confounds the immersion children's competence in arithmetic with their ability to demonstrate this competence when tested through their weaker language.

Tsushima & Hogan (1975) report that grade 4 and 5 Japanese–English bilinguals performed at a significantly lower level on measures of verbal and academic skills than a unilingual group matched on non-verbal IQ. The bilingual group was comprised of children whose mothers were Japanese and whose fathers were born and raised in the United States. All the parents of children in the unilingual group were born and raised in the United States. Tsushima and Hogan report that the bilingual children had been exposed to both English and Japanese in the home from infancy. However, they give no details of the present pattern of bilingual usage in the home nor of the bilinguals' relative competence in both languages. Thus, while this study provides evidence of an increasing deficit in verbal skills among bilingual children between grades 3 and 5, it fails to provide any information about the bilingual learning conditions under which such a deficit might occur.

The same criticism can be made of a study conducted in Singapore by Torrance, Gowan, Wu & Aliotti (1970) who report that grades 3, 4 and 5 children attending English (L2) medium schools performed at a significantly lower level than unilingual children on the fluency and flexibility scales of the Torrance Tests of Creative Thinking, a measure of divergent thinking. Although the study involves more than a thousand subjects little detail is given regarding the comparability of the groups in terms of IQ or SES nor about the level of bilingualism of the bilingual subjects.

In studies involving middle-class Hebrew–English and Spanish–English lower-class children, Ben Zeev (1977 *a*, *b*) reported lower vocabulary scores for bilinguals in comparison to unilinguals when matched for IQ. A similar finding has been reported with pre-school French–English bilinguals (Doyle, Champagne & Segalowitz, 1977).

Studies reporting positive associations

A variety of cognitive advantages have been reported in association with bilingualism. Some studies have reported higher levels of linguistic skills. A positive association has also been reported between bilingualism and both general intellectual skills and divergent thinking. In addition, several studies have reported evidence that bilingualism promotes an analytic orientation to linguistic and perceptual structures and increases sensitivity to feedback cues.

Linguistic skills

Several studies conducted within the context of primary immersion programmes have reported that the immersion students performed better than children in regular programmes on measures of L1 skills despite considerably less instruction through the medium of L1. Barik and Swain (1978), for example, report that by grade 5 children in the Ottawa early total French immersion programmes were performing better than control *S*s on some aspects of English skills. Swain (1975) has also reported that French immersion students used more complex syntactic structures in written English composition than regular programme students. Tremaine (1975) compared the syntactical development of grades 1, 2 and 3 children in a total French immersion programme with that of children who were given 75 minutes of French instruction per day. As would be expected there were large differences between the groups in French syntactical development; however, differences in favour of the immersion group in English syntactical development were also significant even when level of Piagetian operations was controlled. Tremaine concludes that intensive exposure to French facilitated the comprehension of certain English syntactic structures.

Ekstrand (1978) also reports preliminary results of an experimental project in Sweden in which elementary school children with an early start in learning English (L2) did significantly better in Swedish (L1) than control children. Enhancement of linguistic skills as a function of intensity of bilingual learning experiences is also suggested in a longitudinal study conducted by Genesee, Tucker & Lambert (1978). Grade 3 and 5 children in a trilingual English–Hebrew–French programme in Montreal performed at the same level in English and significantly better in Hebrew when compared to children in a bilingual English–Hebrew programme. Genesee *et al.* point out that the Hebrew curriculum in experimental and control schools was essentially the same.

Where the development of both languages is promoted by the school programme, there is also evidence of positive linguistic effects. Dubé & Hébert (1975), for example, report that minority francophone children in a French–English bilingual education project in Maine developed higher levels of English skills than a control group of children in an English-only programme.

Orientation to linguistic and perceptual structures

Several studies have reported evidence that bilingualism can promote an analytic orientation to language and increase aspects of metalinguistic awareness. Feldman & Shen (1971), for example, reported that five-year-old bilingual Head Start children were superior to unilinguals in their ability to switch labels, and in their use of common names and nonsense names in relational statements.

Ianco-Worrall (1972), in a study conducted in South Africa, reported that bilingual children, brought up in a one-person, one-language home environment, were significantly more sensitive than unilingual children, matched on IQ, to semantic relations between words and were also more advanced in realising the arbitrary assignment of names to referents. Unilingual children were more likely to interpret similarity between words in terms of an acoustic rather than a semantic dimension (e.g. *cap–can* rather than *cap–hat*) and felt that the names of objects could not be interchanged.

Ianco-Worrall's finding that bilinguals were more aware of the arbitrary assignment of words to referents was supported by Cummins (1978) in a study involving grades 3 and 6 Irish–English bilinguals matched on IQ with a unilingual group. However, a subsequent study (Cummins & Mulcahy, 1978a) involving grades 1 and 3 Ukrainian–English bilinguals found no differences between bilingual and unilingual groups on this task. Cummins and Mulcahy suggest that the equivocal nature of the findings may be a reflection of the relative crudeness of the measures used to assess aspects of children's metalinguistic awareness.

The results of several studies are consistent with the hypothesis that bilingualism can increase children's ability to analyse linguistic input. Cummins (1978b) reported that both grade 3 and grade 6 bilingual children were significantly better able than unilingual children to evaluate nonempirical contradictory statements (e.g. *The poker chip (hidden) in my hand is blue and it is not blue – True, False or Can't tell?*). Cummins & Mulcahy (1978a) reported that grades 1 and 3 Ukrainian–English bilingual children were significantly better able to analyse ambiguities in sentence structure than a control group of unilingual children matched for IQ, SES and school.

In two studies involving middle-class Hebrew–English bilinguals and lower-class Spanish–English bilinguals, Ben-Zeev (1977a, b) reported that in comparison to unilingual children matched on IQ, bilingual children were better able to treat sentence structure analytically and also performed better on several nonverbal tasks which required perceptual analysis. She suggested that bilingual children develop an analytic strategy of linguistic processing in order to overcome interlingual interference. Bilingual–unilingual differences on the perceptual tasks were interpreted as evidence for the generalisation of bilinguals' analytic strategy towards language to other kinds of structures.

Ben-Zeev (1977 *a*) also reports higher latency of paradigmatic responses by bilingual children on a word association task. Cummins & Mulcahy (1978 *b*) have also reported that Ukrainian–English bilingual children took significantly longer than unilingual children to respond on a word association task. The longer latency of the word association responses may be a result of the increased semantic processing necessary to overcome interlingual interference.

Superior performance by bilinguals on tasks involving an ability to restructure linguistic and perceptual schemata has also been reported by Balkan (1970). In a study conducted in Switzerland, Balkan matched bilinguals and unilinguals on nonverbal intelligence and found that the bilingual group performed significantly better on two variables which he claims measure cognitive flexibility. One of these tests was similar to the Embedded Figures Test, and involved an ability to restructure a perceptual situation. The other test required a sensitivity to the different meanings of words. Bruck, Lambert & Tucker (in press) also found large differences between experimental and control groups on the Embedded Figures Test at the grade 6 level in the St Lambert French immersion programme.

A possible neuropsychological basis for findings of a more analytic orientation to linguistic and perceptual structures among bilingual children is provided in the results of a study carried out by Starck, Genessee, Lambert & Seitz (1977). Starck *et al.* demonstrated more reliable ear asymmetry effects on a dichotic listening task among children attending a trilingual Hebrew–French–English programme as compared to a control group of children whose instruction was totally in English. The significance of this finding is that right ear advantage on dichotic listening tasks reflects greater development of the more analytic left hemisphere functions in comparison to right hemisphere functions.

The findings that bilingual children display a more analytic orientation to language than unilingual children are consistent with the views of Vygotsky (1962) who argued that being able to express the same thought in different languages will enable the child to 'see his language as one particular system among many, to view its phenomena under more general categories, and this leads to awareness of his linguistic operations' (p. 110). Lambert & Tucker (1972) argued that a similar process was likely to operate among children in immersion programmes. They suggested that as children develop high-level bilingual skills they are likely to practice a form of 'incipient contrastive linguistics' by comparing the syntax and vocabulary of their two languages.

Sensitivity to feedback cues

Several studies provide evidence of both greater social sensitivity and greater ability to react more flexibly to cognitive feedback among bilinguals. Ben-Zeev (1977 *b*) suggests that increased attention to feedback cues has adaptive significance for bilingual children in that it might help them understand the communication of others, make them aware of mistakes in their own speech and provide them with information regarding the appropriate times for switching languages. In both Spanish–English and Hebrew–English studies, Ben-Zeev (1977 *a*, *b*) reports that bilinguals were significantly more susceptible to the verbal transformation illusion (Warren & Warren, 1966). In this task a nonsense word is repeated continuously by means of a tape loop and adults typically perceive the verbal stimulus as repeatedly changing. Ben-Zeev interprets the fact that bilinguals perceived a higher number of auditory changes as indicating increased processing effort on their part and increased attention to cues from linguistic input in order to achieve satisfactory closure. However, this interpretation is questioned by Cummins & Mulcahy (1978 *b*) who found no differences between bilinguals and unilinguals on the verbal transformation illusion.

Ben-Zeev also reports that the Spanish–English bilinguals were significantly better able to use hints as cues to successful restructuring on classification tasks. Cummins & Mulcahy (1978 *a*) similarly report that bilingual children made significantly better use of prompts in interpreting ambiguous sentences. However, differences between bilinguals and unilinguals on the ambiguities task remained significant even when the prompting data were eliminated.

The findings of several investigations suggest that bilinguals may be more sensitive to interpersonal feedback and more adept at certain kinds of communication tasks. Genesee, Tucker & Lambert (1976), for example, asked children in immersion classes and regular programme classes to explain how to play a game to two different listeners, one blindfolded and the other not blindfolded. The immersion group was found to be the most sensitive to the needs of listeners and responded most differentially, showing the largest difference between sighted and blindfolded conditions. The authors suggest that the immersion children's school experiences may have made them more aware of possible difficulties in communicating as well as provided them with some experience in coping with such difficulties.

Bain (1975) and Bain & Yu (1978) have undertaken several studies which examined bilingual–unilingual differences in sensitivity to facial expressions. Bain (1975) found significant differences between bilingual and unilingual children at grades 1 and 6 on the Portrait Sensitivity Test in which children were required to identify the facial expressions on a series of 24 portraits painted by famous artists. This finding was replicated cross-culturally by Bain & Yu (1978).

Swain & Cummins: Bilingualism

General intellectual development

Peal & Lambert (1962) reported that ten-year-old French–English bilingual children showed a higher level of both verbal and nonverbal intelligence than a comparison group of unilingual children matched on SES and sex. In addition, factor analysis of the cognitive measures revealed a more differentiated subtest profile in the bilingual group. Cummins & Gulutsan (1974) also reported significantly higher levels of verbal and nonverbal ability among bilingual children.

Two further studies involving French–English bilinguals attending bilingual schools in western Canada have reported that bilingual children performed better than unilinguals on measures of concept formation. Liedke & Nelson (1968) found that bilingual grade 1 children performed significantly better on a Piagetian concept-formation task than a unilingual group matched for age, SES, sex and IQ. The authors hypothesised that the bilingual child is exposed to a wider range of experiences due to the greater amount of social interaction involved in learning two languages as compared to one. Bain (1975) reported significant differences between grade 1 bilinguals and unilinguals on a rule-discovery task at the grade 1 level. Bilingual and unilingual groups were matched for SES, sex, IQ and developmental level of operations. Although in the same direction, differences at the grade 6 level did not reach significance.

Using longitudinal data from the Ottawa and Toronto French immersion programmes, Barik & Swain (1976) investigated the hypothesis that cognitive advantages are associated with the attainment of high levels of bilingual skills. It was found that children who had attained high levels of French skills performed significantly better than low French achievers on two of the three Otis-Lennon IQ subtests when scores were adjusted for initial IQ and age differences between the two groups. The IQ scores of the low French achievers remained unchanged over the three year period whereas the IQ scores of the high French achievers increased, suggesting that the attainment of high levels of L2 skills is associated with greater cognitive growth.

Divergent thinking

Cummins & Gulutsan (1974) reported significant differences between bilingual and unilingual grade 6 children on a verbal originality measure. When intelligence was partialled out the level of significance was reduced but the difference was still significant. However, no differences were found on four other measures of divergent thinking. Further analysis of the data (Cummins, 1977 a) suggested that only those bilinguals who had attained a relatively high level of second-language competence performed at a higher level on the verbal originality task (administered in L1) while children who remained dominant in their home language were at a disadvantage in relation to unilingual children on verbal fluency and flexibility skills. Torrance *et al.* (1970) have also reported that bilingual children in Singapore performed at a higher level than unilingual children on originality and elaboration scales of the Torrance Tests of Creative Thinking. Landry (1974) reported that grade 6 children attending schools where a FLES programme (i.e. between 20 and 45 minutes of second-language instruction per day) was operative, scored significantly higher than a unilingual control group on both the verbal and figural parts of the Torrance Tests of Creative Thinking. Differences between FLES and non-FLES schools at the grade 1 and grade 4 levels were non-significant.

Scott (1973) reported significant differences in divergent thinking between the experimental children in the St Lambert bilingual programme in Montreal and unilingual comparison groups. She also reports that the French speaking skills of the experimental children at the grade 6 level were significantly predicted by earlier (grade 3) divergent thinking abilities. Scott concludes that higher levels of divergent thinking may be either an effect or a causal element in the attainment of functional bilingualism.

A study conducted in Mexico by Carringer (1974) reported that 24 Spanish–English bilinguals performed at a significantly higher level than 24 Spanish-speaking unilinguals on several measures of divergent thinking.

Although, in general, these recent studies are better controlled than the earlier studies which reported negative findings, few are without methodological limitations. A problem in many of these studies (Bain & Yu, 1978; Carringer, 1974; Cummins & Gulutsan, 1974; Feldman & Shen, 1971; Landry, 1974; Peal & Lambert, 1962) is lack of adequate controls for possible background differences between bilingual and unilingual groups. An index of SES based on parental occupation provides inadequate protection against bias. Also, matching only on overall stage of cognitive development (e.g. preoperational, concrete operational, etc.) is insufficient since there can be extremely large individual differences on cognitive variables within stages. Although the remaining studies have matched bilingual and unilingual groups on IQ in addition to SES, the validity of some of the dependent measures used to assess constructs such as 'analytic orientation to language' or 'sensitivity to feedback cues' is open to question. Also, some studies are difficult to evaluate because of inadequate descriptions either of the bilingual learning situation or of the levels of L1 and L2 competence attained by the bilingual Ss.

Factors differentiating positive and negative results

Several factors may be extracted from the studies cited above which in part account for the contradictory results.

For the most part, positive findings are associated with children from majority-language groups whereas negative findings are associated with minority-language groups (Lambert, 1977; Burnaby, 1976). One exception to this generalisation as it relates to majority group children is Macnamara's (1966) study of English–Irish bilinguals. This study, however, has been criticised on methodological grounds (Cummins, 1977 *b*). Other exceptions, but which relate to minority-language children (e.g. Dubé & Hébert, 1975), indicate that the minority-group factor can be overcome through the reinforcement and development of high levels of L1 proficiency.

Another factor, related in part to the first, is the perceived value and prestige of the L1 and L2 in the home and community (Fishman, 1976; Tucker, 1977; Swain, in press). Positive results tend to be associated with situations where both the L1 and L2 have perceived social and economic value.

A third factor, again in part related to the first, is socio-economic status. Higher SES children tend to perform well (Paulston, 1975). Lower SES bilingual children tend not to perform as well as higher SES children, although they do perform as well or better than unilingual groups of a similar SES level (e.g. Bruck, Jakimik & Tucker, in press).

Finally, school programme variables play an important role. Positive results tend to be associated with immersion programmes while negative results tend to be associated with submersion programmes. The nature of the programme differences are outlined in Cohen & Swain, 1976; Burnaby, 1976; Swain, in press.

Research in this area will continue to uncover additional factors, and examine the effects of their interaction. Currently, however, the factors mentioned above have been summarised by the notions of additive and subtractive forms of bilingualism (Lambert, 1977).

Lambert points out that the majority of positive studies have involved bilingual Ss whose L1 was dominant and prestigious and in no danger of replacement by L2. The resulting form of bilingualism is termed 'additive' in that the bilingual is adding another socially relevant language to his repertoire of skills at no cost to his L1 competence. Thus the bilingual Ss in studies which have reported cognitive advantages associated with bilingualism have generally attained a high level of competence in both languages.

In contrast, many of the negative studies involved bilingual Ss from minority-language groups whose L1 was gradually being replaced by a more prestigious L2. Lambert (1977) terms the resulting form of bilingualism 'subtractive' since the bilingual's competence in his two languages at any point in time is likely to reflect some stage in the 'subtraction' of L1 and its replacement by L2. Consequently, many of the bilingual Ss in these studies may be characterised by less than native-like competence in both languages.

On the basis of this analysis it has been suggested (Cummins, 1976, 1978 *a*, in press; Toukomaa & Skutnabb-Kangas, 1977) that there may be threshold levels of linguistic competence which a bilingual child must attain both in order to avoid cognitive disadvantages and allow the potentially beneficial aspects of becoming bilingual to influence his cognitive functioning. In other words, the level of competence bilingual children achieve in their two languages may act as an intervening variable in mediating the effects of bilingual learning experiences on cognitive functioning.

Educational implications

One major educational implication of the threshold hypothesis is that if *optimal* development of minority-language children's academic and cognitive potential is a goal, then the school programme must aim to promote an additive form of bilingualism (Cummins, in press). Attainment of this goal will necessarily involve a home–school language switch at some stage in the educational process, but when and how must be determined in relation to the linguistic and socio-economic characteristics of the learner and of the learning environment (Swain, in press). Specifically when the home language is different from the school language and the home language tends to be denigrated by others and selves, and where the children come from socio-economically deprived homes, it would appear appropriate to begin initial instruction in the child's first language, switching at a later stage to instruction in the school language. On the other hand, where the home language is a majority language valued by the community, and where literacy is encouraged in the home, then the most efficient means of promoting an additive form of bilingualism is to provide initial instruction in the second language (Tucker, 1977; Swain & Bruck, 1976).

January 1979

References

Bain, B. C. (1975). Toward an integration of Piaget and Vygotsky: bilingual considerations. *Linguistics*, **160**, 5–20.

Bain, B. C. & Yu, A. (1978). Toward an integration of Piaget and Vygotsky: a cross-cultural replication (France, Germany, Canada) concerning cognitive consequences of bilinguality. In M. Paradis (ed.), *Aspects of Bilingualism*. Columbia, S.C.: Hornbeam Press.

Balkan, L. (1970). *Les effets du bilinguisme Français-Anglais sur les aptitudes intellectuelles*. Bruxelles: AIMAV.

Barik, H. C. & Swain, M. (1976). A longitudinal study of bilingual and cognitive development. *International Journal of Psychology*, **11**, 251–63.

Barik, H. C. & Swain, M. (1978). Evaluation of a French immersion program: the Ottawa study through grade five. *Canadian Journal of Behavioural Science*, **10**, 192–201.

Ben-Zeev, S. (1977a). The influence of bilingualism on cognitive development and cognitive strategy. *Child Development*, **48**, 1009–18.

Ben-Zeev, S. (1977b). The effect of Spanish–English bilingualism in children from less privileged neighborhoods on cognitive development and cognitive strategy. *Working Papers on Bilingualism*, **14**, 83–122.

Bloomfield, L. (1933). *Language*. New York: Holt, Rinehart & Winston.

Bruck, M., Jakimik, H. & Tucker, G. R. (in press). Are French programs suitable for working class children? In W. Engel (ed.), *Prospects in Child Language*. Amsterdam: Royal Vangorcum.

Bruck, M., Lambert, W. E. & Tucker, G. R. (in press). Cognitive and attitudinal consequences of bilingual schooling: the St Lambert project through grade six. *International Journal of Psycholinguistics*.

Burnaby, B. (1976). Language in native education. In M. Swain (ed.), *Bilingualism in Canadian education: issues and research*. Yearbook of the Canadian Society for the Study of Education, Volume 3. Edmonton, Alta: Western Industrial Research Centre, 62–85.

Carringer, D. C. (1974). Creative thinking abilities of Mexican youth: the relationship of bilingualism. *Journal of Cross-Cultural Psychology*, **5**, 492–504.

Cohen, A. D. & Swain, M. (1976). Bilingual education: the immersion model in the North American context. *TESOL Quarterly*, **10**, 45–53. Reprinted in J. E. Alatis & K. Twaddell (eds), *English as a Second Language in Bilingual Education*. Washington, D.C.: TESOL, 55–63.

Cummins, J. (1976). The influence of bilingualism on cognitive growth: a synthesis of research findings and explanatory hypotheses. *Working Papers on Bilingualism*, **9**, 1–43.

Cummins, J. (1977a). Cognitive factors associated with the attainment of intermediate levels of bilingual skills. *Modern Language Journal*, **61**, 3–12.

Cummins, J. (1977b). Immersion education in Ireland: a critical review of Macnamara's findings. *Working Papers on Bilingualism*, **13**, 121–7.

Cummins, J. (1977c). A comparison of reading achievement in Irish and English medium schools. In V. Greaney (ed.), *Studies in reading*. Dublin: Educational Company of Ireland.

Cummins, J. (1978a). Educational implications of mother tongue maintenance in minority-language groups. *The Canadian Modern Language Review*, **34**, 395–416.

Cummins, J. (1978b). Bilingualism and the development of metalinguistic awareness. *Journal of Cross-Cultural Psychology*, **9**, 131–49.

Cummins, J. (in press). Linguistic interdependence and the educational development of bilingual children. *Review of Educational Research*.

Cummins, J. & Gulutsan, M. (1974). Some effects of bilingualism on cognitive functioning. In S. T. Carey (ed.), *Bilingualism, biculturalism and education*. Edmonton: The University of Alberta Press.

Cummins, J. & Mulcahy, R. (1978a). Orientation to language in Ukrainian–English bilingual children. *Child Development*.

Cummins, J. & Mulcahy, R. (1978b). Orientation to language among children in the Ukrainian–English bilingual program. Report submitted to the Edmonton Public School Board.

Darcy, N. (1953). A review of the literature on the effects of bilingualism upon the measurement of intelligence. *Journal of Genetic Psychology*, **82**, 21–57.

Doyle, A., Champagne, M. & Segalowitz, N. (1977). Some issues in the assessment of linguistic consequences of early bilingualism. *Working Papers on Bilingualism*, **14**, 21–30.

Dubé, N. C. & Hébert, G. (1975). *St John Valley Bilingual Education Project: Five-Year Evaluation Report 1970–1975* (Prepared for U.S. Department of Health, Education and Welfare).

Ekstrand, L. H. Bilingual and bicultural adaptation. Unpublished doctoral dissertation, University of Stockholm, 1978.

Feldman, —. & Shen, M. (1971). Some language-related cognitive advantages of bilingual five-year-olds. *Journal of Genetic Psychology*, **118**, 235–44.

Fishman, J. A. (1968). Sociolinguistic perspective on the study of bilingualism. *Linguistics*, **39**, 21–50.

Fishman, J. A. (1976). *Bilingual education: an international sociological perspective.* Rowley, Mass.: Newbury House.

Genesee, F., Tucker, G. R. & Lambert, W. E. (1976). Communication skills of bilingual children. *Child Development,* **46,** 1010–14.

Genesee, F., Tucker, G. R. & Lambert, W. E. (1978). An experiment in trilingual education: report 3. *The Canadian Modern Language Review,* **34,** 621–43.

Haugen, E. (1953). *The Norwegian language in America: a study in bilingual behavior.* Philadelphia: University of Pennsylvania Press.

Ianco-Worrall, A. (1972). Bilingualism and cognitive development. *Child Development,* **43,** 1390–1400.

Lambert, W. E. (1977). The effects of bilingualism on the individual: cognitive and sociocultural consequences. In P. A. Hornby (ed.), *Bilingualism: psychological, social and educational implications.* New York: Academic Press, 15–27.

Lambert, W. E. & Tucker, G. R. (1972). *Bilingual education of Children: the St Lambert experiment.* Rowley, Mass.: Newbury House.

Landry, R. G. (1974). A comparison of second language learners and monolinguals on divergent thinking tasks at the elementary school level. *Modern Language Journal,* **58,** 1/2, 10–15.

Liedke, W. W. & Nelson, L. D. (1968). Concept formation and bilingualism. *Alberta Journal of Educational Research,* **14,** 225–32.

Macnamara, J. (1966). *Bilingualism and primary education.* Edinburgh: Edinburgh University Press.

Macnamara, J. (ed.) (1967). *Problems of bilingualism. Journal of Social Issues.* Special issue, **23,** no. 2.

Oeistreicher, J. P. (1974). The early teaching of a modern language. *Review of the Council for Cultural Cooperation of the Council of Europe,* **24,** 9–16.

Oksaar, E. (1971). Språkpolitiken och minoriteterna. In D. Schwartz (ed.), *Identitet och Minoritet.* Stockholm: 164–75.

Osgood, C. & Sebeok, T. (eds.) (1965). *Psycholinguistics: a survey of theory and research problems.* Bloomington: Indiana University Press. (First published in 1954 by Indiana University Publications in Anthropology and Linguistics, Mem. 10.)

Paulston, C. B. (1975). Ethnic relations and bilingual education: accounting for contradictory data. *Working Papers on Bilingualism,* **6,** 1–44.

Peal, E. & Lambert, W. E. (1962). The relation of bilingualism to intelligence. *Psychological Monographs,* **76,** 546.

Pohl, J. (1965). Bilinguismes. *Revue Roumaine de Linguistique,* **10,** 343–9.

Scott, S. (1973). The relation of divergent thinking to bilingualism: cause or effect. Research report, McGill University.

Skutnabb-Kangas, T. & Toukomaa, P. (1976). *Teaching migrant children mother tongue and learning the language of the host country in the context of the socio-cultural situation of the migrant family.* Tampere, Finland: University of Tampere. (Tutkimuksia Research Reports, 15, 1976.)

Starck, R., Genesee, F., Lambert, W. E. & Seitz, M. (1977). Multiple language experience and the development of cerebral dominance. In S. J. Segalowitz and F. A. Gruber (eds.), *Language development and neurological theory.* New York: Academic Press.

Stern, H. H. (1973). *Report on bilingual education.* Study E7 of Studies prepared for The Commission of Inquiry on the position of the French language and on language rights in Quebec. Quebec: The Quebec Official Publisher.

Swain, M. (1975). Writing skills of grade three French immersion pupils. *Working Papers on Bilingualism,* **7,** 1–38.

35

Swain, M. (1978). Home–school language switching. In J. C. Richards (ed.), *Understanding second and foreign language learning: issues and approaches.* Rowley, Mass.: Newbury House, 238–50.

Swain, M. & Bruck, M. (eds.) (1976). Immersion education for the majority child. *Canadian Modern Language Review,* 32, entire no. 5.

Torrance, E. P., Gowan, J. C., Wu, J. M. & Aliotti, N. C. (1970). Creative functioning of monolingual and bilingual children in Singapore. *Journal of Educational Psychology,* 61, 72–5.

Toukomaa, P. & Skutnabb-Kangas, T. (1977). *The intensive teaching of the mother tongue to migrant children of pre-school age.* Helsinki: The Finnish National Commission for UNESCO.

Tremaine, R. V. (1975). *Syntax and Piagetian operational thought.* Washington, D.C.: Georgetown University Press.

Tsushima, W. T. & Hogan, T. P. (1975). Verbal ability and school achievement of bilingual and monolingual children of different ages. *Journal of Educational Research,* 68, 349–53.

Tucker, G. R. (1977). The linguistic perspective. In *Bilingual education: current perspective.* Vol. 2: *Linguistics.* Arlington Va.: Center for Applied Linguistics, 1–40.

Vygotsky, L. S. (1962). *Thought and language.* Cambridge, Mass.: M.I.T. Press.

Warren, R. M. & Warren, R. P. (1966). A comparison of speech perception in childhood, maturity and old age by means of the verbal transformation effect. *Journal of Verbal Learning and Verbal Behavior,* 5, 142–6.

Weinreich, M. (1953). *Languages in contact.* The Hague: Mouton.

The following additional references are appended for those interested in extending their studies further.

Alatis, J. E. (ed.) (1970). *Bilingualism and language contact: anthropological, linguistic, psychological, and social aspects.* Report of the twenty-first annual Round Table Meeting on Linguistics and Language Studies. Washington, DC: Georgetown University Press. (Georgetown University Monograph Series on Language and Linguistics, 23.)

Canadian American Conference on Bilingualism, 1976. (1977). Bilingualism: psychological, social and educational implications: (proceedings of a conference . . . held March 12–13, 1976, at the State University of New York); edited by Peter A. Hornby. New York: Academic Press.

Centre for Information on Language Teaching and Research. (1976). Bilingualism and British education: the dimensions of diversity. Papers from a conference convened in January, 1976. (CILT Reports and Papers 14.)

Dodson, C. J. (1967). *Language teaching and the bilingual method.* London: Pitman.

Dodson, C. J. and others. (1968). *Towards bilingualism: studies in language teaching methods.* Cardiff: University of Wales Press.

Elias, G. C. & Ingram, D. E. (1977). Cultural components of reading: an examination of psycholinguistic processes in reading and implications for the bilingual classroom. Singapore: Singapore University Press for SEAMEO Regional Language Centre.

Jones, W. R. (1959). *Bilingualism and intelligence.* Cardiff: University of Wales Press.

Kelly, L. G. (ed.) (1969). *Description and measurement of bilingualism: an international seminar* (University of Moncton, June 1967). Toronto: University of Toronto Press in association with the Canadian National Commission for UNESCO.

Lambert, W. E. (1972). *Language, psychology and culture: essays, selected and introduced by A. S. Dil.* Stanford: Stanford University Press.
Leopold, W. F. (1939–49). *Speech development of a bilingual child.* 4 vols. Evanston, Illinois: Northwestern University Press.
Mackey, W. F. (ed.) (1972). *International bibliography on bilingualism.* Quebec: Presses de l'Université Laval (for the International Centre for Research on Bilingualism, Laval University).
Mackey, W. F. & Andersson, T. (eds.) (1977). *Bilingualism in early childhood.* Rowley, Mass.: Newbury House.
Mackinnon, Kenneth (1977). *Language, education and social processes in a Gaelic community.* London: Routledge & Kegan Paul.
Ney, J. W. & Eberle, D. K. (1975). *A selected bibliography on bilingual/bicultural education.* Arlington, Virginia: Center for Applied Linguistics, ERIC Clearinghouse on Languages and Linguistics.
Saville-Troike, M. (1973). *Bilingual children: a resource document.* Arlington, Virginia: Center for Applied Linguistics.
Schneider, S. G. (1976). *Revolution, reaction or reform: the 1974 Bilingual Education Act.* New York: Las Americas Publishing Co.
Schools Council. Bilingual Education Project (1978). Bilingual education in Wales 5–11: report by Eurwin Price, Schools Council Bilingual Education Project 1968–77, with an independent evaluation by C. J. Dodson. Evans, Methuen Education.
Sharp, D. (1973). *Language in bilingual communities.* London: Edward Arnold (Explorations in Language Study).
Sharp, D. and others. (1973). Attitudes to Welsh and English in the schools of Wales: a full report. London: Macmillan Education (Schools Council Research Studies).

RECENT DEVELOPMENTS IN SYSTEMIC LINGUISTICS

C. S. Butler
Department of English, University of Nottingham

1. Aims and scope

The purpose of this paper is to review work done within the framework of systemic linguistics, developed largely by Halliday over the last 20 years or so. The evolution of the model in the late '50s and '60s will be dealt with only briefly, since this is already covered in the editorial introductions to a useful recent collection of Halliday's writings up to about 1970 (Kress/Halliday, 1976). We shall be concerned principally with the development of Halliday's thinking in the '70s, and with recent proposals by others working within a systemic framework.

2. The background: systemic linguistics up to 1970

Halliday's work can be traced directly back to that of Firth (see e.g. Firth, 1951, 1957 *a*, *b*) and via Firth, to Malinowski (1923, 1935). Two Malinowskian concepts have most influenced Halliday's thinking: that of 'meaning as function in context', and the view of language as performing a number of functions related to the culture in which it operates. Malinowski's concern was with meaning as the function of the largest linguistic items (i.e. texts) in social contexts: Firth's major contribution was to suggest that the same principle might be applied to smaller linguistic units, if the notion of context was extended to cover the linguistic context as well as the context of situation. The key concept here, which was later to become the corner-stone of Halliday's model, was that of the system. A system, for Firth, was simply a set of choices available in a particular context, this context being definable in two ways. The paradigmatic context for a particular 'term' in a system consists of the other choices with which that term contrasts; the system itself, however, operates at a particular point in the syntagmatic structure of linguistic items. A further type of context, which is not developed fully by Firth but plays an important part in Halliday's model, is the place of a particular system in relation to other systems of the language.

Firth's work, insightful though it may have been in many respects, suffered from a lack of explicitness, especially in the formulation of the relationships between the contexts of units at different levels of description. Halliday's work has provided a unified model within which Firth's insights, often somewhat modified, are captured in a systematic manner. The earliest exposition of the theory (Halliday, 1956/1976)[1] takes the categories of 'unit', 'element' and 'class' as theoretical primes. Units are segments of language, of varying sizes, about which descriptive statements are to be made (e.g. sentence, clause); elements are components which occupy structural places within units; classes are exhaustive lists of forms which can operate as particular elements at given places in the structure of the unit next above (e.g. the class 'verbal group' brings together all forms which can operate at the V element of clause structure). The term 'system' does occur, but is used only to describe classes, and is not a fundamental category of the theory at this stage.

The paper 'Categories of the theory of grammar' (Halliday, 1961/1976) provides a fuller and more coherent account of the theory, in which the term 'element' is secondary to that of 'structure', and 'system' also becomes a primary category, along with unit and class. Structures are set up to account for similarities between units, and themselves consist of an ordered arrangement of places, filled by 'elements of structure'. The clause, for example, consists of ordered places filled by four possible structural elements, labelled Subject, Predicator, Complement and Adjunct. Since 'system' is now the term used for a list of choices available at a particular element of structure, 'class' can be redefined as a grouping of units which share potentiality of occurrence at a particular element in the structure of the next largest unit. The four primary categories of system, structure, unit and class are related by the three scales of rank, delicacy and exponence. Rank refers to the hierarchical ordering of units at a particular level (e.g. sentence, clause, group, word and morpheme for the grammatical level of English and many other languages); delicacy refers to the degree of detail to which a description is pursued (e.g. the recognition of secondary and tertiary structuring within primary elements of structure); exponence refers to the representation of one abstract category by another (e.g. of elements of structure by classes of unit), and ultimately by concrete exponents (i.e. actual formal items). A condensed and more readable account of the early '60s theory can be found in Halliday, McIntosh & Strevens (1964).

In Halliday's work from 1961 to 1966, system emerges as the central category of the theory and, concomitantly, there is increasing emphasis on the semantic significance of systemic choice. In the 'Categories' paper, system is treated as being of the same degree of importance as the other three primary categories. Similarly, in Halliday's discussion of 'Class in relation to the axes of chain and choice in language' (Halliday, 1963/1976), system is defined simply as a closed set of options, and is not elevated above the other categories. The paper on '"Deep" grammar' (Halliday, 1966a/1976), however, marks an important turning point in the evolution of the model. Here, Halliday explicitly states that he regards the systemic description of a linguistic item as representing the fundamental, underlying properties of that item, structural properties being ultimately derivable from such a description, by processes of 'realisation' (the term now used to replace the earlier 'exponence'). It is here, too, that the concept of delicacy, previously applied chiefly to the amount of detail in a structural description, is extended to cover the hierarchical ordering of systems in dependency relationships. Systemic description is now seen as representing the 'deep' grammar of linguistic items, while the arrangements of classes in sequence (or 'syntagms') represent surface patterning. In the area of structure, too, this paper shows a shift from a previously relatively surface account to a deeper account, in which structures are interpreted as configurations of 'functions' related to the deep grammar of linguistic items. This notion is, as we shall see, explored further in later papers. A further notable feature of the 1966 article is the recognition that deep grammar is 'semantically significant grammar', representing that part of the grammar which has the most direct relationships with meaning. Also noteworthy here is the influence of Lamb (1964), to whose stratificational model Halliday acknowledges a particular debt.

The emphasis on systemic choice and its semantic significance in the work of the late '60s brings with it increasing attention to the functional basis of the model. Linguistic items are now seen as being multi-layered in their structure, each layer consisting of configurations of 'functional roles' related to some primary functional component of the language system. In various publications at about this time (see especially Halliday, 1968, 1969a, 1970a) Halliday recognises three basic functional components, the ideational, the interpersonal and the textual. The ideational component embodies choices relating to our experience of the world outside and inside us, and can be split into 'experiential' and 'logical' sub-components, the latter dealing with such phenomena as co-ordination, apposition and the like. The interpersonal component is concerned with the intrusion of the speaker into the speech event, by the taking up of roles vis-à-vis the hearer, and the expression of personal attitude. The textual component is concerned with the way in which language makes links with itself and with the situation in which it is used, to form coherent texts with particular patterns of cohesion, information distribution and the like. Halliday's claim that these functions are reflected in the grammar itself, as relatively discrete blocks of related options within the overall systemic description of a language, should probably be regarded merely as an interesting hypothesis in our present state of descriptive knowledge of the world's languages, although added plausibility has been given to the syntactic significance of the components by the suggestion (see e.g. Halliday, 1977a) that they are reflected by different types of grammatical structure (e.g. the logical component by recursive structure). Whatever its theoretical status may turn out to be, however, the notion of functional components remains insightful and stimulating in its attempt to demonstrate a deterministic relationship between the form of language and the functions (ultimately social) which language is designed to serve.

It is within the framework of a functional 'semantic grammar', as outlined above, that most of Halliday's most illuminating descriptive work on English is situated. Particularly important are the descriptions of transitivity and theme (Halliday, 1967a, 1967b, 1968), the study of modal and related meanings and forms under the headings of mood, modality and modulation (Halliday, 1970b/1976), an account of the English verbal group (Halliday, 1966b/1976), and descriptions of intonation which integrate this area of supra-segmental phonology with the grammatical choices realised (Halliday, 1967c, 1970c/1976).

In this necessarily rather sketchy survey of Halliday's work up to 1970, there has not been space to mention any but the most significant publications. For a full list, the reader is referred to the bibliography in the collection of papers mentioned earlier (Kress/Halliday, 1976). Neither have we been able to discuss the (rather few) contributions to systemic theory made by scholars other than Halliday (e.g. Huddleston, 1965, on rank and depth; Hudson, 1967, on constituency in systemic grammars), or the debate between Matthews and Halliday over the concept of rank (Matthews, 1966; Halliday, 1966c; see also Anderson, 1969). Mention should also be made, at this point, of the two-volume introductory text on systemic linguistics by Berry (1975, 1977) which is based largely on Halliday's work up to 1970, although it also makes some original contributions to the theory, notably in the sections on realisation, which develop the ideas put forward in a very condensed form in Halliday (1967d, 1969a).

3. Semantic networks in a social perspective

3.1 Trends in Halliday's post-1970 work

The work of Halliday after 1970 is dominated by two trends: a further increase in the importance, within the model, of semantic choice as such; and a renewed emphasis on the social functioning of language. One product of this combination of factors is Halliday's interest in the acquisition of 'meaning potential' by the child, viewed in relation to the socialisation of the child rather than from the more usual psycholinguistic angle. In what follows, we shall first discuss briefly Halliday's views on language acquisition and its functional basis. We shall then go on to look at the functional organisation of the adult linguistic system, and its relation to the child's model of language. Finally, we shall outline Halliday's proposals for the specification of the 'meaning potential' of the adult language.

3.2 Language acquisition as 'learning how to mean'

Halliday's functional view of language acquisition is encapsulated in the following quotation from his article on 'The functional basis of language' (Halliday, 1973 *a*/1973 *b*: 24):[2] 'Learning one's mother tongue is learning the uses of language, and the meanings, or rather the meaning potential, associated with them. The structures, the words and the sounds are the realisation of this meaning potential. Learning language is learning how to mean.'

Halliday's studies of child language are thus strongly bound up with the functional explanation of the particular forms taken by language.

In 'Relevant models of language' (Halliday, 1969 *b*/1973 *b*) Halliday puts forward seven types of model which, he proposes, the child internalises as a result of his own experience. These are the instrumental ('I want') function, the regulatory ('do as I tell you') function, the interactional ('me and you') function, the personal ('here I come') function, the heuristic ('tell me why') function, the imaginative ('let's pretend') function and the representational ('I've got something to tell you') function. Halliday hypothesises that the utterances of the young child are monofunctional, each serving just one of the functions just listed. This, as we shall see, contrasts strongly with the model of the adult language proposed by Halliday.

The meaning potential associated with three of the seven functions (instrumental, regulatory and interactional) in the language of one 19-month-old is discussed briefly in 'The functional basis of language' (Halliday, 1973 *a*/1973 *b*: 27–34). Halliday shows how this meaning potential can be represented in the form of a network of options, and how each such option is realised by some structural element. The meaning potentials and structural realisations at various stages in the child's linguistic development are discussed in much greater detail in Halliday's book *Learning how to mean* (Halliday, 1975 *a*), which has been hailed by some as his most important work to date.

3.3 The functional organisation of the adult linguistic system

Having proposed that each utterance in the language of the young child fulfils just one of seven key functions, Halliday goes on to ask what there might be in the adult language which corresponds to these functions. The functions of the adult language, unlike those of the child, cannot simply be equated with uses. The adult puts language to many more specific and differentiated uses than the child; but underlying these uses, according to Halliday, are a few highly abstract 'macrofunctions' which characterise almost the whole of adult language use, and are reflexes of the social uses to which language is put.

These 'macrofunctions' are the 'functional components' we discussed earlier: ideational, interpersonal and textual. Unlike child utterances, the utterances of the adult language are multifunctional, in that they draw on all three components of the language system at once. Almost whatever is said by the adult will be about something (ideational function), will express the taking up of a role with respect to the hearer in terms of statement, question, command and the like (interpersonal function), and will show cohesive, information-structuring and other such types of pattern (textual function). Halliday sees the change from the child to the adult system as one of 'functional reduction', in which a set of essentially separate functions, equatable with uses of language, is replaced by a more abstract, but simpler, set of functional components.

3.4 The meaning potential of the adult language

In the papers in *Explorations* and in his later work. Halliday is concerned with language as a form of social behaviour. The study of language from this viewpoint is 'in the last resort an account of semantic options deriving from the social structure' (Halliday, 1971*a*/1973*b*: 64). The whole 'behaviour potential' conditioned by the social structure (that is, what someone 'can do') encompasses non-linguistic as well as linguistic behaviour. What interests Halliday is what the speaker 'can do' with language, and this is equated with what the speaker 'can mean', that is with the 'meaning potential' of the language. This meaning potential is represented in the actual forms of language as what the speaker 'can say'. The position is set out clearly in the following quotation from 'Language in a social perspective' (Halliday, 1971*a*/1973*b*: 51):
'The potential of language is a meaning potential. This meaning potential is the linguistic realisation of the behaviour potential; "can mean" is "can do" when translated into language. The meaning potential is in turn realised in the language system as lexico-grammatical potential, which is what the speaker "can say".'

In this model, then, the semantics, or 'meaning potential', is related both 'upwards', to social factors regulating behaviour, and 'downwards', to the syntax and lexis of the language, the relationships involved being realisational in nature.

In order to ensure a sound basis for such a 'sociological semantics', Halliday insists that meaning choices should relate to behavioural options which are interpretable, and are predicted to be important, on the basis of some social theory. As we shall see, the theory on which Halliday bases his discussions is that of Bernstein (see e.g. Bernstein, 1971), concerned largely with child socialisation. Halliday's aim is to provide accounts of meaning potentials available in defined social contexts (such as mother/child interaction) or settings (such as a buying/selling transaction, or a doctor/patient interview) which are chosen because of their significance as predicted by a social theory.

In other words, 'in sociological linguistics the criteria for selecting the areas of study are sociological' (Halliday, 1972a/1973b: 80).

The social input to the semantics is thus a set of specific contexts and settings. The linguistic output, however, is seen in terms of the general grammatical functional component options in transitivity, mood, theme and so on which, as we have seen, are claimed to underlie nearly all uses of language. The task as envisaged by Halliday is, then, to provide meaning potentials for specific (classes of) context and setting, and to specify the lexicogrammatical realisations of the options in meaning potential.

The options in meaning potential, as well as those in lexicogrammatical potential (and indeed the extralinguistic behavioural options realised by the semantic choices, and the phonological contrasts which realise lexicogrammatical choices) are seen in terms of system networks. We are centrally concerned here, then, with two sets of networks, one specifying the (socio)-semantic potentials available to speakers in defined contexts, the other specifying the lexicogrammatical potential common to almost all uses of language. The task is to identify which options in the functional component networks of transitivity, mood, theme and the like are systematic realisations of the sociosemantic options. There will not, Halliday points out, be a one-to-one correspondence between semantic and grammatical options, but this is a general feature of relationships between levels. The relationship between the semantic and grammatical networks is one of 'pre-selection': that is, a particular choice, or combination of choices, in the sociosemantic network automatically predetermines a choice, or set of choices, from the grammatical networks.

The most detailed example of such a sociosemantic network, with pre-selection realisation rules, is to be found in 'Towards a sociological semantics' (Halliday, 1972a/1973b: 74–96). Here, Halliday develops further an area sketched briefly in an earlier paper (Halliday, 1971a/1973b: 58–62), that of the control of a child by its mother, a context of particular importance in Bernstein's social theory. Halliday formulates a meaning potential for threats and warnings in mother/child interaction. For each feature in the sociosemantic network, a lexicogrammatical realisation is provided in terms of options in transitivity, mood, voice, person, aspect, and lexical categories specified as selections from particular sections of Roget's thesaurus. To give an idea of the type of network and realisation statement involved, the parts relating specifically to threats are given below. (Note that the notational convention

$$\left.\begin{array}{c}a\\b\end{array}\right\}\!\!\longrightarrow\!\!\left[\begin{array}{c}c\\d\end{array}\right.$$

means that if *either* a *or* b is chosen, then a choice must be made between c and d.)

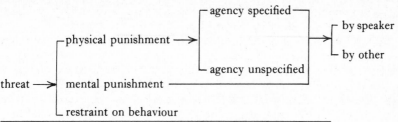

Term in sociosemantics	Lexicogrammatical realisation
Physical punishment	Clause: action: voluntary (*do* type); effective (2-participant): goal= *you*; future tense; positive; verb from Roget §972 (or 972, 276)[3]
Agency specified	Voice: active
Agency unspecified	Voice: passive
By speaker	Actor/Attribuend = *I*
By other	Actor/Attribuend = *Daddy* etc.
Mental punishment	Clause: relational: attributive: Attribute = adj. from Roget §900
Restraint on behaviour	Clause: action: modulation: necessity; Actor = *you*

Further examples of meaning potentials for regulative contexts can be found in the work of Geoffrey Turner (1973).

In two further papers (Halliday, 1972 *b*/1978, 1975 *b*/1978), extracts from which are most readily available in the recent book *Language as social semiotic* (Halliday, 1978),[4] Halliday expands on the notion of a 'sociological semantics' developed in the *Explorations* papers, and sets it within the framework of an overall sociolinguistic theory. This theory is based on 'an interpretation of the social system as a *social semiotic*: a system of meanings that constitutes the "reality" of the culture' (Halliday, 1975 *b*/1978: 123).

The basic elements in Halliday's sketch of a sociolinguistic theory are: the linguistic system, text, situation, register, code (in Bernstein's sense) and the social structure.

The linguistic system is seen as tristratal, with levels of semantics, lexicogrammar and phonology, related realisationally, as in earlier accounts. There is, however, something of a shift from the position taken in 'Towards a sociological semantics', in that the functional components (now called 'metafunctions') are now components of the *semantic* stratum, being seen as 'modes of meaning that are present in every use of language in every social context' (Halliday, 1975 *b*/1978: 112). These semantic components are,

45

however, said to be 'reflected in the lexicogrammatical system in the form of discrete networks of options'. Reading this account (and, indeed, the earlier *Explorations* accounts) of the functional components, one cannot help noticing a certain degree of ambivalence about the relationship between the components and the levels of the model. In the 1975 account, Halliday explicitly states that the functional components belong to the semantic system, and yet it is the lexicogrammar which is labelled in functional terms.

Text, in Halliday's sociolinguistic model, is viewed as the actualisation of choices made from the range of meaning potential specifiable at the semantic level for particular types of situation.

The situation itself is seen as reducible to a number of 'situation types', each of which is 'a constellation of meanings deriving from the semiotic system that constitutes the culture' (Halliday, 1975b/1978: 109). Situation types, or rather the semiotic structures which constitute them, can be characterised in terms of the three dimensions of 'field' (the field of social activity, including the subject-matter), 'tenor' (the role relationships between participants) and 'mode' (the channel of communication, including the medium). These dimensions derive from earlier work by Halliday and others on the classification of language varieties (see § 7).

Register is seen as that range of meaning potential which is available within a particular social context, as defined by certain configurations of field, tenor and mode parameters. Here, as in 'Towards a sociological semantics', Halliday envisages that semantic descriptions should take the form, not of a general description of the language as a whole, but of 'a set of context-specific semantic descriptions, each one characterising the meaning potential that is typically associated with a given situation type. In other words a semantic description is the description of a register' (Halliday, 1975b/1978: 114). Halliday goes on to make interesting, and testable, hypotheses concerning the relationship between situational parameters and the parts of the meaning potential most likely to be activated by them. He suggests that ideational systems are largely activated by field, interpersonal systems by tenor, and textual systems by mode.

Codes are a kind of filter through which the activation of meaning potential by situation types operates. Bernstein's elaborated and restricted codes would be examples here, acting to regulate the availability of parts of the meaning potential.

Finally, the social structure is the source of situation types, of critical socialising contexts such as the family, of hierarchical social class systems, and of the codes which regulate access to the meaning potential.

In concluding this survey of Halliday's views on the meaning potential of the adult language, we should note that in a recent paper (Halliday, 1977b/1978), he appears to have moved away from the sociosemantic model to some extent. The activation of particular components of the meaning potential by situational parameters is discussed, and the functional components are still seen as belonging to the semantic level. In this account, however, the system networks of transitivity mood, theme, and so on, seem to be seen as constituting the semantic stratum, rather than as 'reflections' of the semantic organisation. This would indeed seem to be the most reasonable viewpoint: however, we are left in considerable doubt as to what the lexicogrammatical networks would now look like.

4. Fawcett's 'systemic functional generative grammar'

Fawcett (1975 a), while recognising the value of work at what Halliday regards as the sociosemantic level, gives detailed reasons for the view that sociosemantic networks are not a level of language, the most important of which is that, on Halliday's own admission (see Halliday, 1971 a/1973 b: 62, 1972 a/1973 b: 92), such networks can cover only a relatively small part of the adult language, since they are to be set up only for social contexts predicted as important by a particular social theory. Some of these points are answered in Butler (in preparation), where it is suggested that they rest, in part, on a particular view of the aims of a grammar which is more restricted than that adopted by Halliday, and that it might turn out that the most serious drawback, namely the limited scope of the model, could be remedied if a meaning potential were drawn up for the language as a whole, but with statements giving the overall probabilities of particular choices, and particular forms of realisation, in different classes of social context.

Fawcett's own 'systemic functional generative' model (see especially Fawcett, 1973 a, b, 1975 a, c, and forthcoming) has much in common with Halliday's latest position, although it differs somewhat in orientation, being 'set within the familiar Chomskyan framework of regarding linguistics as in principle a branch of cognitive psychology' (Fawcett, 1973 a: 1), and related to recent work in Artificial Intelligence (see e.g. Winograd, 1972). This, Fawcett makes clear, does not represent a rejection of Halliday's sociological preoccupations, but is rather an attempt to reconcile sociological and psychological orientations. Thus Fawcett's overall model includes not only a model of the language system itself, but also other codes, affective states, our 'knowledge of the universe' (including knowledge about social relations and contexts, and the addressee's current state of information), and a 'problem solver', whose job it is to decide on appropriate strategies of communication, calling on other components of the model.

The linguistic component of Fawcett's model (see Fawcett, 1975 a: 26) conforms in part to the traditional three-level model having semantics, form (syntax and 'items') and (micro)phonology. From the semantic viewpoint, however, intonation ('macrophonology') is parallel to form, since, like form, intonation can realise meanings directly. The semantic level consists of the functional component networks, so that in this respect Fawcett's views accord with those expressed in Halliday (1977*b*/1978). The number of functional components, however, is expanded, in Fawcett (1973*a*, *b*) to six, since he splits not only the ideational component (into 'experiential' and 'logical', as in Halliday's scheme), but also the interpersonal (into 'interactional' and 'expressive') and the textual (into 'thematic' and 'informational'). More recently, as a result of trying to make the criteria for recognising components more explicit, he has recognised eight: experiential, logical relationships, negativity, interactional, affective, modality, thematic and informational, with networks in all but three (negativity, modality and thematic) contributing to group as well as clause structure (see Fawcett, 1978 and forthcoming).

For Fawcett, semantics is the central level, the generative base from which syntactic structures are ultimately derived. While Halliday sometimes hints (e.g. Halliday, 1972*a*/1973*b*: 100) that a full model of language would have system networks at various levels, with a relationship of 'pre-selection' between them, Fawcett makes the simpler proposal that a systemic generative grammar can operate successfully with a single layer of networks, i.e. in the semantics, without making use of the patterns of contrast at the 'lower' levels (even though they may, if one wishes, be modelled by 'systemic networks').

The semantic options are linked to syntactic structures and to grammatical and lexical 'items' by means of realisation rules, which differ somewhat from those proposed by Halliday (1967*d*, 1969*a*) and developed by Berry, (1975, 1977), and also from those put forward by Hudson (1971). Fawcett uses, as a basis for realisation statements, a 'starting structure' for each syntactic unit, consisting of elements of structure which can occur in that unit, and 'places' at which these elements can appear (see Fawcett 1973*a*: 27–9; 1973*b*: 16–19, and forthcoming). The advantages claimed by Fawcett for this scheme are that it gives recognition to the psychological reality of the level of form (see next section), that only one kind of realisation rule is needed (by contrast with Hudson's three (Hudson, 1971)), and that no rule ordering is required.

Thoroughly reworked versions of Fawcett's most important papers, together with a considerable amount of new material (e.g. on illocutionary force) are included in Fawcett (forthcoming). He has also presented detailed proposals for systemic syntax, which will be reviewed in §5, and has made available a selected bibliography of systemic linguistics (Fawcett, 1976*b*).

5. Systemic syntax

As we have seen, much of Halliday's own work claims to be syntactic: indeed, grammar is said to be 'a purely formal level of coding' (Halliday, 1972*a*/1973*b*: 98). Halliday himself, however, never treats syntax as purely formal since, even when working within a model with a separate semantic or sociosemantic level, he always sees the lexicogrammar as organised in such a way as to reflect its role as servant to the semantics. This viewpoint is brought out clearly in a discussion with Herman Parret (Halliday, 1974/1978: 45), where Halliday claims that a sentence, in its grammatical aspect, 'represents a configuration of roles, or syntactic functions, a configuration which is not arbitrary since it represents very clearly the meaning of the sentence as a set of options in the semantic system'. It is probably fair to say that Halliday's concern with the underlying meanings encoded in grammatical forms has led him to be less interested in those aspects of syntax whose semantic significance is less readily apparent. The same could be said of the model of syntax proposed by Fawcett (1974, 1975 b, 1976 a), where the criteria for proposing syntactic categories are that they would be 'needed to state with the greatest economy the realisation rules that express options in the semantics' (Fawcett, 1974: 4).

Fawcett's model of syntax, which is based on extensive textual analysis and is intended as an 'applicable' model, relates back to Halliday's 'Categories' (Halliday, 1961). The terms 'unit' and 'element of structure' retain similar roles to those played in Halliday's model. A 'class', however, is defined not in terms of the operation of its members at a structural element in the next higher unit, but in terms of their own structural 'componence' (i.e. 'class' for Fawcett corresponds to 'type' as discussed in Halliday (1963)).[5] In this way, Fawcett is able to avoid the difficulty, inherent in Halliday's approach, of having to recognise a given stretch of language as belonging to two or more different classes of unit if it can operate at more than one structural element in the next higher unit. By defining class on purely internal criteria, Fawcett is able to show what he believes to be one of the most elegant features of language, namely that a given element of structure can typically be filled by a range of classes of unit.

The rank scale in Fawcett's model is very much reduced in extent, only three ranks of unit being recognised: clause, group and a new unit, the 'cluster', set up to account for (among other things) the structure of genitival constructions. Words and 'grammatical' morphemes are regarded, not as syntactic units at all, but as 'items'. The scale of delicacy is seen in much the same way as in Halliday, but is not treated as a primary part of the theory. The scale of exponence is, however, developed in a more detailed way by Fawcett, who breaks it down into three parts: a unit is composed of elements of structure ('componence'), each of which, in a given syntactic structure, is filled by a particular class of unit ('filling'), and this process operates cyclically until the elements are eventually represented by particular formal items ('exponence' proper).

A very different view of systemic syntax from those put forward by Halliday and Fawcett is seen in the work of Hudson (see especially Hudson, 1971, 1974, 1976). Hudson argues strongly for an autonomous treatment of syntax, believing that 'it is only if you start from the assumption that syntax and semantics are separate that you can really find out how closely they are related, and be impressed by the many points at which they are in one–one relationship' (Hudson, 1976: 7). Hudson, more than other systemicists, has confronted systemic linguistics with the kinds of problem in which transformational generative linguists would be interested, attempting to show that in a variety of syntactic areas systemic grammar can cope with the same problems as transformational grammar, and often in a more elegant and satisfying manner. The result has been a long-needed emphasis on the generative properties of the model, and on formalisation (see also Martin (forthcoming); McCord (1975)). In the course of evolution of Hudson's thinking, however, his approach has become more and more unlike Halliday's, to the extent that the latest version, Hudson's 'daughter dependency theory', might well be regarded as a separate model, though with clear links to early systemic theory.

Hudson's conception of system goes back to the early Hallidayan approach (Halliday, 1961/1976), terms in systems being seen simply as classes and sub-classes of linguistic item. Hudson, however, abandons the Firthian 'polysystemic' approach, in which systems showing paradigmatic contrasts are formulated for particular environments in the syntagmatic structure. Instead, Hudson (1971: 44) treats the environments themselves as being in paradigmatic relationship. This has important consequences for the shape of the grammar: the scale of rank is no longer an important component of the theory, the various syntactic units simply forming the least delicate classes of 'syntactic item'; and the distinction between 'features' (e.g. singular/plural) and 'category labels' (e.g. NP, clause) is thus removed, both types appearing as class labels in system networks. For Hudson, then, there is just one super-network of syntactic options, and this contrasts with a Hallidayan grammar, in which each unit (and sometimes class of unit) acts as the 'point of origin' for a set of networks.

Syntagmatic relations of constituency and sequence are shown by structural tree diagrams in all versions of Hudson's model. Dependency relations between syntactic items, however, are treated rather differently in successive versions. In Hudson's detailed grammar of English complex sentences (Hudson, 1971), dependency relations (e.g. in subject–verb concord, or the *have*+ *-en* relationship in perfective forms) are left implicit, being deducible from the functional labels attached to linguistic items. These function labels (e.g. SUBJECT, PROCESS, MOOD-FOCUS), showing the way in which an item is being used in a sentence, rather than its internal structural properties, are proliferated in the 1971 model to an extent which threatens to make the grammar too powerful. In Hudson's later account of 'systemic generative grammar' (Hudson, 1974), this defect is remedied by the abolition of explicit function labels, the function of an item now being deduced from its configuration of features.

The latest version of Hudson's grammar (Hudson, 1976) treats dependency relations as central to the theory. Two types of dependency are proposed:

'daughter dependency' relations between mothers (wholes) and daughters (parts which are constituents of the wholes); and 'sister-dependency' relations between parts of the same whole (e.g. between verb and object NP in a transitive clause). Structural tree diagrams showing these two kinds of dependency succeed in incorporating both 'deep' and 'surface' information into a single representation.

The generative apparatus of a daughter-dependency grammar consists of two basic parts: the system network (or 'classification rules'), and a set of structure-building rules of several types. These two components operate cyclically: in the generation of structure for a given item (say, a clause) features are selected for that item from the network, and structure building rules then operate on these features to build up features for each constituent or 'daughter' of the item. The cycle is then repeated for each daughter, and the process continues until no more rules can be applied. A lexical matching procedure then gives the final lexicalised syntactic structure.

6. Discourse analysis and the systemic model

The systemic model has also been a strong influence on certain recent attempts to formulate a model of discourse interaction. In their work on teacher/pupil talk in the classroom, Sinclair & Coulthard (1975) set up a model of the discourse level based on the early 'scale and category' approach. This new level has its own rank scale, with the units 'act', 'move', 'exchange', 'transaction' and 'interaction' (or for the classroom, 'lesson'). Classes of the various units (e.g. 'answering move', 'teaching exchange') show a range of structures defined in terms of structural elements occupying places in the syntagm. Each such element can be realised by a class, or classes, of the unit next below on the rank scale. For example, the 'head' element of an answering move can be realised by an act belonging to one of the classes labelled 'reply', 'react', 'acknowledge'. Recent work in this area is summarised in an earlier review in the present series (Coulthard, 1975).

7. Applications of systemic theory

This review has concentrated on the evolution of systemic theory (or, perhaps rather more accurately, systemic theories); it would not, however, be complete without a mention of applications of systemic linguistics, mainly to the description of English, and in particular to a range of varieties or styles of the language. Proponents of systemic theory have themselves paid more attention to descriptive and textual matters than have most grammarians in the transformational generative tradition, and there is a very real sense in which systemic linguistics, especially in its more heavily semanticised versions, with their emphasis on function, is better equipped than most other models to deal with such problems.

Among descriptions of English grammar and semantics which are based on, or strongly influenced by, the systemic model, particular mention should be made of Leech's (1969) account of the semantics of English, the grammar of spoken English by Sinclair (1972), the grammars by Scott, Bowley, Brockett, Brown & Goddard (1968) and by Muir (1972), Halliday & Hasan's (1976) description of cohesion in English, and Halliday's new book on the meaning of modern English (Halliday, forthcoming). The introduction to systemic linguistics by Berry (1975, 1977) also contains valuable descriptions of English structures and systems. Recently, systemic models have also been applied to the description of non-European languages (see e.g. Owens (1977) for an account of Nubi drawing on daughter dependency theory, and El-Rabbat (1978) for a description of transitivity phenomena in Egyptian Colloquial Arabic).

Work on language variety has been particularly dominated by the Hallidayan approach. In addition to Halliday's own contributions to this area (Halliday *et al.*, 1964; Halliday, 1975*b*/1978, and at various points in many other publications), we should mention the work of Gregory and his colleagues (Spencer & Gregory, 1964; Gregory, 1967; Gregory & Carroll, 1978). Within the specific area of literary varieties of English, Halliday's contributions have again been considerable (see Halliday, 1962, 1964, 1971*b*/1973*b*), and the work of Sinclair is also noteworthy (Sinclair, 1966, 1968).

Finally, we should mention the fascinating work of Winograd (1972), which takes early systemic theory as the basis for formulation of a computer model of communication.

8. Concluding remarks

This short review has certainly failed to do justice to the wide range of interest revealed in the writings of Halliday and others in what has been called the 'Neo-Firthian' tradition. (For a detailed critical account of the contribution of this tradition to general linguistics the reader is referred to Monaghan (forthcoming).) In limiting ourselves to the consideration of developments within the systemic model itself, we have excluded discussion of Halliday's insightful views on language in education, and on many other aspects of language as a social phenomenon. Fortunately, these areas are well represented in his most recent publication (Halliday, 1978).

It is almost certainly within the perspective of language as social semiotic that we can expect Halliday's future contributions to lie. We may also confidently predict exciting developments in the work of Hudson and others interested in purely intralinguistic studies within a modified systemic framework. These two approaches, which Halliday has dubbed the 'inter-organism' and 'intra-organism' viewpoints, will no doubt continue to provide complementary information leading to a deeper understanding both of the mechanisms of the language system itself and of the functioning of that system within the social environment of man.

The author wishes to thank colleagues and friends, especially Margaret Berry and Robin Fawcett, for valuable comments and discussion.

[1] References given in the form (Halliday 19—/1976) are to the Kress/Halliday book *Halliday: System and function in language.*
[2] References given in the form (Halliday, 19—/1973 b) are to articles reprinted (and most readily available) in the book *Explorations in the functions of language* (Halliday, 1973 b – see bibliography). All page references to such articles are to *Explorations* rather than to the original article.
[3] The section numbers appear to be in error here, the relevant sections actually being 963, 279.
[4] Page references are given to the 1978 book, rather than to the original articles. It should be emphasised that this book is largely a collection of extracts rather than complete papers.
[5] This discussion is not included in the excerpt from this paper reprinted in Kress/Halliday, 1976.

April 1979

Addendum, December 1981

Since this review was written there have been important additions to the literature linking systemic linguistics to discourse analysis and artificial intelligence:

Berry, M. (1981). Systemic linguistics and discourse analysis: a multi-layered approach to exchange structure. In Coulthard & Montgomery (eds.), 120–45.
Berry, M. (forthcoming). *Layers of exchange structure.* Discourse Analysis Monographs, No. 7, University of Birmingham, English Language Research.
Coulthard, R. M. & Brazil, D. C. (1979). *Exchange structure.* Discourse Analysis Monographs, No. 5, University of Birmingham, English Language Research.
Coulthard, M. & Montgomery, M. (eds.) (1981). *Studies in discourse analysis.* London, Boston & Henley: Routledge & Kegan Paul.
Davey, A. (1978). *Discourse production.* Edinburgh: Edinburgh University Press.

References

Anderson, J. (1969). A note on 'rank' and 'delicacy'. *Journal of Linguistics,* **5**, 1, 129–35.
Bernstein, B. (1971). *Class, codes and control, Vol. 1: Theoretical studies towards a sociology of language.* London: Routledge & Kegan Paul.
Berry, M. (1975). *An introduction to systemic linguistics, Vol. 1: Structures and systems.* London: Batsford.
Berry, M. (1977). *An introduction to systemic linguistics, Vol. 2: Levels and links.* London: Batsford.
Butler, C. S. (1981). The directive function of the English modals. Ph.D. thesis, University of Nottingham.

Coulthard, R. M. (1975). Discourse analysis in English – a short review of the literature. *Language Teaching and Linguistics: Abstracts*, **8**, 2, 73–89.

El-Rabbat, A. H. (1978). The major clause types of Egyptial Colloquial Arabic – a participant-process approach. Ph.D. thesis, University of London.

Fawcett, R. P. (1973 a). Systemic functional grammar in a cognitive model of language. University College London, mimeo. (Available from CIU/ELLD, British Council.)

Fawcett, R. P. (1973 b). Generating a sentence in systemic functional grammar. University College London, mimeo. (Available from CIU/ELLD, British Council.) Revised version to appear in M. A. K. Halliday and J. R. Martin (eds.), *Readings in systemic linguistics 1956–1974.*

Fawcett, R. P. (1974). Some proposals for systemic syntax: Part 1. *MALS Journal*, **1**, 2, 1–15.

Fawcett, R. P. (1975 a). Summary of 'Some issues concerning levels in systemic models of language' (paper read to Nottingham Linguistic Circle, Dec. 1973). *Nottingham Linguistic Circular*, **4**, 1, 24–37.

Fawcett, R. P. (1975 b). Some proposals for systemic syntax: Part 2. *MALS Journal*, **2**, 1, 43–68.

Fawcett, R. P. (1975 c). System networks, codes, and knowledge of the universe: a cognitive perspective on the relationship between language and culture. Paper presented to Burg Wartenstein Symposium No. 66. Semiotics of Culture and Language. Revised version to appear in M. A. K. Halliday, S. M. Lamb and A. Makkai (eds.), *The semiotics of culture and language.* SUNY, Buffalo: The Press at Twin Willows.

Fawcett, R. P. (1976 a). Some proposals for systemic syntax: Part 3. *MALS Journal*, **2**, 2, 35–68.

Fawcett, R. P. (1976 b). *A selected systemic bibliography.* Available through ETIC Archives.

Fawcett, R. P. (1978). How many functional components in a systemic functional grammar? Paper read to the meeting of the Linguistics Association of Great Britain. Sheffield, September 1978.

Fawcett, R. P. (1980). *Cognitive linguistics and social interaction: towards an integrated model of a systemic functional grammar and the other components of a communicating mind.* Heidelberg & Exeter: Julius Groos Verlag & Exeter University.

Firth, J. R. (1951). General linguistics and descriptive grammar. *Transactions of the Philological Society*, 1951, 69–87.

Firth, J. R. (1957 a). *Papers in Linguistics, 1934–1951.* London: Oxford University Press.

Firth, J. R. (1957 b). A synopsis of linguistic theory. *Studies in Linguistic Analysis.* Oxford: Blackwell.

Gregory, M. (1967). Aspects of varieties differentiation. *Journal of Linguistics*, **3**, 177–98.

Gregory, M. & Carroll, S. (1978). *Language and situation – language varieties and their social contexts.* London: Routledge & Kegan Paul.

Halliday, M. A. K. (1956/1976). Grammatical categories in Modern Chinese. *Transactions of the Philological Society 1956*, 177–224.

Halliday, M. A. K. (1961/1976). Categories of the theory of grammar, *Word*, **17**, 3, 241–92.

Halliday, M. A. K. (1962). The linguistic study of literary texts. In H. Lunt (ed.), *Proceedings of the Ninth International Congress of Linguists.* The Hague: Mouton. Reprinted in S. Chatman and S. R. Levin (eds.), *Essays on the language of literature.* Boston: Houghton Mifflin, 1967, 217–23.

Halliday, M. A. K. (1963/1976). Class in relation to the axes of chain and choice in language. *Linguistics*, **2**, 5–15.

Halliday, M. A. K. (1964). Descriptive linguistics in literary studies. In A. Duthie (ed.),

English studies today: third series. Edinburgh: Edinburgh University Press. Reprinted in D. C. Freeman (ed.), *Linguistics and literary style.* New York: Holt, Rinehart & Winston, 1970.

Halliday, M. A. K., McIntosh, A. & Strevens, P. D. (1964). *The linguistic sciences and language teaching.* London: Longman.

Halliday, M. A. K. (1966a/1976). Some notes on 'deep' grammar. *Journal of Linguistics,* **2**, 1, 56–67.

Halliday, M. A. K. (1966b/1976). The English verbal group. (Nuffield Programme Work Paper, published for the first time in Kress/Halliday, 1976.)

Halliday, M. A. K. (1966c). The concept of rank: a reply. *Journal of Linguistics,* **2**, 1, 110–18.

Halliday, M. A. K. (1967a). Notes on transitivity and theme in English: Part 1. *Journal of Linguistics,* **3**, 1, 37–81.

Halliday, M. A. K. (1967b). Notes on transitivity and theme in English: Part 2. *Journal of Linguistics,* **3**, 2, 199–244.

Halliday, M. A. K. (1967c). *Intonation and grammar in British English.* The Hague: Mouton (Janua Linguarum Series Practica 48).

Halliday, M. A. K. (1967d). Talk given to Nottingham Linguistic Circle, May, 1967.

Halliday, M. A. K. (1968). Notes on transitivity and theme: Part 3. *Journal of Linguistics,* **4**, 2, 179–215.

Halliday, M. A. K. (1969a). Options and functions in the English clause. *Brno Studies in English,* **8**, 81–8. Reprinted in F. W. Householder (ed.), *Syntactic theory 1.* Harmondsworth: Penguin, 1972, pp. 248–57.

Halliday, M. A. K. (1969b/1973b). Relevant models of language. *Educational Review,* **22**, 1, 26–37.

Halliday, M. A. K. (1970a). Language structure and language function, in J. Lyons (ed.), *New horizons in linguistics.* Harmondsworth: Penguin, 140–65.

Halliday, M. A. K. (1970b/1976). Functional diversity in language, as seen from a consideration of modality and mood in English. *Foundations of Language,* **6**, 3, 140–65.

Halliday, M. A. K. (1970c/1976). *A course in spoken English: intonation.* London: Oxford University Press.

Halliday, M. A. K. (1971a/1973b). Language in a social perspective. *Educational Review,* **23**, 3, 165–88.

Halliday, M. A. K. (1971b/1973b). Linguistic function and literary style: an inquiry into the language of William Golding's *The Inheritors.* In. S. Chatman (ed.), *Literary style: a symposium.* London and New York: Oxford University Press, 330–65.

Halliday, M. A. K. (1972a/1973b). Towards a sociological semantics. *Working papers and prepublications* (series C, no. 14). Centro Internazionale di Semiotica e di Linguistica, Università di Urbino.

Halliday, M. A. K. (1972b/1978). Sociological aspects of language change. In L. Heilmann (ed.), *Proceedings of the 11th International Congress of Linguists.* Bologna: Il Mulino. Vol. **2**, 853–79.

Halliday, M. A. K. (1973a/1973b). The functional basis of language. In B. Bernstein (ed.), *Class, codes and control. Vol. 2: Applied studies towards a sociology of language.* London: Routledge & Kegan Paul, 343–66.

Halliday, M. A. K. (1973b). *Explorations in the functions of language.* London: Edward Arnold.

Halliday, M. A. K. (1974/1978). Discussion with Herman Parret. In H. Parret, *Discussing language.* The Hague: Mouton.

Halliday, M. A. K. (1975a). *Learning how to mean.* London: Edward Arnold.

C. S. Butler: Systemic linguistics

Halliday, M. A. K. (1975 b/1978). Language as social semiotic. In A. Makkai and V. B. Makkai (eds.), *The first LACUS forum*. Columbia, S. Carolina: Hornbeam Press, 17–46.

Halliday, M. A. K. & Hasan, R. (1976). *Cohesion in English*. London: Longman.

Halliday, M. A. K. (1977 a). Types of linguistic structure, and their functional origins. Mimeo.

Halliday, M. A. K. (1977 b/1978). Text as semantic choice in social contexts. In T. A. van Dijk and J. S. Petöfi (eds.), *Grammars and descriptions*. Berlin: de Gruyter, 176–225.

Halliday, M. A. K. (1978). *Language as social semiotic: the social interpretation of language and meaning*. London: Edward Arnold.

Halliday, M. A. K. (forthcoming). *The meaning of modern English*. London: Oxford University Press.

Halliday, M. A. K. & Fawcett, R. P. (eds.) (forthcoming). *Current papers in systemic linguistics*.

Huddleston, R. D. (1965). Rank and depth. *Language*, **41**, 574–86.

Hudson, R. A. (1967). Constituency in a systemic description of the English clause. *Lingua*, **18**, 225–50.

Hudson, R. A. (1971). *English complex sentences: an introduction to systemic grammar*. Amsterdam: North Holland.

Hudson, R. A. (1974). Systemic generative grammar. *Linguistics*, **139**, 5–42.

Hudson, R. A. (1976). *Arguments for a non-transformational grammar*. Chicago and London: University of Chicago Press.

Kress, G./Halliday, M. A. K. (1976). *Halliday: system and function in language*. London: Oxford University Press.

Lamb, S. M. (1964). The sememic approach to structural semantics. *American Anthropologist*, **66**, 57–78.

Leech, G. N. (1969). *Towards a semantic description of English*. London: Longman.

Malinowski, B. (1923). The problem of meaning in primitive languages. In C. K. Ogden and I. A. Richards, *The meaning of meaning*. London: Routledge & Kegan Paul.

Malinowski, B. (1935). *Coral gardens and their magic, Vol. 2*. London: Allen & Unwin. New York: American Book Co.

Martin, J. R. (forthcoming). The meaning of features in systemic linguistics. To appear in M. A. K. Halliday and R. P. Fawcett, *Current papers in systemic theory*.

Matthews, P. H. (1966). The concept of rank in 'neo-Firthian' grammar, *Journal of Linguistics*, **2**, 101–10.

McCord, M. C. (1975). On the form of a systemic grammar. *Journal of Linguistics*, **11**, 2, 195–212.

Monaghan, J. (1979). *The neo-Firthian tradition and its contribution to general linguistics*. Tübingen: Max Niemeyer Verlag.

Muir, J. (1972). *A modern approach to English grammar – an introduction to systemic grammar*. London: Batsford.

Owens, J. (1977). Aspects of Nubi grammar. Ph.D. thesis, University of London.

Sinclair, J. McH. (1966). Taking a poem to pieces. In R. Fowler (ed.), *Essays in style and language*. London: Routledge & Kegan Paul, 68–81.

Sinclair, J. McH. (1968). A technique of stylistic description. *Language and Style*, **1**, 215–42.

Sinclair, J. McH. (1972). *A course in spoken English: grammar*. London: Oxford University Press.

Sinclair, J. McH. & Coulthard, R. M. (1975). *Towards an analysis of discourse – the English used by teachers and pupils*. London: Oxford University Press.

Scott, F. S., Bowley, C. C., Brockett, C. S., Brown, J. G. & Goddard, P. R. (1968). *English grammar – a linguistic study of its classes and structures*. London: Heinemann.

Spencer, J. & Gregory, M. J. (1964). An approach to the study of style. In N. E. Enqvist, J. Spencer and M. J. Gregory, *Linguistics and style*. London: Oxford University Press.

Turner, G. J. (1973). Social class and children's language of control at age five and seven. In B. Bernstein (ed.), *Class, codes and control. Vol. 2: Applied studies towards a sociology of language*. London: Routledge & Kegan Paul, 135–201.

Winograd, T. (1972). *Understanding natural language*. New York and London: Academic Press.

CATEGORIES OF SITUATIONAL CONTEXT FROM THE PERSPECTIVE OF STYLISTICS

Nils Erik Enkvist
Åbo Akademi, Åbo, Finland

Different attitudes to language varieties and context

In recent linguistics there has been a polarity reminiscent of that between the ancient analogists and anomalists. At one pole are the reductionists. They want to study imaginary ideal speakers in imaginary, ideal, homogeneous speech communities and to view language as a code, while deliberately excluding the real world in which communication takes place. At the other extreme are those who insist that no linguistic inquiry can be meaningful unless it comes to terms with the whole complexity, variation, flux and categorial fuzziness of natural languages. But students of language varieties are at once committed to the study of contexts: only contexts can show when each variant is used.

The reductionists have been highly successful in producing tidy fragments of linguistic description, no doubt thanks to their consciously simplified working hypotheses. All the same, we can never describe a natural language completely as long as we go on dissecting it in decontextualised or (purportedly) contextually neutral conditions. One of the assets all of us use when producing and interpreting texts is our knowledge of our fellow men and of the world. A full study of a natural language must therefore be concerned with the contexts in which that language actually occurs.

'Context', however, can be an awkward term. Sometimes it refers merely to the syntagmatic environment of a sound, phoneme, letter, morpheme, word, phrase, clause, sentence, or text unit, within the text itself. But it has often been used in a wider sense to signify the total socio-physical envelope of utterance. In this paper I shall conform to the latter tradition and use 'context' as an abbreviation of 'context of situation', except in the section on Riffaterre's stylistics which operates with intratextual contexts. Those who deplore this usage can console themselves with other terms such as 'situational envelope' or simply 'envelope' (Enkvist, 1973:55); for French, the term *situation de discours* has been suggested to avoid the same ambiguity (Ducrot & Todorov, 1972). There are also several related problems which must be neglected in this paper. Thus the medium and narrative mode may affect the division of labour between text and context. In a face-to-face speech situation, exophoric references and deictics can express information by pointing directly at the situational context; in a decontextualised written report, relevant contextual features must be made explicit through verbal description and thus moved from context into the text. Another problem ignored here concerns the borderline between linguistic, paralinguistic, and contextual features: should tempo, voice colour, loudness, gesture and other paralinguistic features (see e.g. Abercrombie, 1968; Birdwhistell, 1973; Crystal, 1969; Crystal & Quirk, 1964; Laver & Hutcheson, 1972) count as linguistic or as contextual? The present writer's answer would be: count them as linguistic if your linguistics is capable of analysing them as part of a linguistic structure. If not, count them as contextual if you need worry about them at all.

The need for context analysis in linguistics

To remind ourselves of the importance, and indeed ubiquity, of contexts, we need only list a number of things linguists try to do. We shall then see at once how readily situational features enter into such pursuits.

To begin with, grammatical descriptions of natural languages must always be sensitive to historical, regional, social, situational and individual variation. Grammarians cannot avoid explaining the contextual range of variation within the language and the use and function of each language variant (Bailey, 1973, 1974; Sankoff, 1978; Shotter, 1978). Anybody who analyses a corpus of linguistic data must also remember that his texts are anchored in speech situations. Even uncontextualised grammatical examples have a context in being uncontextualised grammatical examples. Then, those who measure acceptability in elicitation experiments know that judgements are never made in a contextual vacuum: they depend on the background and personality of the jurors, on the setting, and on the testing methods. Stylistic judgements are even more firmly tied to contexts because stylistic appropriateness is the same as contextual acceptability. In semantics it has long been a truism that meanings are affected by both syntagmatic and situational context. Utterances are apt to change or lose their meaning when torn out of their envelopes, and the disambiguation of ambiguous sentences is based on contextual cues. The illocutionary and perlocutionary force of an utterance also depend on context: to say "I do" will only make somebody married under very specific contextual conditions. Actually, the very interpretability of a text presupposes a context. Texts are interpretable only if we can imagine a possible world in which they might be true, either as such or after possible editing and normalisation. And imagining possible worlds around a text is just another expression for contextualisation. Finally, truth values of sentences containing deictic shifters also depend on contexts. If somebody says, 'Yesterday I saw a lot of elephants here,' the truth of the proposition depends on who says it, when, and where.

All these reasons have conspired to turn the tide and bring in a new wave of interest in contexts, as seen in studies of linguistic variation (e.g. Bailey & Shuy, 1973). Thus many of today's linguists live in an antireductionist climate, even to a point where they have been thought to need warnings against contextual chimaeras (Bickerton, 1973). Actually, it is interesting to see how even confessedly reductionist grammarians have had to admit contexts into their work, though covertly and under various technical labels. Thus performative super-structures brought in contextual features: message sender, receptor, modalities. Concepts such as speech acts, illocutionary and perlocution-ary force, conversational and conventional implicature, presupposition, sincerity conditions, felicity conditions, factivity, distinctions between old and new information, topic and comment, theme and rheme, metephor, irony, and allusion all share one characteristic: they bring certain aspects of context into the analysis and description of sentences and texts. Thus allusions are explicable in terms of a 'vertical context system' (Schaar, 1978). A number of very recent studies in syntax and semantics have also begun more explicitly to recognise contextual categories where they happen to be relevant, usually, however, without worrying about complete theories of context. A more systematic concern with contexts appears in movements such as text linguistics, discourse analysis, and pragmalinguistics. On the applied side, the increasing emphasis on communicative competence has similarly brought in descriptions of speech acts and contexts (Edwards, 1968; Kirstein, 1975; Müller, 1970, 1971). More generally, views of linguistic activity as co-operative interaction have given us new insights into the context-bound motivations of utterances, either in general (Allwood, 1976; Arndt, 1978; Goody, 1978; Grice, 1975), or in specific ethno-methodological frames such as group dynamics or turn-taking in con-versation (e.g. Sacks, Schegloff & Jefferson, 1975; Schegloff & Sacks, 1973; Rasper, Rudigkeit, Schäfer & Wenner, 1978).

Students of style have been particularly interested in contexts (e.g. Enkvist, 1964; Spencer & Gregory, 1964; Gregory, 1967; Gregory & Carroll, 1978). It is easy to see why, for styles have often been defined as those varieties of languages that correlate with situational features. If, however, style is defined thus broadly, many types of language variants come to fit under the umbrella of style. This is true of historical forms, dialects, sociolects, registers (if indeed they differ from styles – see Ure, 1969 and Ure & Ellis, 1977) and idiolects. Such a situation should not worry us because it merely shows that different kinds of language varieties can be used in a stylistic function. For instance, in religion and law, the frozen language of old texts readily turns into a present-day biblical or legal style. In some communities where people use standard language in formal contexts and regional dialect in informal ones, these different sublanguages become styles, functionally speaking. And when different languages are used in different situations within the same speech community, these languages too turn into styles. This explains why it is idle to argue whether a certain variant of a language is a style or something else: it can actually be both. For the same reason, arguments about the place of stylistics in the hierarchy of linguistic subdisciplines readily become barren. The answers tend to reflect our own purpose and point of attack rather than anything inherent in the language itself.

Some historical landmarks in context analysis

With the turning tide, we are once again apt to hail early analysts of contexts as pioneers, instead of dismissing them as people working with concepts too nebulous for stringent formalisation. We might recall in passing that linguists such as Sir Alan Gardiner (Gardiner, 1932: 71 ff.) and Leonard Bloomfield (Bloomfield, 1957: 22 ff.) gave us glimpses of contextualised tableaux of speech acts: Gardiner cited a domestic interlude where one James Hawkins said "Rain!" to his wife May, and Bloomfield produced a behaviourist playlet involving Jack, Jill and an apple. More systematic attention was paid to contexts in Denmark (Hjelmslev, 1961), Czechoslovakia (Beneš & Vachek, 1971; Fried, 1972; Vachek & Dubský, 1966, s.v. *fonction*), and in the Soviet Union (Amonosova, 1968; Kolšanskij, 1969); an overview has been attempted by Rozkovcová (1973). Most prominently, however, contexts came to the fore in the linguistics of Firth in Britain (Firth, 1957; Langendoen, 1968; Mitchell, 1975). Under the inspiration of Philipp Wegener's theory of contexts and of Malinowski, Firth used to emphasise that the only way to understand how language really works is

to establish with certainty that the facts of speech we are studying can be observed or regarded in actual patterns of behaviour. We must take our facts from speech sequences, verbally complete in themselves and operating in contexts of situation which are typical, recurrent, and repeatedly observable. Such contexts of situation should themselves be placed in categories of some sort, sociological and linguistic, within the wider context of culture. (Firth, 1957:35.)

Firth also illustrated the process of contextualisation with a diagram (Firth, 1957:36):

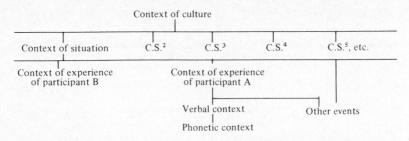

Firth's followers have continued the traditions of their master (Mitchell, 1975). A determination to integrate contexts into linguistic theory and language description also permeates the works of Halliday, whose systematic rigour has made them highly influential (Berry, 1975; Halliday, 1973, 1977, 1978). A rich array of context categories has been developed by Coseriu (1955–56, 1962); the full significance of its environments, *entornos*, can be understood only in the frame of Coseriu's theory of language, into which it is fully integrated. The Romanian linguist Slama-Cazacu has also made good use of context in her writings ever since the early 1960s (Slama-Cazacu, 1961, 1967, 1977). Anthropological linguists and ethnolinguists have always had to reckon with contextual features (for a recent example, see Voegelin & Yamamoto, 1977). These traditions, usually derived from Boas and Sapir, were fused into a comprehensive view of language in relation to human behaviour by Pike (Pike, 1967), and they have been profitably applied by his followers (e.g. Grimes, 1975; Longacre, 1976). Sociolinguists have been preoccupied with contexts too; some of their works will be referred to below.

Context description and classification in studies of style

The context analyst's first embarrassment is richness. There is an infinite number of speech situations and contexts, each of which can be described in terms of an infinite number of contextual features. From among these, the analyst must extract those features which correlate with the stylistically significant choices in the language. For instance, when two people converse it will presumably make no difference to their language whether they wear red or blue ties or black or brown shoes, or whether the conversation takes place in rain or in sunshine. But the language of husband and wife is likely to be different from that of, say, two company directors who meet for the first time. The student of context must therefore learn to distinguish between two classes of contextual features: those that are stylistically significant and those that are not. Stylistically significant context features have the same distribution as style markers in language: they co-occur with a set of stylistically significant features of language. Stylistically non-significant contextual features fail to show such patterns of co-occurrence.

In trying to discover whether a given feature in the context is stylistically significant or not, we can proceed in two ways. Either we start out from a given linguistic form which is recognised as being stylistically significant and then make an inventory of the contexts in which it occurs, finally trying to identify the feature or features which all these contexts have in common. Or we start out from a certain context or range of contexts and make an inventory of the linguistic forms that occur in it. In the latter approach, these forms must then be compared with those that occur in other, contrasting situations: otherwise we cannot know which forms are characteristic of the context. In practice, these approaches supplement each other. The former method enables us to look into the contextual spread of well-defined style markers such as politeness formulae or pronouns of address (e.g. Ahlgren, 1978; Bates & Benigni, 1975; Brown & Gilman, 1960; Ferguson, 1976; Friedrich, 1972; Lambert & Tucker, 1976; Paulston, 1975; Sievert, 1976). The latter method will give us a start in studies of literary styles and in the quest for major style categories in an entire language.

After the stylistically relevant features in the context have been found, they must be described with the aid of some specific theories and models of language. In principle, a student of style should be free to choose whatever descriptive model best suits his purpose, and even to profit from several models. Stylistics, like applied linguistics in general, ought to be an eclectic discipline.

The reason why there is no universal inventory of stylistically relevant context features is simple: in different cultures and in different situations, different contextual features may have stylistic significance. This appears most clearly when we compare distant cultures. Context categories and their stylistic markers may be so alien that they are hard to translate from one culture and language into another. This is true, for instance, if we try to render linguistic etiquette in Japanese or Javanese into English (Geerz, 1968). Hence the only possible policy for students of context is to start from suitably abstract lists of potentially significant categories of contextual features. From among these, the investigator should then pick the ones that prove useful for his particular purpose.

Indeed the very degree of determinism in the relation between text and context can vary. Some contexts determine language to the point of complete predictability. Such 'frozen' language (to use a term from Joos, 1962) occurs in unalterable ceremonial formulae, military commands, traditional prayers, performative language whose efficacy depends on wordings, and so forth. In conventional types of literary contexts such as sonnet-writing, the writer is constrained to choose one among a small set of forms (definable in terms of rhyme schemes, line length and stress pattern). At the other end of the spectrum are the contexts that set linguistic freedom and innovation at a premium. In some kinds of poetry, for instance, linguistic liberties rate above the rules of normal syntax. Thus the range of permissible variation can become a stylistically significant characteristic of the context.

Taxonomies of context features

When getting down to actual context classification, students of style will do wisely in consulting works by sociolinguists. For obvious reasons the relations between stylistics and sociolinguistics have become close. Both study language varieties in context, and are therefore committed to similar methodologies. Whether an investigation claims to be stylistic or sociolinguistic may sometimes be merely a matter of academic expediency: the word 'style' has traditional literary overtones and comes naturally to students in departments of languages and literatures, whereas people in sociology and linguistics prefer to speak of social variation. Thus, though the character of the data may differ, the problems and methods are closely related.

There is today no dearth of sociolinguistic texts dealing with contextually conditioned variation (e.g. Fishman, 1968, 1972; Giglioli, 1972; Gumperz & Hymes, 1972; Hymes, 1964, 1967, 1977; Labov, 1970, 1972; Leodolter, 1975; Marková, 1978; Pride & Holmes, 1972). To cite just one conceptual frame, Fishman, 1972, defines the smallest sociolinguistic unit as the speech, which is part of a larger speech event such as a conversation, prayer or lecture. The first task is to find connection between speech acts and events, and types of language. This is done by consulting people from the speech community concerned. When the connections have been found, they must be correlated with contextual variables. One group of such variables consists of role relationships recognised in that particular community: husband/wife, father/son, clergyman/layman, employer/employee, friend/friend. Some such relationships are more stable than others: the king/subject relation, for instance, is more invariant than that between shopkeeper and customer, because a shopkeeper may also meet customers in roles of equality. The situational context in time and place may similarly affect the situation.

Another of Fishman's useful concepts is the distinction between congruent and incongruent behaviour. Lovers, he says, may meet at a time and place proper for love-making, but may behave incongruently by quarrelling or discussing politics. Incongruent behaviour may lead to reinterpretations of role relationships: quarrelling lovers may relapse into, say, an employer/employee relation. Situations need not be discontinuous: some situational variables can form a scale. By metaphorical switching, Fishman denotes an intentional and conscious change of language without a corresponding change in the social situation. If, for instance, a speaker switches to Cockney in the midst of a situation normally calling for Standard English, he does so for special effect. Metaphorical switching of course involves risks of misinterpretation.

When moving from the micro-level to the macro-level, Fishman introduces another important concept, that of domain. 'There are,' he says, 'classes of events recognised by each speech network or community in which several seemingly different situations are classed as being of the same kind' (Fishman, 1972: 51). Such sets of equivalent situations form a domain.

Fishman summarises his contextual variables with the aid of an acrostic list:

(S) Setting or scene: time and place, psychological setting and cultural definition of the type of scene.
(P) Participants or personnel: addressor-addressee-audience.
(E) Ends: ends and goals in view and in outcome.
(A) Art characteristics: the form and content of what is said.
(K) Key: tone, manner or spirit in which an act is done.
(I) Instrumentalities: channel and code or subcode.
(N) Norms of interaction and interpretation.
(G) Genres: traditional categories of speech acts and events.

This is a heterogeneous list in that some variables are accessible to objective description, whereas others such as 'ends' and 'key' must be based on more subjective judgements.

Fishman wrote about speech events and speech acts; indeed the study of speech acts and of pragmatics has become one of the focal areas of linguistics in the past decade (see e.g. Austin, 1962; Bates, 1976; Bayer, 1977; Cole, 1978; Cole & Morgan, 1975; van Dijk, 1976, 1977b; Holcroft, 1978; Mackey, 1978; Moles & Rohmer, 1977; Sadock, 1974; Searle, 1969, 1976; Stalnaker, 1970; Wunderlich, 1976a, 1976b; bibliography in Verschueren, 1978, 1978–9). There have been some attempts to link context categories, viewed in terms of speech acts, with strategies of cognition and comprehension (e.g. van Dijk, 1977b). Van Dijk has suggested that when interpreting speech acts we first apply to them our store of general semantic information (memory, frames). We then add information coming from immediately preceding events and acts, and make use of global macro-information about the whole previous interaction process. The general social context which is relevant at all stages of interpretation depends on distinctions between private and public and between institutional, formal and informal categories; particular contexts are defined by positions (roles, status), properties (sex, age), relations (dominance, authority), and functions ('father', 'waitress'). One of the most consistent attempts at basing stylistics on a pragma-linguistic basis comes from Barbara Sandig (Sandig, 1970, 1978).

There is no dearth of explicit lists of context features. The following, which includes both an intratextual and an extratextual part, comes from Enkvist (1964):

textual context	extratextual context
linguistic frame	period
phonetic context (voice quality, tempo, etc.)	text type, genre
	speaker/writer
phonemic context	listener/reader
morphemic context (he sings/he singeth)	relationship between speaker/writer and listener/reader in terms of sex,
syntactic context (including sentence length and complexity)	age, familiarity, education, class and status, authority, common stock of
lexical context	experience, etc.
punctuation, capitalization	situation and environment
compositional frame	gesture, physical action
beginning/middle/end of utterance, paragraph, poems, play, etc.	dialect and language
relationships of text to surrounding textual portions	
metre, literary form, typography	

Another influential approach to grouping contextual dimensions is that of Spencer and Gregory (1964), which relates to the linguistic theory of Halliday. Spencer and Gregory first 'place' a text in its historical and dialectical setting. Then each text is analysed in terms of field, mode and tenor. Field relates a text to its subject matter: a love-letter and an article on abdominal surgery differ in field. Mode relates the discourse to its channel and medium. Tenor is the term for the relations between the sender and the receptor of the message, degrees of formality being one of the most important factors affecting tenor. All categories interact: certain fields usually go together with certain tenors. Scientific articles, for instance, are usually dressed in formal style. A more elaborate discussion of these matters is now available in Gregory and Carroll (1978).

Another inventory of dimensions of situational constraint has been presented by Crystal and Davy (1969). In their view, certain linguistic features belong to a common core of language and are stylistically neutral as they can occur in all styles. (This view, by the way, can be contested: frequencies, or rather densities, even of items such as *and* may turn out to be style markers.) The other potentially style-discriminating features are situationally restricted along the following dimensions:

(A) Individuality, Dialect, Time.
(B) Discourse:
   (*a*) Medium: Simple versus Complex (speech, writing, or a combination of speech and writing).
   (*b*) Participation: Simple versus Complex (monologue, dialogue).
(C) Province, Status, Modality, Singularity.

By individuality, Crystal and Davy mean the relatively permanent features of speech and writing habits that appear in the unselfconscious utterances of every individual. Dialect includes both regional and social variation. Time places the text in its chronological frame. Province relates the utterance to variables in occupational and professional activity which are independent of individual characteristics. Status covers variation in the social standing of the participants. Modality is here used to indicate the choice of conventional spoken or written formats for the utterances, such as letter, postcard, note, telegram, memo, lecture, report, essay, monograph, textbook. Singularity refers to personal idiosyncrasies of a more occasional, non-systematic and transitory type.

Crystal and Davy too are careful to add that relations between these variables are of interest. Thus certain combinations of medium, participation and province tend to be linked to certain features of status, and so forth. One of the useful parts of their book is a battery of diagnostic questions helping us to find stylistically relevant features in a text. 'Apart from the message being communicated,' we should ask to begin with, 'what other kinds of information does the utterance give us?' This query can in turn be broken into a set of more specific subquestions:

Does it tell us which specific person used it? (Individuality.)
Does it tell us where in the country he is from? (Regional dialect.)
Does it tell us which social class he belongs to? (Class dialect.)
Does it tell us which period of English he spoke or wrote it, or how old he was? (Time.)
Does it tell us whether he was writing or speaking? (Discourse, Medium.)
Does it tell us whether he was speaking or writing as an end in itself, or as a means to a further end? (Simple versus Complex Discourse Medium.)
Does it tell us whether there was only one participant in the utterance, or whether there was more than one? (Discourse Participation.)

Does it tell us whether the monologue and dialogue are independent, or are to be considered as a part of a wider type of discourse? (Simple versus Complex Discourse Participation.)
Does it tell us which specific occupational activity the user is engaged in? (Province.)
Does it tell us about the social relationship existing between the user and his interlocutors? (Status.)
Does it tell us about the purpose he had in mind when conveying the message? (Modality.)
Does it tell us that the user was being deliberately idiosyncratic? (Singularity.)
Does it tell us none of these things? (Common Core.)
Having specified the number of distinct categories within each of these dimensions, the student may then find out to what extent the same constellation of categories tends to reappear in the language. A variety of language 'will then be seen as a unique configuration of linguistic features...which displays a stable formal–functional correspondence ...' (Crystal & Davy, 1969: 64–83).

To cite yet another example from another linguistic tradition, we might go to Gläser's *Habilitationsschrift* for the University of Leipzig (Gläser, 1969). Her *Situationsforschung* or *Situationik* is a typology of contextual forces that influence the coding and decoding of a text. In an abbreviated translation, her major categories of situational variables are groupable as follows:

(a) the psychological motivation of an utterance (emotional factors, attitudes to conversation partner),
(b) personality factors (age, sex, education, social background),
(c) norms of behaviour (collectively accepted rules of behaviour in institutionalised contexts such as administration, education, the military, law, the press, business, industry, advertising, traffic, the police, etc.),
(d) cultural background (the collective stock of information within the speech community, which can be activated by reference and allusion: for instance, national literature, history, the Bible, classical mythology),
(e) the special pragmatic motivation of the utterance (not in terms of individual psychological motives but in terms of social motive categories such as the forming of opinions, the increase of consumption, teaching people to obey traffic rules, etc.).

Gläser emphasises that these situational variables may affect the choice of linguistic features at all levels of language. She also cites Trojan (Trojan, 1952) to connect intonation patterns with subjective situational features: surprise, joy, disappointment, disgust. Thus there may be links between psychological motivation (which Gläser counts among her situational variables) and the phonetic surface shape of an utterance. This once again brings up the problem of the relation between contextual and paralinguistic features.

It would be easy to go on listing further examples of catalogues or taxonomies of potentially significant contextual features (e.g. van Dijk, 1977*b*; Scherfer, 1976; Taylor, 1975, etc.). Most of these present kaleidoscopic rearrangements of features and feature categories already exemplified in the lists quoted above. And most context taxonomists make clear that it is up to each investigator to pick from them those categories that he needs, to simplify or to elaborate them as indicated. As always in linguistic and social research, the crux of the method is to find the optimal delicacy level – the level where all important distinctions are made and all unimportant ones omitted. As an example of a study where a low delicacy level proved useful we should recall Labov's study of correlations between sociolect and situational context in New York City English. Labov chose to range his styles on one single scale ranging from most spontaneous and casual speech to most deliberate speech, and he distinguished five levels of self-consciousness or formality: casual speech, careful speech, reading, word lists, and minimal pairs (Labov, 1970). In the work of Basil Bernstein and his collaborators, styles range on a scale between two extremes, the elaborated code and the restricted code, which originally claimed to correlate with the social background and stratification of English schoolchildren (Bernstein, 1971–3). Such approaches, isolating small sets of carefully chosen contextual features which correlate with styles, could be termed 'correlational'. The opposite approach, which seeks to isolate culturally significant categories of speech events and communication situations and which was illustrated above through Fishman and others, might be called 'interactional' (Oskaar, 1974).

In a wealth of instances, we know who originally generated the text. There are therefore certain types of studies which expressly connect the speaker/writer, as a part of the context, to his or her text. Two kinds of such studies deserve special mention, apart of course from those discussions of period and genre styles and individual styles which abound in any work on literary history and literary criticism. One deals with women's styles. With the recent wave of interest in woman's social position, we have gained a number of studies on sex differences in language (e.g. Brouwer, Gerritsen & de Haan, 1979; Crosby & Nyquist, 1977; Edelsky, 1979; Lakoff, 1973, 1975; Yaguello, 1978). Another well established genre is the determination of authorship, that is, the attribution of anonymous texts to specific authors through stylostatistical analysis. In addition to their methodological interest, attribution studies have also been important because they show us something of the essence of a style as a set of style markers that make it different from other styles. Some methodologically suggestive examples are Ellegård (1962), Moerk (1970), Mosteller and Wallace (1964) and O'Donnell (1970). Some stylistic attribution studies have been carried out as part of criminal investigations: we can then speak of forensic stylistics (e.g. Johannisson, 1973; Svartvik, 1968).

In the grouping of texts into such categories as correspond to specific contexts it may be useful to verify intuitions through numerical taxonomy or factorial analysis. A suggestive study on vectors of style was published by Carroll (Carroll, 1960); the methods developed by Osgood and his collaborators (Osgood, Suci & Tannenbaum, 1957) are also potentially applicable to the scaling of stylistic responses.

Functional stylistics and context

The term 'functional stylistics' has sometimes been used for approaches that start out from a small set of predetermined social functions of language, and then describe the language used in each function (e.g. Kožina, 1968). An underlying assumption is that the purpose of language is to serve socially definable goals, i.e. functions, which need specific forms of language, i.e. functional styles. Operationally, functions can be defined as sets of socially equivalent contexts. A functional style is marked by that set of linguistic features which co-occurs with a function. To translate a statement by Fleischer, an East German linguist:

The linguistic system does not exist for its own sake. 'Language does not function because it is a system: on the contrary, language is a system in order to function.' This function is extralinguistic and social: language is what makes it possible for human beings to be productive. It serves cognition and communication as well as education and training, the control of behaviour and the development of sensibilities... (Fleischer, 1970: 23, translated by the present writer; the quotation within the quotation comes from the Soviet linguist, Ščerba.)

Understandably, protagonists of such views are apt to discuss styles in terms of a few major functional categories. In *Stylistics*, a textbook for Soviet students of English at college level, Gal'perin (1971: 18–19) thus lists

(1) The belles-lettres style: (*a*) poetry proper, (*b*) emotive prose, (*c*) drama.
(2) The publicistic style: (*a*) speeches (oratory), (*b*) essays, (*c*) articles in journals and newspapers.
(3) The newspaper style: (*a*) newspaper headlines, (*b*) brief news items and communiqués, (*c*) advertisements.

(4) The scientific prose style: (*a*) humanities, (*b*) exact sciences.

(5) The style of official documents: (*a*) commercial, (*b*) diplomatic, (*c*) legal, (*d*) military.

Whether a functionalist presents a smaller or larger number of functional styles, he too will of course be tempted to pose the fundamental question as to what factors actually determine his categories (e.g. Kitaxova & Kitaxov, 1978; Trojanskaja, 1979). And if he proceeds to break down his 'functions' into their constituent features, his list of such features may come to look very much like that of everybody else. Functional stylistics has been a characteristic of the Prague School, one of its pioneers being Havránek. It is therefore appropriate to cite a survey article on Prague views of context (Dubský, 1972: 116–17):

The fundamental stylistic factor in functional stylistics is the concrete purpose of the utterance and this is determined by the conditions in which the act of speech takes place in a concrete area of human activity. We can distinguish four main aspects: the content of the discourse, the situation, the attitude of the speaker to reality, and his relation to the listener.

The different objective styles of standard language are determined by objective factors. The main objective factors can be summarised in three principal groups:

(1) The factors connected with meaning:
   (*a*) the function of communication, which can be communicative (colloquial style), practically professional (style of the official, technical and professional language), theoretically professional (the scientific language), function of mass communications (journalistic style), aesthetically communicative (works of art);
   (*b*) the purpose of the act of speech, which can be an objective statement (the interpretative style) or an appeal (in the journalistic style);
   (*c*) the speaker's attitude to the theme: it can be serious (official style), humorous (the comical nature of the utterance), deprecating (ironical or invective nature of the utterance);
   (*d*) the mode of theme: dynamic (narration) or static (description);
   (*e*) the degree of spontaneity (from the style of entirely spontaneous and that of prepared utterances).

(2) The elements connected with the situation of the utterance:
   (*a*) private or official setting (the style of the private or official utterances);
   (*b*) bilateral (the style of dialogues) or unilateral speech (the style of monologues);
   (*c*) the contact between the author and the addressee (in the colloquial utterance), whether the addressee is present (style of situational utterances) or absent (broadcasting style).

(3) The language substance used: phonic (the style of spoken utterances) or graphic (the style of written or printed utterances).

In trying to set up major functional style categories for a language, of the type of 'publicistic style' and 'newspaper style' and 'scientific style', the question arises to what extent such labels are actually justified by the linguistic hallmarks available in texts. Can a distinction between, say, five major style categories do justice to the endless variety of styles and substyles and to the infinite range of stylistic overlaps, blends and switches? One reply is that what matters is approach, the actual number of styles being of secondary importance (Fleischer, 1970: 24). Another reply cites the need for simplifications in teaching. A third avenue is to build in more variation into the theory, for instance by granting each style a characteristic core but also a variable periphery. The most convincing validation would be empirical: if distributional analysis of the clustering of linguistic features in a stylistically heterogeneous corpus of texts reveals categories corresponding to functional styles, their existence has been supported through empirical testing. An example of such analysis is available in Šajkevič's computer study of a set of English seventeenth-century texts (Šajkevič, 1968).

Nor is there any reason why the definition of language functions could not be carried out at a far more delicate level. To help language teachers to chart objectives, contents, methods and testing techniques, Freihoff and Takala (1974) have provided us with a taxonomy of language functions and communicative tasks. Starting out from the four classic subskills (listening, reading, speaking, writing) and four non-linguistic channels (perceiving, thinking, acting, storing in memory), they classify communication situations into approximately one hundred different types. A monolingual processing of a message may for instance involve reading and storing in memory, or repeating phrase for phrase, or commenting and expanding with the aid of notes, and so on. Creative language functions express the speaker/writer's own thoughts or perceptions and include tasks such as eye-witness reporting. One category of tasks involves physical activity beside linguistic behaviour, as when people carry out certain actions while reading an instruction. Bilingual activities comprise written translation, simultaneous oral interpretation, and so forth. Combinations of language functions in communication can then be expressed in a taxonomic code. The designation 12-P-41e, for instance, indicates a successive (P) translation of a message heard in a foreign language (12) into spoken native language (41) with additional comments by the translator (e).

Trying to avoid situational context: Riffaterre

Among students of stylistic context, Michael Riffaterre stands out for trying to avoid viewing style as deviance from a norm external to the text itself (Riffaterre, 1971). Riffaterre therefore appeals to intratextual context rather than to situation. What constitutes style, he says, is the appearance of units which become stylistically marked because they contrast with other units in their textual environment. In developing his argument, Riffaterre distinguishes between a microcontext comprising a single stylistically marked item or structure and its contrasting environment, and a macrocontext comprising the total sequence of units or structures in the text. The microcontexts are of two kinds. One is based on the reader's general knowledge of semantic plausibilities. Thus Corneille's collocation *obscure clarté* makes us react to the oxymoron even without access to further context. The other kind of microcontext occurs when the stylistically marked item stands out only within its own textual envelope, as in Voltaire's

il était décidé par l'université de Coimbre que le spectacle de quelques personnes brulées *à petit feu, en grande cérémonie*, est un secret infaillible pour empecher le terre de trembler.

À petit feu and *en grande cérémonie* are, as such, perfectly normal and compatible collocations. Their stylistic effect thus does not reside in themselves as such but in their being placed in a certain textual envelope.

Microcontext, then, enables us to study the stylistic markedness of individual linguistic units or structures. Macrocontext is

la partie du message littéraire qui précède le procédé stylistique et qui lui est extérieure (ce sens de *contexte* est le plus proche l'acception courante). (Riffaterre, 1971: 80).

Of macrocontexts there are two types. One follows the pattern *contexte → procédé stylistique → contexte*. Here the text returns to the same contextual pattern that prevailed before the appearance of the contrastive, and therefore stylistically marked, item. The other has the pattern *context → procédé stylistique point de départ d'un nouveau contexte → procédé stylistique*. This latter scheme appears in texts which contain a whole series of stylistically marked items of the same kind: archaisms, for instance. The ensuing saturation makes these items lose their contrastive power and turns them into a new context, which in turn serves as the background for new contrasts. Thus the first type of macrocontext is apparently a characteristic of more homogeneous texts, the second of texts with shifts of style. To the crucial question as to how one is to spot contrasts, polarities and stylistic markedness, Riffaterre answers by appealing to informant responses obtained from an *archilecteur* (in an earlier paper, the term was 'average reader', AR). The archi-reader's responses can be elicited directly, or reconstructed from a set of statements by, for instance, literary critics. They are not based on statistical assessments of collocational or transitional probabilities. Riffaterre does discuss in detail the limitations of his *archilecteur* as a basic criterion in stylistic analysis. But he does not give explicit models explaining how the archi-reader arrives at his responses. In fact one might ask at this point whether the archi-reader does not consciously or unconsciously match the emerging text with his experiences of a network of contextually related texts.

Epilogue

The purpose of this survey has been to show that those who must study or describe the contextual background and spread of varieties of language, such as styles, need no longer despair or start from scratch. A number of principles have been suggested for the description and classification of contexts, and particularly for the extraction of their linguistically relevant features. There are long lists of contextual factors we ought to think of. The problem is that the world offers such an endless variety of situations: we must learn to concentrate on those features that are relevant to our purpose, and to ignore the rest. A knowledge of the cultural and social milieu of the text, together with a good portion of common sense, will best help the prospective context analyst to profit from the principles rehearsed in this paper.

References

Abercrombie, D. (1968). Paralanguage. *British Journal of Disorders of Communication*, **3**, 55–9. Also in Laver & Hutcheson (1972), 64–70.

Ahlgren, P. (1978). *Tilltalsordet ni. Dess semantik och användning i historiskt perspektiv*. Uppsala: Almqvist & Wiksell.

Allwood, J. (1976). *Linguistic communication as action and cooperation. A study in pragmatics*. Gothenburg Monographs in Linguistics 2. Department of Linguistics, University of Gothenburg.

Amonosova, N. N. (1968). *Anglijskaja kontekstologija*. Leningrad.

Arndt, H. (1978). Determinanten sprachlicher Interaktion: Gruppen- und Interaktionstypen. *Die neueren Sprachen*, 77. **27** Neue Folge, 300–25.

Austin, J. L. (1962). *How to do things with words*. Oxford: Clarendon Press.

Bailey, C.-J. N. (1973). *Variation and linguistic theory*. Washington: Center of Applied Linguistics.

Bailey, C.-J. N. (1974). Contributions of the study of variation to the framework of the new linguistics. *Linguistische Berichte*, **29**, 1–10.

Bailey, C.-J. N. & Shuy, R. W. (1973). *New ways of analyzing variation in English*. Washington D.C.: Georgetown University Press.

Bates, E. (1976). *Language and context. The acquisition of pragmatics*. New York, San Francisco & London: Academic Press.

Bates, E. & Benigni, L. (1975). Rules of address in Italy: a sociological survey. *Language in Society*, **4**, 271–88.

Bayer, K. (1977). *Sprechen und Situation*. Tübingen: Niemeyer.

Beneš, E. & Vachek, J. (eds.) (1971). *Stilistik und Soziolinguistik*. Beiträge der Prager Schule zur strukturellen Sprachbetrachtung und Spracherziehung. Munich: List.

Bernstein, B. (1971–3). *Class, codes and control*, I–II. Primary Socialization, Language and Education, IV. London: Routledge & Kegan Paul.

Berry, M. (1975–7). *Introduction to systemic linguistics*, I–II. London: Batsford.

Bickerton, D. (1973). The chimaera of context. *University of Hawaii Working Papers in Linguistics*, **5/6**, 1–21.
Birdwhistell, R. L. (1973). *Kinesics and context*. Essays on body-motion communication. Harmondsworth: Penguin Books.
Bloomfield, L. (1975). *Language* (revised ed.). London: Allen & Unwin.
Brouwer, D., Gerritsen, M. & de Haan, D. (1979). Speech differences between women and men: on the wrong track? *Language in Society*, **8**, 33–50.
Brown, R. & Gilman, A. (1960). The pronouns of power and solidarity. In T. A. Sebeok (1960), *Style in language*. Cambridge, Mass.: M.I.T. Press, 253–76.
Carroll, J. P. (1960). Vectors of prose style. In T. A. Sebeok (1960), *Style in language*. Cambridge, Mass.: M.I.T. Press, 283–92.
Cole, P. (ed.) (1978). *Syntax and semantics, 9. Pragmatics*. New York: Academic Press.
Cole, P. & Morgan, J. L. (eds.) (1975). *Syntax and semantics, 3. Speech acts*. New York: Academic Press.
Coseriu, E. (1955–6). Determinación y entorno. Dos problemas da una lingüistica del hablar. *Romanistisches Jahrbuch*, **7**, 29–54. Reprinted in Coseriu (1962), 282–323.
Coseriu, E. (1962). *Teoria del lenguaje y lingüistica general*. Biblioteca románica hispánica, II. Estudios y essayos 61. Madrid.
Crosby, F. & Nyquist, L. (1977). The female register: an empirical study of Lakoff's hypotheses. *Language in Society*, **6**, 313–22.
Crystal, D. & Quirk, C. R. (1964). *Systems of prosodic and paralinguistic features in English*. Janua Linguarum series minor, 39. The Hague: Mouton.
Crystal, D. & Davy, D. (1969). *Investigating English style*. London: Longmans.
van Dijk, T. A. (1977*a*). *Text and context: some explorations in the semantics and pragmatics of discourse*. London: Longmans.
van Dijk, T. A. (1977*b*). Context and cognition: knowledge frames and speech act comprehension. *Journal of Pragmatics*, **1**, 211–32.
van Dijk, T. A. (ed.) (1976). *Pragmatics of language and literature*. Amsterdam: North-Holland.
Dubský, J. (1972). The Prague conception of functional style. In Fried (1972), 112–27.
Ducrot, O. & Todorov, T. (1972). *Dictionnaire encyclopédique des sciences du langage*. Paris: Éditions du Seuil.
Edelsky, C. (1979). Question intonation and sex roles. *Language in Society*, **8**, 15–32.
Edwards, P. (1968). Meaning and context: an exercise in practical stylistics. *English Language Teaching*, **22**, 272–7.
Elllegård, A. (1962). *A statistical method for determining authorship*. Gothenburg: University of Gothenburg.
Enkvist, N. E. (1964). On defining style. In Enkvist *et al.* (1964), 3–56.
Enkvist, N. E., Spencer, J. & Gregory, M. (1964). *Linguistics and style*. Language and Language Learning, 6. London: Oxford University Press.
Enkvist, N. E. (1973). *Linguistic stylistics*. Janua Linguarum series critica 5. The Hague and Paris: Mouton.
Ferguson, C. A. (1976). The structure and use of politeness formulas. *Language in Society*, **5**, 137–51.
Firth, J. R. (1957). *Papers in linguistics, 1934–1951*. London: Oxford University Press.
Fishman, J. A. (1968). *Readings in the sociology of language*. The Hague and Paris: Mouton.
Fishman, J. A. (1972). *The sociology of language*. Rowley, Mass.: Newbury House.
Fleischer, W. (1970). Grundfragen der Stilklassifikation unter funktionalen Aspekt. *Wissenschaftliche Zeitschrift der Pädagogischen Hochschule 'Dr Theodor Neubauer' Erfurt Mühlhausen*. Gesellschaft- und sprachwissenschaftliche Reihe **7**, 2, 23–28.

N. E. Enkvist: Stylistics

Freihoff, R. & Takala, S. (1974). *Kielenkäyttötilanteiden esittelyyn perustuva kielenopetuksen tavoitekuvausjärjestelmä.* [A system of goal description for language teaching based on presentations of situations of language use.] Reports from the Language Centre, University of Jyväskylä, number 2, separate English summary in number 3, German summary in number 4.

Fried, V. (1972). *The Prague School of linguistics and language teaching.* London: Oxford University Press.

Friedrich, P. (1972). Social context and semantic feature: the Russian pronominal usage. In Gumperz & Hymes (1972), 270–300.

Gal'perin, I. R. (1971). *Stylistics.* Moscow: Higher School Publishing House.

Gardiner, Sir A. H. (1932). *The theory of speech and language.* Oxford: Clarendon Press.

Geertz, C. (1968). Linguistic etiquette. In Fishman (1968), 282–95.

Giglioli, P. P. (ed.) (1972). *Language and social context.* Harmondsworth: Penguin Books.

Gläser, R. (1969). *Linguistische Kriterien der Stilbeschreibung.* Typescript of Habilitationsschrift, Leipzig: Karl-Marx-Universität, Sektion Theoretische und angewandte Sprachwissenschaft.

Goody, E. N. (ed). (1978). *Questions of politeness. Strategies in social interaction.* Cambridge Papers in Social Anthropology, 8. Cambridge: Cambridge University Press.

Gregory, M. (1967). Aspects of varieties differentiation. *Journal of Linguistics*, **3**, 177–98.

Gregory, M. & Carroll, S. (1978). *Language and situation. Language varieties and their social contexts.* London, etc.: Routledge & Kegan Paul.

Grice, H. P. (1975). Logic and conversation. In Cole & Morgan (1975), 41–58.

Grimes, J. (1975). *The thread of discourse.* Janua Linguarum Series minor 207. The Hague and Paris: Mouton.

Gumperz, J. J. & Hymes, D. (eds.) (1972). *Directions in sociolinguistics: the ethnography of communication.* New York, etc.: Holt, Rinehart & Winston.

Halliday, M. A. K. (1973). *Explorations in the functions of language.* London: Edward Arnold.

Halliday, M. A. K. (1977). *System and function in language: selected papers.* G. Kress, ed. Oxford: Oxford University Press.

Halliday, M. A. K. (1978). *Language as a social semiotic.* London: Edward Arnold.

Hjelmslev, L. (1966). *Omkring Sprogteoriens Grundlaeggelse.* Copenhagen: Akademisk Forlag.

Holcroft, D. (1978). *Words and deeds. Problems in the theory of speech acts.* Oxford: Oxford University Press.

Hymes, D. (1964). *Language in culture and society. A reader in linguistics and anthropology.* New York: Harper & Row.

Hymes, D. (1967). Models of interaction of language and social setting. *Journal of Social Issues*, **33**, 8–28.

Hymes, D. (1977). *Foundations in sociolinguistics. An ethnographic approach.* London: Tavistock.

Johannisson, T. (1973). *Ett språkligt signalement.* English summary: 'A linguistic signalement'. Nordistica Gothoburgensia 6. Acta Universitatis Gothoburgensis. Gothenburg: Almqvist & Wiksell.

Joos, M. (1962). *The five clocks.* Bloomington: Indiana University Research Center in Anthropology, Folklore and Linguistics. The Hague: Mouton.

Kirstein, B. (1975). Toward a situational grammar. *Linguistische Berichte*, **39**, 28–38.

Kitaxova, Z. Ju. & Kitaxov, K. (1978). Problemy klassifikacij funkcional'nyx stilej v jazykax različnyx tipov. [On the problem of classifying functional styles in languages of different types.] *Voprosy jazykoznanija*, **1**, 3–17.

Kolšanskij, G. V. (1959). O prirode konteksta. [About the nature of context.] *Voprosy jazykoznanija*, **4**, 47–9.
Kožina, M. (1968). *K osnovanijam funkcional'noj stilistiki.* [Towards the foundations of functional stylistics.] Perm': Universitet im. A.M. Gor'kogo.
Labov, W. (1970). The study of language in its social context. *Studium Generale*, **23**, 30–87. Also in Giglioli (1972), 283–308 and in Pride & Holmes (1972), 180–202.
Labov, W. (1972). The isolation of contextual styles. In Labov (1972), *Sociolinguistic patterns*. Philadelphia: University of Pennsylvania Press.
Lakoff, R. (1973). Language and woman's place. *Language in Society*, **2**, 45–80.
Lakoff, R. (1975). *Language and woman's place.* New York: Harper & Row.
Lambert, W. E. & Tucker, G. R. (1976). *Tu, vous, usted: a social-psychological study of address patterns.* Rowley, Mass.: Newbury House.
Langendoen, D. T. (1968). *The London School of linguistics.* The Hague: Mouton.
Laver, J. & Hutcheson, S. (eds.) (1972). *Communication in face to face interaction.* Harmondsworth: Penguin Books.
Leodolter, R. (1975). Die Kategorie der 'Sprechsituation': Zur soziolinguistischen Theoriebildung (Zusammenfassung). *Grazer Linguistische Studien*, **1**, 142–49.
Lock, A. (ed.) (1978). *Action, gesture and symbol. The emergence of language.* London, New York and San Francisco: Academic Press.
Longacre, R. E. (1976). *An anatomy of speech notions.* Amsterdam: de Ridder.
Mackey, W. F. (1978). Pragmalinguistics in context. *Die neueren Sprachen*, 77. **27** Neue Folge, 194–223.
Marková, I. (ed.) (1978). *The social context of language.* Chichester and New York: Wiley.
Mitchell, T. F. (1975). *Principles of Firthian linguistics.* London: Longmans.
Moerk, E. L. (1970). Quantitative analysis of writing styles. *Journal of Linguistics*, **6**, 223–30.
Moles, A. A. & Rohmer, E. (1977). *Théorie des actes. Vers une écologie des actions.* Tournai: Casterman.
Mosteller, F. & Wallace, D. L. (1964). *Inference and disputed authorship: the federalist papers.* Reading, Mass.: Addison & Wesley.
Müller, R. M. (1970). Situation und Lehrbuchtexte: die Kontextualisierbarkeitsprobe. *Praxis des neusprachlichen Unterrichts*, **17**, 3, 229–42.
Müller, R. M. (1971). Was ist 'situational teaching': ein Vorschlag zur Systematisierung. *Praxis des neusprachlichen Unterrichts* **18**, 229–39.
O'Donnell, B. (1970). *An analysis of prose style to determine authorship. "The O'Ruddy", a novel by Stephen Crane and Robert Barr.* Studies in General and Comparative Literature, IV. The Hague and Paris: Mouton.
Oksaar, E. (1974). Sprache und Denken. *Zeitschrift für germanistische Linguistik*, **1**, 317–30.
Osgood, C. A., Suci, G. J. & Tannenbaum, P. H. (1957). *The measurement of meaning.* Urbana, Chicago and London: University of Illinois Press.
Paulston, C. B. (1975). Language and social class: pronouns of address in Swedish. *Working Papers in Sociolinguistics*, **29**, 1–19.
Pike, K. (1967). *Language in relation to a unified theory of the structure of human behavior.* Janua Linguarum series maior, 24. The Hague: Mouton.
Pride, J. B. & Holmes, J. (eds.) (1972). *Sociolinguistics.* Harmondsworth: Penguin Books.
Rasper, Chr., Rudigkeit, R., Schäfer, G. & Wenner, D. (1978). Die Beziehung zwischen Turn-Taking Verhalten und sozialem Rang. *Linguistische Berichte*, **56**, 1–22.
Riffaterre, M. (1971). *Essais de stylistique structurale.* Paris: Flammarion.

Rozkovcová, L. (1973). On theories of context in linguistics. *Philologia Pragensia*, **16**, 94–106.

Sacks, H., Schegloff, E. A. & Jefferson, G. (1975). A simplest systematics for turn-taking for conversation. *Language*, **50**, 696–735.

Sadock, J. M. (1974). *Towards a linguistic theory of speech acts*. New York, San Francisco and London: Academic Press.

Šajkevič, A. Ja. (1968). Opyt statističeskogo vydelenija funkcional'nyx stilej. [An attempt at statistical determination of functional styles.] *Voprosy jazykoznanija*, **1**, 64–76.

Sandig, B. (1970). Probleme einer linguistischen Stilistik. *Linguistik und Didaktik*, **1**, 3, 177–94.

Sandig, B. (1978). *Stilistik. Sprachpragmatische Grundlegung der Stilbeschreibung*. Berlin and New York: Walter de Gruyter.

Sankoff, D. (ed.) (1978). *Linguistic variation. Models and methods*. New York, San Francisco and London: Academic Press.

Schaar, C. (1978). Linear sequence, spatial structure, complex sign, and vertical context system. *Poetics*, **7**, 377–88.

Schegloff, E. A. & Sacks, H. (1973). Opening up closings. *Semiotica*, **8**, 289–327.

Scherfer, P. (1976). Über funktionale Varietäten des Französischen. *Linguistische Berichte*, **46**, 1–15.

Searle, J. A. (1969). *Speech acts: an essay in the philosophy of language*. Cambridge: Cambridge University Press.

Searle, J. A. (1976). A classification of illocutionary acts. *Language and Society*, **5**, 1–23.

Shotter, J. (1978). The cultural context of communication studies: theoretical and methodological issues. In Lock (1978), 43–78.

Sievert, H.-J. (1976). Zum Gebrauch von Anredeformen: Gruss- und Verabschiedungsformeln in der deutschen Sprache der Gegenwart in der DDR. *Deutsch als Fremdsprache*, **13**, 297–300.

Slama-Cazacu, T. (1961). *Langage et contexte*. The Hague: Mouton.

Slama-Cazacu, T. (1967). Sur les rapports entre la stylistique et la psycholinguistique. *Revue Roumaine de Linguistique*, **12**, 4, 309–30.

Slama-Cazacu, T. (1977). Convergent and divergent aspects of psycholinguistics and sociolinguistics. In Uribe-Villegas (1977), 169–95.

Spencer, J. & Gregory, M. (1964). An approach to the study of style. In Enkvist *et al.* (1964), 59–105.

Stalnaker, R. C. (1970). Pragmatics. *Synthese*, **22**, 272–89.

Svartvik, J. (1968). *The Evans statements. A case for forensic linguistics*. Gothenburg Studies in English 20. Gothenburg: University of Gothenburg; Almqvist & Wiksell.

Taylor, C. V. (1975). A schema for the contextual study of language. *Linguistics*, **164**, 45–61.

Trojan, F. (1952). *Der Ausdruck der Sprachstimme*. Vienna and Düsseldorf: Maudrich.

Trojanskaja, E. S. (1979). Aktual'nye problemy issledovanija funkcional'nyx stilej. [Topical problems in the study of functional styles.] In M. Ja. Cvilling *et al.* (eds.), *Lingvostilističeskie issledovanija naučnoj reči*. Moscow: Izdatel'stvo "Nauka".

Ure, J. (1969). Practical registers. *English Language Teaching*, **23**, 107–14 and 206–15.

Ure, J. & Ellis, J. (1977). Register in descriptive linguistics and linguistic sociology. In Uribe-Villegas (1977), 197–243.

Uribe-Villegas, O. (ed.) (1977). *Issues in sociolinguistics: contributions to the sociology of language*. The Hague, Paris and New York: Mouton.

Vachek, J. & Dubský, J. (1966). *Dictionnaire linguistique de l'École de Prague*. Utrecht and Anvers: Spectrum Publishers.

Verschueren, J. (1978). *Pragmatics : an annotated bibliography with particular reference to speech act theory*. Library and Information Sources in Linguistics, 4. Amsterdam: Benjamins.

Verschueren, J. (1978–9). Pragmatics: an annotated bibliography. Part I, *Journal of Pragmatics*, **2**, 373–400. Part II, *Journal of Pragmatics*, **3**, 99–125.

Voegelin, C. F., Yamamoto, F. Y., A. Y. and F. M. (1977). Presuppositional culture spaces. *Anthropological Linguistics*, **19**, 320–53.

Wunderlich, D. (ed.) (1976 a). *Linguistische Pragmatik*, 2nd edition. Wiesbaden: Akademische Verlagsgesellschaft Athenaion.

Wunderlich, D. (1976 b). *Studien zur Sprechakttheorie*. Frankfurt: Suhrkamp.

Yaguello, M. (1978). *Les mots et les femmes*. Paris: Payot.

MOTHER-TONGUE TEACHING FOR THE CHILDREN OF MIGRANTS

Arturo Tosi

Oxford Polytechnic. Formerly Co-ordinator, EEC/Bedfordshire Pilot Project for Mother-Tongue Teaching.

In the US in the mid '60s a debate began to question the principles of monolingual English schooling and the effectiveness of compensatory education for children whose mother tongue was not English. The alternative provision suggested consisted of a system offering simultaneous teaching in both ESL and the children's L1: the two languages being referred to as those of the 'majority' and the 'minority' groups. Literature on this subject has since adopted the term 'bilingual education' (see the U.S. Civil Rights Report on Bilingual Education and the critique of it by Hines, 1976). More recently a similar debate has developed in some Northern European countries where large numbers of foreign workers are employed. Under the increasingly popular title 'mother-tongue teaching' research projects and pilot schemes concerned with the first language of migrants' children have emerged. Although initial interest was stimulated by UNESCO and the Council of Europe, as well as the impact of American research findings, a major impetus to the European debate was provided by the 1977 EEC Directive on the education of children of migrant workers. The purpose of this article is to survey recent studies on the philosophy, objectives and implications of bilingual education, and to outline their relevance in the context of the migration of workers in Europe. This survey is, however, subject to the following restrictions: (1) it deals only with recent migration to Europe; (2) it includes materials on some aspects of bilingualism simply to introduce the linguistic situation of migrants' children and does not claim to be comprehensive on this topic; (3) it does not consider studies on minorities with privileged background, and (4) it deals mainly with articles in English and materials obtainable in England.

Terminology

As Swain and Cummins (1979) point out in a recent review, the term 'bilingualism' is not used consistently. Scholars, while disagreeing as to its definition, tend to define it in their work, whereas practitioners and administrators tend to do so less. However, there is more consensus in the definition of 'bilingual education'. Basically the term refers to the use of two languages and study of their corresponding cultures. Most scholars (Gaarder, 1967 a; John & Horner, 1971; Rado, 1974; Cohen, 1975; Fishman, 1975, 1976, 1977 a; Mackey & Beebe, 1977) have agreed that bilingual schooling offers two languages as the media of instruction, i.e. some subjects are taught in both media as well as language skills themselves. Further definitions specify that neither 'smattering' primary and secondary FL courses (Fishman, 1976), nor instruction in the vernacular as a bridge to another language, constitute bilingual education (Gaarder, 1967 a; John & Horner, 1971). Fishman (1977 a) and Cohen (1975) indicate that bilingual instruction may involve either subjects closely allied to language (e.g. culture, literature, social studies) or completely unrelated to it (e.g. mathematics). The same scholars also distinguish between two-way and one-way bilingual programmes. In the former, children of each ethnic group use both an L1 and an L2 to learn the curriculum. In the latter, children of only one group learn bilingually. Paulston (1975) also terms as bilingual those education programmes which do not involve both languages as media of instruction. Her definition includes both (1) programmes taught in the mother tongue with an L2 component (being the target language and normally the official language), and (2) those where all schooling is in L2 except for a component in L 1 skills. Paulston (1975), using Gaarder's distinction between 'folk bilingualism' and 'élitist bilingualism', differentiates between 'folk bilingual education' and 'élitist bilingual education'. The new distinction, as we shall see later, will be justified by the need to account for contradictory findings produced by traditional approaches in which bilingual education is evaluated as an independent variable (Paulston, 1974, 1975).

'Immigrants' can also be an ambiguous term. In North America, 'immigrants' and 'immigrant languages' mean non-English speaking populations and their languages. Fishman (1966) has, among others, documented the efforts of these communities to maintain their languages. 'Migrants' usually refers to farm workers who come from neighbouring countries and move periodically from place to place to find work. While in the U.S. the terms 'immigrant' and 'migrant' are normally used consistently, this is not true for other countries. In Australia (see Rado, 1974) and Scandinavia (see Skutnabb-Kangas & Toukomaa, 1976; Toukomaa & Seppo, 1978) they are used interchangeably. In British studies, 'migrant' normally designates a non-indigenous population temporarily hosted in a new country: seasonal labourers, for example, or those on a limited contract. Long-term migrants and settlers are referred to as 'immigrants'. The European Commission uses the term 'migrants' to cover all foreign populations whether from the EEC states or overseas (European Communities Commission, 1975 a, b). UNESCO and the Council of Europe in official documents, studies and reports also refer to all foreign workers as 'migrants' (UNESCO, 1978; Council of Europe, 1975 a, b) and this is how the term is used in this paper.

81

A. Tosi: Mother-tongue teaching

In Europe, by 'linguistic minority groups', ethnologists (Heraud, 1968; Salvi, 1975; Stephens, 1976) usually mean those communities (a) whose language – whatever its status – is not the official language in any state (e.g. Basque in Spain), and (b) whose languages are official languages elsewhere, but which are spoken by minorities where they are living (e.g. French speakers in Aosta Valley in Italy). Stephens (1976) explains further that, since 'linguistic minorities' designates 'well established communities', the term excludes immigrant populations. In Britain, however, it quite often refers to communities of foreign workers (Community Relation Commission, 1974; Campbell-Platt, 1976; Khan, 1976; Perren, 1976, 1977, 1979).

'Mother tongue' or 'native language', as defined in the 1953 UNESCO Report, is 'the language acquired in early years...which normally becomes the natural instrument of thought and communication'. In Europe it is common to use this term to refer to both the languages spoken in the migrants' communities and the minority languages taught in the classroom, i.e. the national standard languages of the countries of origin.

The term 'dialect' can also produce some confusion. In most European languages (French – see Littré, 1956, Martinet, 1960; English – see Haugen, 1966), 'dialects' is often used to mean regional or locally based varieties of the national language. But in Italy 'dialect' does not usually refer to different varieties of the national language (Lepschy, A. L. & G., 1977). Although in both English and Italian the word tends to be associated with a lower-class language, the degree of structural similarities and mutual intelligibility between these standard languages and their dialects may vary considerably. This is, of course, of particular importance in identifying the minority child's L 1 (standard language or dialect), and can create misunderstandings in analysing the L 1 and L 2 learning processes, ultimately affecting evaluation of achievement in bilingual programmes.

Children's bilingualism in a multiethnic society

Unlike middle-class children educated bilingually, bilingualism has been foisted upon migrant workers and their children (Fishman, 1967; Paulston, 1974, 1975; Toukomaa & Skutnabb-Kangas, 1977). Northern European countries, with the exception of Sweden, generally overlook the fact that at home a child speaks a different language from that used in the school: he/she is either taught together with majority-language speakers or receives auxiliary tuition in the majority language. Toukomaa and Skutnabb-Kangas stress that education systems operated by the majority attempt to adapt the minority child to their own socio-cultural models by using such compensatory education. As pointed out by Angel (1971), in the resulting competition the minority child can be seen as handicapped. Gaarder (1967 b) explains that 'minority children have been cheated or damaged or both, by well-intentioned but ill-informed educational policies, which have made of their bilingualism an ugly disadvantage in their lives'. Rado (1974) also points out that these pupils are made educationally disadvantaged by the school when not allowed to use their whole linguistic repertoire. She suggests that, compared with the monolingual, the bilingual child, who can function in two language environments, is more skilled. Several investigations, however, report that these children perform badly in verbal intelligence tests, whichever language they are tested in, so affecting their academic performance (Darcy, 1953, 1963; Saville-Troike, 1975; Skutnabb-Kangas & Toukomaa, 1976; Swain & Cummins, 1979). Such low achievement Skutnabb-Kangas and Toukomaa attribute to conditions of 'semilingualism' or 'double semilingualism'.

The notion of semilingualism

The term 'semilingualism' was introduced by Hansegård to describe someone who can 'function' in two languages, but is not really proficient in either (1968). Toukomaa (1975) defined it at two interdependent levels: (1) the standard of linguistic competence demanded by the community and (2) individual abilities. Skutnabb-Kangas and Toukomaa say that the diglossic community of Torne Valley in Sweden exemplifies this notion. Natives of this area who are speakers of a Finnish dialect, illiterate in Standard Finnish but educated in Swedish, experience difficulties in monoglottic Swedish areas. In monoglottic Finnish areas their linguistic competence is below that of a local eight-year-old who can read and write. At home they are not semilingual, but outside they are. Communities differ considerably in the demands they make on their members' linguistic skills and competence. This social factor, as well as the positive or negative associations between bilingualism and cognitive functioning (see survey article by Swain & Cummins, 1979), seems relevant in evaluating the linguistic competence of people who seek membership of two different communities, such as migrant families. Conditions similar to those recorded in the Torne Valley are being investigated among Italian workers in Britain (Tosi, 1979). The first generation was recruited by a British brick factory from secluded Italian villages in the '50s and early '60s. They were all speakers of Southern Italian dialect. A few had a little competence in speaking Standard Italian, the vast majority were illiterate. The second generation – native speakers of their parents' dialect, educated in English – on the whole achieved poor standards at school, and cannot speak, read or write Standard Italian. The competence in each language of the intermediate generation (those who entered the country with their parents while of school age) is proportional to the time spent in schools in each country. All three have standards of linguistic competence which are below those required for social emancipation in the new country, or re-integration in the old. Changes in the country of origin, like rapid industrialisation and urban growth which displace agricultural traditions, may result in social and linguistic emancipation for migrants' co-villagers from which they are cut off. In this case, retention of native dialects and local traditions which are no longer dominant in their linguistic communities may increase the linguistic isolation and result in one more difficulty for the migrant wishing to return (Tosi, 1978 *b*).

Semilingualism, from the point of view of individual abilities, has been tentatively divided by Hansegård (1968) into various aspects: (*a*) size of vocabulary, (*b*) correctness, (*c*) automatism, (*d*) creative and neologising ability, (*e*) mastery of cognitive and performative functions, (*f*) degree of richness in individual meanings. Further investigations in these components have produced some contradictory findings, either because they attempt to measure different things, or because they are concerned with aspects of language only partially affected by semilingualism (Skutnabb-Kangas, 1975; Jaakkola, 1976). Different researchers agree, however, about the functional and cognitive limitations of the minority children's L1. Rado (1974) refers to domain-specific language use and uneven vocabulary development as affecting both vocabulary power and expansions of existing meanings. She suggests that these conditions, while normal in bilinguals, can be made into handicaps by schools, which fail to develop both languages, and compare these pupils' standard of achievements in L2 with those of monolinguals. The school, in only a few years of L2 instruction, seems to develop opposing and uninterchangeable uses of two languages. Children appear to be backward in cognitive development and literacy skills in the school language, while the home language, which remains only a medium for family communication, will not develop from the level of a repetitive, descriptive jargon, tied to informal situations. These conditions, it has been agreed by most scholars, can justify the adoption of the notion of semilingualism (Paulston, 1975; Skutnabb-Kangas & Toukomaa, 1976; Cummins, 1976; Toukomaa & Skutnabb-Kangas, 1977). Brent-Palmer (1979) has made a recent attempt to integrate and evaluate such a notion within a sociological framework of community relations.

In analysing children's first language, Rado (1974) also points to the question of lexical and syntactic borrowings which affect L 1 development as a result of frequent transference and language contacts. Titone (1977) stresses the socio-/psycholinguistic character of these interferences and analyses the nature and mechanism of this phenomenon in a multicultural context of SL learning. Such changes in migrants' languages are studied by many investigators. Most of these works are reviewed by Albin and Ronelle (1972), who analyse morphological and semantic interferences in a community of Yugoslav immigrants in California. More recent studies concentrate on phonological and morphological interferences in the Greek spoken by Greek Canadians (Seaman, 1972; Orlowsky, 1974), in Spanish (Harris, 1974; Saltarelli, 1975) and Italian

(Tosi, forthcoming). All these studies indicate that changes are due to a sociolinguistic environment which does not reinforce generally accepted standards and correct norms. This phenomenon has been shown to have two major implications, one social and one individual. At the social level, where one generation's language provides the limited data for the succeeding generation's grammar-building process, progressive changes in norms and meaning lead inevitably to the extinction of the migrants' language (Saltarelli & Gonzo, 1977), when it is not developed by formal education. At the individual level, most investigators have indicated that inconsistent linguistic models in the family, lack of reinforcement of accepted norms in the community, and exclusion from exposure to the standard language are responsible for weakening children's L 1 development (Rado, 1974; Skutnabb-Kangas & Toukomaa, 1976; Cummins, 1976; Toukomaa & Skutnabb-Kangas, 1977; Tosi, 1979). Since these affect, in turn, acquisition and performance in an L2, they argue that minority children's L1 should be developed and reinforced by the school.

Language planning in a multi-ethnic society

The arguments for mother-tongue teaching

To the question 'why should children of migrant workers be taught their mother tongue?' there are various answers. The findings of several studies show it to be a two-fold problem. Following Fishman's analysis of societal bilingualism and language change in multilingual communities (1972), some scholars relate 'mother-tongue teaching' in bilingual programmes to new linguistic objectives and to forward-looking social policies. Such studies (1) tend to focus on minority languages' new status and their culture-carrying nature, in a society looking for alternatives to the melting-pot hypothesis. Others (2) concentrate on the therapeutic effect of teaching in the mother tongue on semilingual children's linguistic–cognitive development. The two positions are obviously interdependent. Both groups, in criticising monolingual schooling and compensatory education, have used research findings interchangeably.

    1. Those particularly concerned with the linguistic needs of semilingual children emphasise the slow linguistic and cognitive development (Skutnabb-Kangas & Toukomaa, 1976) and emotional disturbances (Lewis, 1970) likely to be suffered by a migrant's child not educated in his/her L1. The Finnish scholars base their arguments on the theories of psychologists such as Vigotsky (1962), and Luria and Yudovich (1956), who maintain that verbal communication between child and adult has the double function of regulating further external communication and reorganising the child's mental process and cognitive abilities. Thus Skutnabb-Kangas and Toukomaa argue that early instruction in L2 threatens L1 development and hinders cognitive growth. Although many studies report advantages in early rather than late L2 learning

A. Tosi: Mother-tongue teaching

(Burstall, 1975; Macnamara, 1976; Titone, 1977), Skutnabb-Kangas and Toukomaa take Malmberg's point (1971) that most of this argument is based on the imitative character of early language learning. Since migrants' children lack satisfactory pre-school verbal interaction with adults, the Finnish scholars maintain that L2 teaching should be delayed until co-operation between cognitive functioning and linguistic operation can be minimised. Discussions on this theory – the threshold hypothesis – and on language shelter programmes (developing L1 before introducing L2) can be found in Cummins (1976), Paulston (1977), Toukomaa and Skutnabb-Kangas (1977), Swain and Cummins (1979), and Brent-Palmer (1979). This argument implies that the school should (a) compensate for the migrant parents' limited opportunities for providing linguistic stimuli and (b) reinforce interaction between linguistic operations and cognitive functions. Such aid could only be given by a system (1) offering migrants' children intensive L1 teaching from pre-school onwards, and (2) delaying L2 teaching until there are well developed L1 structures on which both L2 and subjects in L2 can be anchored. Lewis (1970), drawing on the work of Luria (1932) and Spoerl (1946), similarly maintains that bilingual children's emotional conflicts result from tensions between linguistic settings. Their emotional maladjustment is not so much generated by the complexity of thinking and speaking in two languages, as by cultural conflict. Lewis concludes that, to prevent this breakdown in both emotional and linguistic development, a school system is needed which fully develops both languages and cultures (see also Vernon Jensen, 1962; Krear, 1969), i.e. aims to establish linguistic and cultural pluralism in the community. Baetens Beardsmore (1977) also supports this conclusion when reviewing studies of anomie in children on the margins of two cultural and linguistic environments.

2. The issues of cultural pluralism and immigrant groups' language rights constitute the central arguments for mother-tongue teaching among those scholars questioning the philosophy of assimilation-orientated monolingual/monocultural education systems. A classic review of the arguments for and against language rights of im/migrant groups can be found in Kloss (1971). He analyses four main arguments for assimilation (e.g. the tacit contract, the 'take and give', the anti-ghettoisation and the national unity theories) and examines seven arguments in support of the opposite view, i.e. im/migrants have the right to retain and cultivate their own languages. He then distinguishes between promotion-orientated and tolerance-orientated language rights, concluding that im/migrant groups can lay no claim to promotion-orientated measures unless they prove that their desire to keep their languages alive lasts more than a generation. On the other hand, Kloss admits that there may be pedagogical arguments in favour of promotion-orientated measures: elementary schools can use the pupils' L1 to speed up their eventual assimilation. Verdoot (1977), analysing Kloss's arguments, adopts Fishman's (1967) distinction between

bilingualism and diglossia. He suggests, from this viewpoint, that the most common relationship in migrant communities is bilingualism without diglossia. In the first generation the two languages show a degree of compartmentalisation, but the second generation, bilingual at an early age, becomes irreversibly monolingual under the pressure of the 'other tongue' which tends to displace the mother tongue. Bilingualism without diglossia, therefore, tends to be a transitional stage, since it provides no support for the development of second-generation bilingualism. When, instead, maintenance support is provided for the mother tongue, the community speech develops into bilingualism with diglossia: the only desirable relationship, according to Verdoot. But Verdoot also warns that not all such support provision is designed to maintain their languages. This point is spelt out by many other scholars who, attempting to analyse the social implications of bilingual programmes, have considered whether they promote language maintenance or language shift. Fishman (1977 b) reviews most models of bilingual education: Spolsky's typology (1974), which distinguishes between seeking to 'salvage the child' (compensatory, language shift) and seeking to 'salvage the language' (pluralistic, language maintenance); the trichotomy model (Fishman, 1975), which includes enrichment programmes also directed towards the majority groups; and that proposed by Paulston (1975), which explains transitional/maintenance orientations in the light of a combination of conflictual/non-conflictual states of inter-ethnic relations. Skutnabb-Kangas and Toukomaa (1976) also propose a typology of minority–majority relations correlated to linguistic policies, based on Paulston's multidimensional model. With this model they claim that unlike the present state of cultural assimilation, a multiethnic society should foster cultural pluralism with economic structural incorporation. To pursue this goal, the education system should give the migrant child 'just as good a command of the mother tongue as he/she would obtain in a school in his/her native land, and as good linguistic skills in the host country's language as the majority children have' (1976). Paulston (1975) additionally warns against viewing bilingual education as an independent variable when evaluating programmes, as may happen in response to the need to show parents and educators immediate results. Only by treating it as a dependent variable (i.e. considering the macrosocial factors which have led to that particular form of bilingual education) can the linguistic outcome be adequately evaluated and its long-term consequences assessed. Similarly Toukomaa and Skutnabb-Kangas (1976) argue that unless we consider these programmes as result of socio-economic factors, the educational and linguistic implications of which language minority children are taught in cannot be understood. They maintain that a primary task is the evaluation of decisions on educational measures which lead to bilingualism, monolingualism and semilingualism ('Semilingualism and the education of migrant children as a means of reproducing the caste of assembly line workers', Skutnabb-Kangas,

A. Tosi: Mother-tongue teaching

1978). In 1971, Kjolseth, analysing assimilationist and pluralistic models, also stressed that no feature of a bilingual programme can be considered as being in itself either shift- or maintenance-orientated. He suggested that any programme feature takes relevance in one or other direction only within the specific socio-economic–cultural context of ethnic relations between the groups concerned.

Policies and politics of mother-tongue teaching

While the dangers of generalising from findings on specific programmes have been widely acknowledged – Mackey first pointed to them in the evaluation of the J. F. Kennedy programme in Berlin (1972) – European researchers have always paid great attention to North American investigations. At the level of policy makers and implementors, however, while efforts are made to maintain that migrants' children are accepted by schools on the children's own terms, this is contradicted by policies towards minorities. These are based on the assumption of the tacit contract theory, i.e. migrants, in return for being permitted to live in the host country, give up claims to minority rights, and adapt culturally and linguistically to the new environment. Willke (1975) provides a comparative analysis of Swedish, British and W. German methods of reception for migrant children, which includes a large bibliography also covering France, the Netherlands and Switzerland. Segers and Van Den Broeck (1978) illustrate pilot bilingual programmes in the province of Limburg in Belgium, and di Luzio (1978) a research project involving children of Italian migrants in W. Germany. Johanneson (1975, 1976), Stockfelt-Hoatson (1976, 1977) and Andersson and Tinghjorn (1978) all report on Sweden, the only country which has since 1973 automatically offered migrants' children reception in L1. In Britain, among those who influence policy, some educational organisations (e.g. National Association of Teachers of English, National Association for Multiracial Education, Co-ordinating Committee for Mother-Tongue Teaching) have shown awareness of the educational problems of migrants' children. But governmental reports either do not discuss the problems of bilingual education (*A language for life* by Sir Alan Bullock) or do not even mention the possibility of teaching such children their mother tongue (*Educational disadvantage and the educational needs of immigrants*, 1974). Many countries profess principles and have policies on the recognition and promotion of minority languages, but most European governments, Britain included, have neither (Perren, 1977).

In Europe, migrants' communities have not so far sought a change of policy in mainstream schools; but they have interpreted the 'tacit contract' to mean that if their languages cannot enjoy promotion-orientated treatment, they should at least benefit from a tolerant atmosphere outside the schools. In Britain, for example, many groups of migrants receive help from their country of origin, e.g. Italians, Spaniards, Portuguese and Turks (Khan, 1976; Verdoot, 1977), and many others from private agencies in the new country, e.g. Chinese, Indian and Pakistani (Khan, 1976). Most Local Education Authorities know little of the organisation and the extent of this provision, and mainstream school teachers are not made aware of the role of the minority children's mother tongue in overall linguistic development (Khan, 1976; Tosi, 1978 *a, c*). Voluntary classes differ in resources, subjects and objectives. All teach the group's language and use it as a medium of instruction; most include culture and social studies of the homeland, and many preserve the language exclusively for religious purposes (Khan, 1976). The more emphasis is placed on non-educational goals – i.e. religious, patriotic, political – the less attention is paid to linguistic aspects (Tosi, 1978 *a*).

In the last few years, the linguistic education of migrants' children has attracted new attention in Europe, resulting from strong pressure from various international advisory and political organisations. In the past, statements on human rights ignored minority groups' linguistic rights (European Convention for the Protection of Human Rights and Fundamental Freedoms) or only referred to national minorities (UN Covenant on Civil and Political Rights and UNESCO Convention against Discrimination in Education), but in 1975 experts' seminars of the Council of Europe (1975 *a, b*) recommended that the teaching of migrants' mother tongues should be promoted by the 'host' country. This was followed by an official Council of Europe recommendation (1976) and an EEC Education Ministers' resolution (1976) 'to provide more such opportunities, if possible in schools and in collaboration with the country of origin'. In the same year, further meetings sponsored by UNESCO and the World Federation of Foreign Language Teachers Associations (FIPLV/UNESCO, 1976) were held on the subject. In addition to the fundamental aspect stressed by the Council of Europe and the EEC – mother-tongue maintenance to allow reintegration into the country of origin – the UNESCO workshops focused on another important objective: enabling children to retain their sense of personal identity and pride in their cultural heritage. Finally, in July 1977, the EEC Council of Ministers adopted a Directive (1977) on the education of the children of migrant workers, stipulating that 'member states must offer reception teaching which will include tuition in the language or in one of the official languages of the host country adapted to the specific needs of foreign children'. It calls on host states 'to take appropriate measures in co-ordination with normal education, and in co-operation with the country of origin, to promote the teaching of the mother tongue and culture of the country of origin'. Although these measures are to be taken 'with a view principally to facilitating the possible reintegration into the member states of origin' of nationals of those states, a subsequent declaration confirms a resolve to achieve this objective for all migrants (EEC

A. Tosi: Mother-tongue teaching

Commission, 1977). The same document specifies that the Directive should be seen 'not only as an important step towards the creation of school structures adapted to real needs of migrants, but also as an important landmark on the way to complete freedom of movement within the Community'. In the EEC's reports in support of mother-tongue teaching, they envisage alternative types of provision: (*a*) the language and culture of the country of origin taught in school hours, (*b*) lessons given in the mother tongue, the language of the host country being taught as a foreign language, (*c*) the language and culture of the country of origin taught outside school hours, and (*d*) the language and culture of the country of origin taught partly within and partly outside school hours (EEC Commission, 1977). The Commission considers (*a*) the most desirable.

Categories of bicultural and bilingual programmes

Two main aspects of bilingual/bicultural programmes have been identified by researchers as most relevant when evaluating their implications for both child and environment. One involves the role of the L1 in the curriculum (how, to what extent, and with what objective it is taught). The other focuses on the impact of minority language maintenance in the overall socio-cultural context (i.e. assimilation or pluralism). Accordingly scholars have devised models to group the different programmes into categories. Fishman (1977*c*), who presents three major socio-curricular models, analyses their relevance in the context of migration in Europe.

(1) *Compensatory/transitional.* The L1 (minority or marked language) is used to enable the poor/non-speaker of the L2 (majority or unmarked) to master subjects until skills in the L2 are developed. The outcome is transitional bilingualism and assimilation – in Fishman's word it is 'self-liquidating'. (2) *Language maintenance.* The marked language is emphasised and introduced as a more stable medium of instruction, while the unmarked language is introduced gradually, until they both become media of instruction for all subjects. The outcome is balanced bilingual co-ordinate competence in individuals and cultural pluralism in the community. The minority group preserves its own language and becomes diglossic for compartmentalised intragroup and intergroup purposes. (3) *Enrichment orientated.* Bilingual education including marked and unmarked languages is offered within the same community. This happens where the majority group seek 'additional cognitive and emotional exposure to that available via monolingual deprivation' (Fishman, 1977*b*). Accounting for the specific situation of children of migrants in Northern Europe, Fishman (1977*c*) warns of the difficulties inherent in the first and second models. The first, designed to be compensatory, is imposed and *absorptive*. The second, though fostering societal bilingualism and cultural pluralism, can become *separative*. This can happen when the majority population

90

may not be interested in learning the marked language or when provisions are offered to encourage segregation and repatriation, e.g. teaching in Turkish to children of Turks in Bavarian schools (Fishman, 1977 c). The solution suggested by Verdoot (1977) of 'bilingualism with diglossia' resulting from language maintenance might therefore produce segregation. Fishman proposes as an alternative relationship, double diglossia, where the school-related language of one group is the home and neighbourhood language of the other and vice versa. Such a programme in the long term is then neither *absorptive* nor *separative*, but an *additive* and enriching one for both the marked and unmarked populations involved.

Some situational factors and final remarks

Some obvious conclusions from these studies are the complexity of bilingual learning, the multi-disciplinary dimension of bilingual education, and the difficulty of using purpose-designed models in new situations. Fishman (1977 c) wonders whether new models will be required to deal with the needs of children of migrant workers in Europe if those previously analysed prove to be inadequate in this context. The transitional model seems unsuitable for programmes aiming to give linguistic support to the European policy of free movement of population: much emphasis is put in Europe on the need to preserve functional command of the marked languages in view of a possible return. Neither does the monoliterate model (where both languages are to be practised through the curriculum, but literacy skills only developed in the unmarked language) look suitable: such programmes would hardly seem worthwhile to the minority community because of the value they place on the marketable nature of literacy in another language. Fluency and literacy in both languages have certainly to be sought in Europe, but it still appears doubtful whether the marked language will be used as a medium of instruction. Obviously the curriculum will impose limits on the use of the minority groups' languages to teach other subjects. Some courses may claim to do this with classes 'on language and culture' or 'language and social studies', while the constraints of time effectively prevent using that medium for activities other than the reinforcement of linguistic skills. Language maintenance will not be achieved if such a programme fails to promote cognitive functioning in both languages and so develop balanced co-ordinate bilingualism.

Solutions are not simple: no scheme can claim to be either bilingual or bicultural in the classic sense – see Fishman's typology (1975, 1977 c) – just because the curriculum includes some teaching of the national language of the country of origin (Tosi, 1978 a). Specific linguistic objectives must be identified within the framework of language policy. Since language policy is integral to social policy, authorities will have to identify specific aims for different minority groups. It has been pointed out (Trim, 1977) that, in planning such education, a social policy should reflect considered goals and a realistic assessment of current community relations. Programmes may well attempt linguistic objectives in disharmony with the community's social development, if the dimension of community relations is overlooked (Fishman & Lovas, 1970). This can apply to those projects aiming at language maintenance in a community undergoing a process of language shift or, conversely, projects attempting language shift among those more determined to maintain their linguistic and cultural heritage. In Britain, for instance, migrants of European origin – in particular EEC nationals like Italians – may still consider themselves only temporarily resident. They will require programmes which develop competence in Standard Italian – an alien language to speakers of a Southern Italian dialect. In this case the main preoccupation of the course would not be the mismatch between home and school. The aim would be to teach Standard Italian, equipping pupils for re-integration into a school at home, so making return less problematic. Such programmes would have only a dubious claim to maintaining the linguistic heritage of the community. On the other hand, Italians elsewhere may wish to settle and identify themselves with the dominant culture. Here, language-shift-orientated programmes could well help children to cope better with the initial linguistic discontinuity by adopting – at least in the early stages – the community's dialects. Other groups, like Punjabis, Commonwealth citizens, may be more definite about settling permanently, but at the same time be more determined to maintain their language and culture. A scheme aiming at language shift for Punjabi children, therefore, would be unlikely to meet the aspirations of that community. Other factors have to be taken into account if programmes aim for enrichment goals. It is likely that the majority group will, at some stage, wish to exploit some of the linguistic resources offered by minorities: in Europe Italian and Spanish, for example, will have an appeal although they are spoken by the more 'mobile' minority groups. Other groups, such as Asians in Britain, though more settled, may find their language considered less prestigious and attractive. Maybe these groups, supported by a well educated, more self-aware middle class, will be able to enforce their rights. Maybe they will be able to obtain enrichment programmes leading from bilingualism with diglossia to a double diglossic situation in the whole community. But should this not happen, language maintenance programmes may result for the lower-class co-members in the separative effect envisaged by Fishman (1977 c) and the ghettoisation implications described by Kloss (1971) and Verdoot (1977).

In reply to Fishman's question, it would appear that Europe will require more than one model to meet the varied needs of groups sharply divided in their demands and aspirations. One warning put forward by Fishman himself and others is certainly relevant in this context: many bilingual programmes fail because they do not develop with the support of the communities themselves. Involving minority groups in policy decisions is not only a due recognition of their 'adulthood' but also a guarantee of correctly interpreting the social and linguistic orientation of their neighbourhood. In 1966 Fishman noted that 'when ethnic languages and cultures are truly foreign, schools are comfortable with them. But as soon as they are found in our own backyards, the schools deny them.' In Europe many authorities and schools still appear to be more interested in promoting studies of foreign rather than ethnic cultures. Although a reaction is now developing among many circles of educators, the ultimate rehabilitation and promotion of ethnic languages largely depends on the will of minorities to reinforce their political position by actively involving themselves in community life. To conclude with Spolsky (1971), one must appreciate the role of linguistic science in that political reality where social and educational changes take place. Applied linguists can greatly help in solving minority children's language problems with discussions and research, but cannot provide final answers. In Europe their contribution with relevant investigations has just started. *October 1979*

Addendum, December 1981

Much discussion on societal bilingualism and language education of im/migrant children has developed in Europe since the publication of this survey article. Whilst the slowness of bilingual innovations and expansions of mother-tongue teaching provision tend now to be more often justified by lack of finance rather than lack of research evidence, both governments and schools still find it difficult to draw practical inspiration from their conclusions. The debate, however, has progressed considerably from its initial stage of theorisation and has recently focused on more solid theoretical ground, on three independent areas of questions. These include (*a*) the definition of the im/migrant child's bilingual state, (*b*) the evaluation of the impact of his/her bilingualism on the school and overall society and (*c*) the design of instruments suitable for the particular conditions of mother-tongue development in the context of second-language learning. The first area (*a*) has involved, as one would expect, much discussion on the notion of semilingualism as a new theory likely to present the language of these children within a new deficit perspective and to elicit further compensatory approaches (Brent-Palmer, 1979). Skutnabb-Kangas and Toukomaa (1980), however, stress that the deficit dimension of semilingualism is not inherent in the im/migrant children's bilingualism, but rather in the monolingual school that utilises the monolingual majority child as the rule against which the minority child is found to be different (or semilingual). Cummins (1979*a* and *b*) specifies that this happens when the school fails adequately to develop cognitive functioning. Distinguishing between BICS (basic interpersonal communicative skills) and CALP (cognitive academic language proficiency), he suggests that such conditions can develop a situation of low CALP which manifests itself in two languages rather than one. Much discussion has also attended the problem of (*b*), the impact of immigrants' bilingualism on the school and overall society. Most of them, however, echo the American literature and show little sensitivity to factors and conditions typical of European countries, their educational systems and their current state of ethnic relations. In Britain, the lucid reports on language diversity among multiethnic school populations by Rosen and Burgess (1980) and that

93

A. Tosi: Mother-tongue teaching

on the bilingualism of ethnic minorities in England (Khan, 1980), are exceptions to this generalisation. Within the dimension of societal bilingualism, attention is also developing in connection with factors of a political nature affecting immigration and education (Tosi, forthcoming), and in particular concerning the relationship between the politics of immigration, language policies and education (Skutnabb-Kangas, 1980, Tosi, 1980 and 1981*a*). At applied level (*c*), projects and investigations are beginning to produce some useful guidelines for instructors, material designers and examiners, as some important questions relating to actual teaching are beginning to be investigated on a more solid theoretical ground. On the one hand, it has been pointed out that there can be no magic formula suitable for a type of language pedagogy different from either L1 and L2 teaching; specific sociolinguistic surveys have shown that the instruction, together with its instruments and methodology, must be carefully planned in relation to the pattern of bilingualism of a specific urban community (Tosi, 1981*b*). On the other hand, more theoretical work attempts to identify all variables characteristic of the process of mother-tongue development in the context of second-language learning, with a view to formulating a model for the planning, design and evaluation of material appropriate for different linguistic and urban communities (Tosi, 1981*a*). [References follow main References section.]

References

A language for life. (1975). Report of the Committee of Inquiry into reading and the use of English, appointed by the Secretary of State for Education and Science under the Chairmanship of Sir Alan Bullock, F.B.A. London: HMSO.

Albin, A. & Ronelle, A. (1972). *The speech of Yugoslav people in S. Pedro, California.* The Hague: Mouton.

Andersson, A. B. & Tinghjorn, G. (1978). The linguistic development of immigrant children in Sweden. In N. Dittmar, H. Haberland, T. Skutnabb-Kangas and U. Teleman (eds.), 259–65.

Angel, F. (1971). Social class or culture? A fundamental issue in the education of culturally different students. In B. Spolsky (1972).

Baetens Beardsmore, H. (1977). Anomie in bicultural education. In M. De Grève & E. Rossel (eds.), 9–23.

Brent-Palmer, C. (1979). A sociolinguistic assessment of the notion 'immigrant semilingualism' from a social conflict perspective. *Working Papers on Bilingualism,* **17,** 135–80.

Burstall, C. (1975). Factors affecting foreign-language learning: a consideration of some recent research findings. *Language Teaching & Linguistics: Abstracts,* **8,** 1, 5–25.

Campbell-Platt, K. (1976). Distribution of linguistic minorities in Britain. In *CILT Reports and Papers,* 14, 15–30. Revised by S. Nicholas (1978). Briefing Paper. London: The Runnymede Trust.

CILT (1976). Bilingualism and British education: the dimensions of diversity. Centre for Information on Language Teaching and Research. Papers from a conference convened in January 1976. *CILT Reports and Papers,* 14.

Cohen, A. D. (1975). *A sociolinguistic approach to bilingual education.* Rowley, Mass.: Newbury House.

Community Relations Commission (1974). D. F. Kohler (ed.), *Ethnic minorities in Britain.* London: CRC.

Council of Europe (1975*a*). Meeting of experts on curricula for children of migrant workers. 26–27 June 1975. Strasbourg.

Council of Europe (1975*b*). Meeting of experts on the teaching of the language of the host country to children of migrant workers. 30–31 October 1975. Strasbourg.

Council of Europe (1976). Parliamentary Assembly of the Council of Europe. Recommendation 786 on the education and cultural development of migrants. Strasbourg.

Council of Europe (1977). Parliamentary Assembly of the Council of Europe. Recommendation 814 on modern languages in Europe.

Cummins, J. (1976). The influence of bilingualism on cognitive growth: a synthesis of research findings and explanatory hypothesis. *Working Papers on Bilingualism*, **9**, 1–43.

Darcy, N. (1953). A review of the literature on the effects of bilingualism upon the measurement of intelligence. *Journal of Genetic Psychology*, **82**, 21–57.

Darcy, N. (1963). Bilingualism and the measurement of intelligence: review of a decade of research. *Journal of Genetic Psychology*, **103**, 259–282.

De Grève, E. & Rossel, E. (eds.) (1977). *Problèmes linguistiques des enfants de travailleurs migrants*. 10e Colloque de l'AIMAV en collaboration avec la Commission des Communautés Européennes. Brussels: AIMAV, Didier.

Dittmar, N., Haberland, H., Skutnabb-Kangas, T. & Teleman, U. (eds.) (1978). Papers from the first Scandinavian-German Symposium on the language of immigrant workers and their children, 19–23 March 1978. Roskilde: Roskilde Universitets Center, Lingvistgruppen.

Educational disadvantage and the educational needs of immigrants (1974). Observation on the report on education of the Select Committee on race relations and immigration presented to Parliament by the Secretary of State for Education and Science by command of Her Majesty. London: HMSO.

European Communities Commission (1975 a). Education of migrant children. Report of the discussions of three meetings of experts (28–29 October 1974, 14–15 August 1975, 16–17 October 1975). Directorate-General for Research, Science and Education, XII/226/76-E, Brussels.

European Communities Commission (1975 b). Education of migrant workers. European Documentation: School Series. Brussels.

European Communities Commission (1976). An education policy for the Community. Resolution of the Council and of the Ministers of Education. Meeting within the Council of 9 February 1976. Background note published 26 March 1976.

European Communities Council (1977). Council Directive on the education of children of migrant workers, 25 July 1977, 77/486/EEC.

European Communities Commission (1977). *The children of migrant workers*. Collection Studies, Education Series No 1, Brussels.

FIPLV/UNESCO (1976). *Teaching children of migrants*. A documentation. Report of the Symposium sponsored by the World Federation of Foreign Language Teachers' Associations and UNESCO. R. Freudenstein (ed.). Brussels: AIMAV, Didier, 1978.

Fishman, J. A. (1966). *Language loyalty in the United States*. The Hague: Mouton.

Fishman, J. A. (1967). Bilingualism with and without diglossia; diglossia with and without bilingualism. *Journal of Social Issues*, **23**, 2, 29–38.

Fishman, J. A. (1972). Language maintenance and language shift revisited. In J. A. Fishman (ed.), *Language in sociocultural change*. Stanford, Calif.: Stanford University Press, 76–134.

Fishman, J. A. (1975). Worldwide perspective on the sociology of bilingual education. In R. C. Troike & N. Modiano (eds.), *Proceedings of the first Interamerican Conference on Bilingual Education*. Arlington, Va.: Center for Applied Linguistics, 4–13.

Fishman, J. A. (1976). *Bilingual education: an international sociological perspective*. Rowley, Mass.: Newbury House.

Fishman, J. A. (1977 a). The sociology of bilingual education. In B. Spolsky & R. Cooper (eds.), *Frontiers of bilingual education*. Rowley, Mass.: Newbury House.

A. Tosi: Mother-tongue teaching

Fishman, J. A. (1977 b). The social science perspective. Keynote. In J. A. Fishman (ed.), *Bilingual education: current perspectives*, Vol. I. Arlington, Va: Center for Applied Linguistics, 1–49.

Fishman, J. A. (1977 c). Bilingual education for the children of migrant workers: the adaptation of general models to a new specific challenge. In M. De Grève & E. Rossell (eds.), 97–105.

Fishman, J. A. & Lovas, J. (1970). Bilingual education in a sociolinguistic perspective. *TESOL Quarterly*, 4, 215–222. Reprinted in B. Spolsky (ed.), (1972), 83–93.

Gaarder, A. B. (1967 a). Organisation of the bilingual school. *Journal of Social Issues*, 23, 110–20.

Gaarder, A. B. (1967 b). Bilingualism and education. Report of the Special Subcommittee on Bilingual Education of the Committee on Labor and Public Welfare, US Senate, Ninetieth Congress. Reprinted in B. Spolsky (ed.) (1972), 51–9.

Hansegård, N. E. (1968). *Tvåspråkighet eller halvspråkighet?* [Bilingualism or semi-lingualism?] Aldusserien 253, Stockholm. 3rd edition.

Harris, J. W. (1974). The morphologization of phonological rules; an example from Chicanos Spanish. In R. J. Campbell, M. G. Goldwin and M. C. Wang (eds.), *Linguistics studies in Romance languages*. Washington, D.C.: Georgetown University Press.

Haugen, E. (1966). Dialect, language, nation. *American Anthropologist*, 68, 922–35.

Heraud, P. (1968). *Peuples et langues d'Europe*. Paris: Denoel.

Hines, M. E. (1976). A critique of the US Commission on Civil Rights Report on Bilingual Bicultural Education. In J. E. Alatis & K. Twaddel (eds.), *ESL in Bilingual Education*. Washington, DC: TESOL, Georgetown University, 21–33.

Jaakkola, M. (1976). Diglossia and bilingualism among two minorities in Sweden. *International Journal of the Sociology of Language*, 10, 67–84.

Johanneson, I. (1975). Bilingual–bicultural education of immigrant children in Sweden. *International Review of Education*, 21, 347–55.

Johanneson, I. (1976). The teaching of immigrants' mother tongue in Sweden. A report prepared for UNESCO. *Pedagogical Reports*, 6, Department of Education, Lund.

John, V. P. & Horner, V. M. (1971). *Early childhood bilingual education*. New York: The Modern Language Association of America.

Khan, V. (1976). Provision by minorities for language maintenance. In *CILT Reports and Papers*, 14, 31–47.

Kjolseth, R. (1971). Bilingual education programs in the United States: for assimilation or pluralism? In B. Spolsky (ed.) (1972), 94–121.

Kloss, H. (1971). Language rights and immigrant groups. *International Migration Review*, 5, 250–68.

Krear, S. E. (1969). The role of the mother tongue at home and at school in the development of bilingualism. *English Language Teaching*, 24, 1, 1–4.

Lasonen, K. & Toukomaa, P. (1978). *Linguistic development and school achievement among Finnish immigrant children in mother-tongue medium classes in Sweden*. Research Reports 70. Department of Education, University of Jyväskylä.

Lepschy, A. L. & G. (1977). *The Italian language today*. London: Hutchinson.

Lewis, E. G. (1970). Immigrants – their languages and development. *Trends in Education*, 18, 25–32.

Littré, E. (1956). *Dictionnaire de la langue française*. Editions Universitaires.

Luria, A. R. (1932). *The nature of human conflicts*. New York edition: Liveright, 1967.

Luria, A. R. & Yudovich, F. Ia. (1956). *Speech and the development of mental processes in the child*. Harmondsworth, Mddx: Penguin Books Ltd (1971).

di Luzio, A. (1978). The bilingualism of the children of Italian workers in W. Germany:

the development of their mother tongue in contact with German. In N. Dittmar, H. Haberland, T. Skutnabb-Kangas & U. Teleman (eds.), 25–34.

Mackey, W. F. (1972). *Bilingual education in a binational school.* Rowley, Mass.: Newbury House.

Mackey, W. F. & Beebe, V. M. (1977). *Bilingual school for a bicultural community.* Rowley, Mass.: Newbury House.

Macnamara, J. (1976). First and second language learning: same or different? *Journal of Education,* **158,** 2, 39–54.

Malmberg, B. (1971). *Språkinlärning. En orientering och ett debattinlägg.* [Learning a language. An orientation and a debate contribution.] Aldusserien 339, Aldus/Bonniers, Stockholm.

Martinet, A. (1960). *Eléments de linguistique générale.* Paris: Armand Colin.

Orlowsky, D. (1974). Language learning and language change: the acquisition of modern Greek by Greek Canadian children. In R. Darnell (ed.), *Linguistic diversity in Canadian society.* Edmonton: Linguistic Research, 201–21.

Paulston, C. B. (1974). Implications of language learning theory for language planning: concerns in bilingual education. Arlington, Va.: Center for Applied Linguistics.

Paulston, C. B. (1975). Ethnic relations and bilingual education: accounting for contradictory data. *Working Papers on Bilingualism,* **6,** 1–44.

Paulston, C. B. (1977). Theoretical perspectives on bilingual education programs. *Working Papers on Bilingualism,* **13,** 130–77.

Perren, G. E. (1976). Bilingualism and British education. In *CILT Reports and Papers,* **14,** 7–14.

Perren, G. E. (1977). The languages of minority groups. Paper from the Specialist Conference on Language and Languages in Education convened by CILT, 1–3 July 1977.

Perren, G. E. (1979). Languages and minority groups. In G. E. Perren (ed.), *The mother tongue and other languages in education.* NCLE Papers and Reports 2, 45–59.

Rado, M. (1974). The implications of bilingualism. Bilingual education. An occasional paper from the Centre for the Study of Teaching, La Trobe University School of Education, Bundoora, Victoria.

Saltarelli, M. (1975). Levelling of paradigms in Chicano Spanish. In W. G. Milan, J. J. Staczek & J. C. Zamora (eds.), *Colloquium on Spanish and Portuguese Linguistics.* Washington, DC: Georgetown University Press.

Saltarelli, M. & Gonzo, S. (1977). Migrant languages: linguistic changes in progress. In M. De Grève & E. Rossel (eds.), 167–86.

Salvi, S. (1975). *Le lingue tagliate.* Milan: Rizzoli.

Saville-Troike, M. R. (1975). Bilingual children: a resource document. *Papers in Applied Linguistics,* Series 2. Arlington, Va.: Center for Applied Linguistics.

Seaman, D. (1972). *Modern Greek and American English in contact.* The Hague: Mouton.

Segers, J. & Van Den Broeck, J. (1978). Bilingual education for the children of migrant workers in the Belgian province of Limburg. *International Journal of the Sociology of Language,* **15,** 77–84.

Skutnabb-Kangas, T. (1975). *Tvåspråkighet eller dubbel halvspråkighetvem utgör normen?* [Bilingualism or double semilingualism – who sets the norms?] Papers from the Second Scandinavian Conference of Linguistics, Lysebu, 19–20 April 1975. E. Hovdhaugen (ed.), Department of Linguistics, University of Oslo, Norway.

Skutnabb-Kangas, T. & Toukomaa, P. (1976). *Teaching migrant children their mother tongue and learning the language of the host country in the context of the socio-cultural situation of the migrant family.* Tampere, Finland: University of Tampere. (Tutkimuksia Research Reports, 1976.)

A. Tosi: Mother-tongue teaching

Skutnabb-Kangas, T. (1978). Semilingualism and the education of migrant children as a means of reproducing the caste of assembly line workers. In N. Dittmar, H. Haberland, T. Skutnabb-Kangas & U. Teleman (eds.) (1978).

Spoerl, D. Y. (1946). Bilinguality and emotional adjustment. *Journal of Abnormal and Social Psychology*, **38**, 37–57.

Spolsky, B. (1971). The limits of language education. *Linguistic Reporter*, **13**, 3, 1–5. Reprinted in B. Spolsky (ed.) (1972).

Spolsky, B. (ed.) (1972). *The language education of minority children*. Rowley, Mass.: Newbury House.

Spolsky, B. (1974). Speech communities and schools. *TESOL Quarterly*, **8**, 17–26.

Stephens, M. (1976). *Linguistic minorities in Western Europe*. Llandysul, Wales: Gomer Press.

Stockfelt-Hoatson, B. I. (1976). Factors which influence the integration of migrants' children into pre-school education in Sweden. Strasbourg: Committee for General and Technical Education. Council of Europe. CCC/EGT (76)19.

Stockfelt-Hoatson, B. I. (1977). The teaching of bilingual infant immigrants in a Swedish town. *International Journal of the Sociology of Language*, **14**, 118–25.

Swain, M. & Cummins, J. (1979). Bilingualism, cognitive functioning and education. *Language Teaching & Linguistics: Abstracts*, **12**, 1, 4–18.

Titone, R. (1977). Teaching a second language in a multilingual/multicultural context. Paper from a meeting of experts on language teaching in a bi- or plurilingual and multicultural environment. Paris: UNESCO.

Tosi, A. (1978 a). *L'insegnamento della lingua madre ai figli dei lavoratori immigrati in Gran Bretagna con particolare riferimento al gruppo italiano.* [The teaching of the mother tongue to children of migrant workers in the U.K.: an analysis of four viewpoints: their motives, interests and objectives.] *Rassegna Italiana di Linguistica Applicata*, **10**, 177–93.

Tosi, A. (1978 b). Linguistic and cultural distance between first and second generations in communities of migrant workers as a factor in the role and educational policy of migrants' community organisations. Paper from the UNESCO Colloquium on the role and educational policy of of migrants' associations. July, 1978.

Tosi, A. (1979). Semilingualism, diglossia and bilingualism: some observations on the sociolinguistic features of a community of Southern Italians in Britain. *Lingua e Contesto: Nuovi Studi di dialettologia, linguistica geografica, sociologica e pragmatica*, **4**, 1979. Manfredonia: Atlantica Ed.

Tosi, A. (forthcoming). *Bilinguismo, transfert e interferenze. Considerazione sul processo di acquisizione dell'italiano in figli di emigrati bilingui in inglise e dialetto campano.* Paper from a Conference on *Linguistica Contrastiva*, May 1979, convened by *Società di Linguistica Italiano*, Asti (forthcoming in *Atti del congresso*).

Toukomaa, P. (1975). *Om svårigheten att definiera halvspråkighet.* [On the difficulty in defining semilingualism.] Nordisk Minoritetsforskning 3.

Toukomaa, P. & Skutnabb-Kangas, T. (1977). *The intensive teaching of the mother tongue to migrant children of pre-school age and children in the lower level of comprehensive school.* Helsinki: The Finnish National Commission for UNESCO. Tampere: University of Tampere.

Toukomaa, P. & Seppo, S. (1978). Vocational aspirations of Finnish immigrant youth in Sweden. Research Reports 2, 1978. Department of Social Psychology, University of Helsinki.

Trim, J. L. M. (1977). Helping migrant children to communicate: some implications of the Council of Europe work in language systems construction. In M. De Grève & E. Rossel (eds.) (1977), 211–20.

UNESCO (1953). *The use of vernacular languages in education.* Monographs on fundamental education. Paris: UNESCO.
UNESCO (1978). The education of migrant workers and their families. Educational studies and documents, 27. Paris: UNESCO.
US Commission on Civil Rights (1975). *A better chance to learn: bilingual bicultural education.* Washington DC: Clearinghouse Publications, 51, of the Commission.
Verdoot, A. (1977). Educational policies on languages: the case of the children of migrant workers. In H. Giles (ed.), *Language ethnicity and intergroup relations.* New York: Academic Press, 241–52.
Vernon Jensen, J. (1962). Effects of childhood bilingualism. *Elementary English,* **39,** 132–43.
Vigotsky, L. S. (1962). *Thought and language.* Cambridge, Mass.: M.I.T. Press.
Willke, I. (1975). Schooling of immigrant children in West Germany–Sweden–England: the educationally disadvantaged. *International Review of Education,* **21,** 357–401.

Addendum references

Cummins, J. (1979*a*). Linguistic interdependence and the educational development of bilingual children. *Review of Educational Research,* **49,** 222–51.
Cummins, J. (1979*b*). Cognitive/academic language proficiency, linguistic interdependence, the optimum age question and some other matters. *Working Papers on Bilingualism,* **19,** 198–205.
Khan, V. (1980). The 'mother tongue' of linguistic minorities in multicultural England. *Journal of Multilingual and Multicultural Development,* **1,** 1, 71–88.
Rosen, H. & Burgess, T. (1980). *Languages and dialect of London schoolchildren.* London: Ward Lock Educational.
Skutnabb-Kangas, T. & Toukomaa, P. (1980). Semilingualism and middle-class bias: a reply to Cora Brent-Palmer. *Working Papers in Bilingualism,* **19,** 182–97.
Skutnabb-Kangas, T. (1980). Guest worker or immigrant: different ways of reproducing an underclass. *Rolig Papir,* 21, 80, Roskilde Universitets Center, Lingvistgruppen.
Tosi, A. (1980). Bilinguismo e immigrazione. Una nota sociolinguistica al piano europeo di mantenimento delle lingue nazionali nelle comunità di emigrati. *Rassegna Italiana di Linguistica Applicata,* **3** (1979)/**1** (1980), 243–63.
Tosi, A. (1981*a*). Issues in im/migrant bilingualism, 'semilingualism' and education. *AILA Bulletin,* **3,** December 1981.
Tosi, A. (1981*b*). Materials for mother-tongue teaching in the context of second-language learning. Criteria for design and evaluation. Paper prepared for the National Congress on Languages in Education, 1980–1982.
Tosi, A. (1981*c*). Between the mother's dialect and English. In A. Davies (ed.), *Language and learning in home and school.* London: Heinemann Educational.
Tosi, A. (forthcoming). *Immigration and bilingual education.* Oxford: Pergamon Press.

VOCABULARY ACQUISITION: A NEGLECTED ASPECT OF LANGUAGE LEARNING

Paul Meara
Birkbeck College, London

Introduction

Vocabulary acquisition is part of the psychology of second-language learning that has received short shrift from applied linguistics, and has been very largely neglected by recent developments in research. This neglect is all the more striking in that learners themselves readily admit that they experience considerable difficulty with vocabulary, and once they have got over the initial stages of acquiring their second language, most learners identify the acquisition of vocabulary as their greatest single source of problems.

This article is an attempt to redress this neglect. It summarises the current work being done on vocabulary acquisition, and draws attention to a number of studies carried out by experimental psychologists which may have implications for the development of vocabulary in a second language. The article ends with a number of questions which have not been investigated in any depth, but which seem to me to be worth looking at more closely.

A: Bibliographies and general works

Despite the comments above about the general level of neglect in the study of vocabulary acquisition, there do exist a number of bibliographies of relevance to anybody working in this field. The most important of these is Dale and Razik (1963), a very extensive work, not primarily concerned with foreign-language acquisition, but containing three relevant subsections with some 150 references. The 1963 edition of this work is actually a reworking of an earlier edition, and this may account for the fact that most of the references relate to second-language work carried out in the 1930s. The most recent bibliography dealing specifically with vocabulary acquisition is Twomey (1979). This work is patchy in its coverage, however, and a fuller bibliography, using a larger database, is in preparation (Meara, in prep.).

The principal impression that emerges from these bibliographies is that research in vocabulary acquisition has been largely atheoretical and unsystematic. There are no clear theories of vocabulary acquisition, and the level of research activity is in general fairly low. Twomey, for instance, contains a large number of references which are short articles aimed at providing practical tips for teachers concerned with particular items of vocabulary for a particular target audience (e.g. Brown, 1974; Martin, 1976; Salt, 1976; Ridout, 1977), and on the whole, research in the field has avoided the serious theoretical questions that arise once one moves away from this very basic level.

A small number of generalised approaches to vocabulary acquisition do exist. Galisson (1970) discusses vocabulary teaching at length, and considers the effectiveness of different types of vocabulary-learning exercises. These ideas are expanded in Galisson (1979). An approach to vocabulary teaching based on contrastive lexical structure is to be found in Holec (1974) (cf. also Dagut, 1977, for a shorter argument on the same lines). Two other large-scale works, Dale, O'Rourke and Bamman (1971) and O'Rourke (1974) are also worth mentioning at this stage. They are both concerned exclusively with first-language vocabulary development, but the ideas discussed are clearly of some relevance to second-language learners.

There also exist a number of shorter articles which draw attention to the need for further work on vocabulary acquisition. Marton (1977) discusses the problem of idioms, which he sees as the biggest obstacle to fluent comprehension in advanced learners. Lord (1974) draws attention to the importance of Leopold's (1948) study of semantic development in a bilingual child (cf. also Yoshida, 1978, for an empirical study along these lines). A brief but excellent critique of vocabulary research is Levenston (1979), who reiterates a number of the points made in this paper, criticising applied linguistics for its general neglect of vocabulary learning in favour of the study of syntactic development. Levenston discusses a number of research projects which have only recently begun, and which are therefore difficult to assess satisfactorily. These include Levenston's own work – Blum and Levenston (1978) and Levenston and Blum (1977), where it is argued that lexical simplification strategies used by learners may follow universal rules; and Linnarud (1979), who suggests that foreign-language learners may have characteristically low levels of vocabulary richness compared to normal speakers. (On this use of Type-token ratios as a measure of learners cf. also Webber, 1977; Philpot, 1977; and Meara, 1978.) All these pieces of work are small-scale, however, and none of them adds up to a coherent and impressive body of knowledge at this stage.

Apart from these general works, and a few small pockets of isolated research work mentioned above, there also exist a number of fields which have been or are being investigated in a fairly systematic fashion, and are thus important because they comprise the bulk of the work on vocabulary acquisition.

101

B. Vocabulary control

The best developed and most systematic work in the field is to be found in attempts to justify the selection of vocabulary items for inclusion in courses and examinations on the basis of frequency counts and similar objective measures. This work is too well known to need discussion here. Good summaries can be found in Bongers, 1947; Mackey, 1965; and Syracuse University Research Corporation, 1973.

Despite their obvious merits, frequency counts are now very much out of favour with applied linguists (cf. Wilkins, 1972, for a fairly typical criticism of this sort of approach). In contrast to the very carefully chosen vocabulary of earlier course books, many modern books appear to rely almost entirely on subjective assessments of the usefulness of words. Van Ek (1977), for instance, contains no discussion of what criteria were used for the inclusion of words in the Threshold Level vocabulary (cf. also Hoffman, 1976). In general, language teachers seem to be unaware of more recent developments in word counts. West's *General service list* (1953) is often cited by publishers and examining boards as guiding their choice of words in readers and examinations for learners of English, for example, despite the fact that both this list and the related Thorndike–Lorge list have now been superseded by the more recent Kučera–Francis count (Kučera & Francis, 1967). Recent counts for a number of other languages commonly taught to learners also exist, and ought to be more widely known. These include Juilland and Chang-Rodriguez (1964) for Spanish; Juilland, Brodin and Davidowitch (1970) for French, and Juilland and Traversa (1973) for Italian. An important feature that differentiates most of these modern counts from their earlier counterparts is the use of computers in their preparation. All the early counts were carried out by hand (the Thorndike–Lorge count was in fact begun during the Depression as a way of providing work for the unemployed), and were accordingly both expensive and slow to reach completion. The rapid processing made possible by computers makes its possible to produce word counts at minimal cost, and to keep them regularly updated.

This use of computers to carry out simple statistical analyses of texts is a development which is likely to be of some importance to language teachers, as it has considerable implications for the preparation of teaching materials. Computer programmes which will do word counts and similar basic statistics on continuous text have existed for some time, but they are now beginning to appear in the form of easy-to-use packages, designed for amateurs with no real experience of computer programming, and require minimal instruction before they can be used. An excellent example of an easy-to-use package of this sort is the Oxford Concordance Project (Hockey & Marriott, 1979–80; Burnard, Hockey

& Marriott, 1979). This package produces basic word counts for texts of any reasonable length, alphabetical listings, frequency listings, concordances with contexts of specified lengths, and so forth. Though the package is primarily aimed at literary scholars, its uses are of course not limited to literary texts. It could also be used, for example, to provide accurate frequency counts of the vocabulary used in 'special purpose' situations or to prepare a glossary to accompany a set text, and so forth. Use of tools of this kind seems likely to become increasingly important in the preparation of teaching materials (cf. Lyne, 1975; Culhane, 1977; and Johnson, 1972. An interesting general introduction to this sort of work is Morton, 1979).

This outline of research into vocabulary control and selection has been deliberately brief, and is not intended to be a comprehensive one. On the whole this work is well known and reasonably familiar. My main reason for raising it here is because work of this type has played such a preponderant part in the study of vocabulary acquisition that no review would be complete without at least a cursory mention. However, the work is also important because it illustrates two aspects of research into vocabulary acquisition which are characteristic of the field as a whole, and therefore deserve further comment. In the first place, this work is characteristic in that it concentrates on what is basically a problem to do with the management of learning, rather than with the learning process itself – i.e. the object of this type of research is to decide what words are to be taught, not to find out how words are actually learned. This is an important point, and will be returned to later at the end of the next section. In the second place, this work also illustrates how easy it is to fall into the trap of accepting uncritically a whole set of assumptions, and to design a large research programme around these assumptions, without ever calling their validity into question. In this case, the central assumption is that it really is necessary to place a severely restricted upper limit on the number of words that a learner can reasonably be expected to acquire in a foreign language. Some simple arithmetic indicates that a vocabulary of 2,000 words could be learned in 11 months if new words were acquired at a rate of six per day. This figure does not appear to be wildly excessive, given what we know about the capacity of the brain to acquire new information. Nevertheless, most teachers would undoubtedly consider 2,000 words to be well beyond the capacity of many learners, even over a five-year course of instruction (cf. for instance Wicklow, 1974, and Barnard, 1971, where these assumptions are made quite explicit). No doubt there is some practical justification, based on experience, for this general belief that learners cannot easily acquire a large foreign-language vocabulary in a short space of time, but the theoretical basis for this agreement is by no means clear. This is obviously an area in which further research would be most useful.

C. Mnemonics

The second major area of research to be discussed is one which has, in a way, addressed itself to this problem, challenging the assumption that massive vocabularies cannot be acquired, by introducing mnemonic techniques into the teaching of vocabulary.

The best studied of these methods is the 'key word' method which has been the object of considerable attention in the last few years, particularly in the United States (Atkinson & Raugh, 1975; Atkinson, 1975; Raugh & Atkinson, 1974; Pressley, 1977; Pressley & Levin, 1978; Pressley (in press); Singer, 1977). In this method, the target-language words are associated with phonetically similar English words (called 'key words') in the first stage of learning, and then, in the second stage, these key words are associated with the English translation of the original target-language word by means of a striking visual image. Thus, for example, Raugh and Atkinson suggest that the Spanish word CABALLO (pronounce cob-eye-oh [*sic*]) might be linked to EYE and EYE to HORSE via the image of a horse with a great cyclopean eye in the middle of its forehead. Or more prosaically, CABALLO might be linked to the English word CAB, which in its turn would be linked to HORSE via the image of a horse drawing a cab. The papers listed above report a number of experiments which compare more traditional ways of learning vocabulary (e.g. list repetition) with this key word method, and despite its initial implausibility, present some impressive results in support of this sort of practice. Raugh and Atkinson (1974), for example, report that learners using the key word method can cope with very long lists of words (60 items) and still get 80 per cent correct on a subsequent test, a figure that is considerably better than that produced by learners using repetition and rehearsal methods. More importantly, the key word groups preserve their advantage over time, and show less evidence of forgetting than is found with control groups.

This evidence is very impressive at first sight, but work of this kind is actually rather problematical at a deeper level, and needs to be treated with some caution. The most obvious problem is that experiments of this sort treat vocabulary items as discrete pairs of translation equivalents, and completely ignore the complex patterns of meaning relationships that characterise a proper, fully formed lexicon, as opposed to a mere word list. Learning vocabulary is not just a matter of acquiring translation equivalents, as it is well known that languages rarely map their lexical items onto each other in a one-to-one fashion. Some lexical structuring must go on when even the shortest word list is learned, and any view of vocabulary acquisition which treats the problem as a simple matter of pairing words with their translation equivalents is an oversimplified one, which cannot adequately account for how these semantic relationships are built up in a foreign-language vocabulary. All the experimental studies of vocabulary acquisition which make use of mnemonic devices are basically subscribing to a model of 'paired associate learning' which does not seem to me to be sufficiently rich to account for what is involved in the acquisition of a second-language vocabulary (cf., for example, Crothers & Suppes, 1967, where a model of vocabulary acquisition based on paired associate learning is explicitly discussed).

A second problem that characterises the key word studies is that they are generally one-off experiments that do not study real language learners in the course of learning a language, but only subjects prepared to take part in a small number of experimental sessions in a laboratory setting. This means that the subjects tested often have an initial vocabulary of zero, and it is unclear how far the results of such experiments might be generalisable to more advanced learners. More importantly, it means that the comparison between the key word method and other methods is usually limited in practice to methods that can also be contained within a single experimental session, such as rote learning by repetition. Whether the key word method is in the long term more effective than other methods which are not readily comparable with it, such as the Silent Way, or Total Immersion, or even methods which place special emphasis on vocabulary acquisition, such as Gouin's Series technique (Gouin, 1880) or Barter's Comparative Method (Barter, 1970; Becker, 1977), is typically a question which is not asked. Indeed, even within its own terms of reference, the comparisons made are rather spurious. It is difficult to imagine that even the most ardent believer in rote learning methods might require his students to use this method with lists containing 60 items. It seems important, then, that these laboratory tests should be complemented by properly controlled longitudinal classroom tests, before their findings are widely accepted.

A third problem is that the key word method is used principally in situations where the target-language word is required to evoke the native-language equivalent. The phonetic link idea seems to work reasonably well in this respect, and the method does seem to have some value as far as recognition vocabulary is concerned. The value of the method for developing active vocabulary is much less clear, however, and it seems likely that the practice of stressing crude phonetic similarities between English words and target-language words would in the long term have a serious detrimental effect on the pronunciation of target-language words.

A final point to be made about this work is that Raugh and Atkinson, at least, have a highly directive approach to the choice of key words. One might have expected that this choice could easily be left to the individual learner, but Raugh and Atkinson actually go to some length to stress that not all key words are equally effective, and only key words shown by extensive research to be effective should be used.

A more recent mnemonic technique is the Hook technique, described by Paivio, 1978, and Paivio and Desrochers, 1979. This research is still in its infancy, but seems to suffer from some of the same problems as the key word method. The same criticism also applies to Ott, Blake and Butler, 1976, who report a number of studies using a variety of 'elaborative techniques' (Lado, Baldwin & Lobo, 1967; Butler, Ott & Blake, 1973; Knop, 1971; Groberg, 1972; Holley, 1971; cf. also Setzler & Clark, 1976).

D. General comments

So far we have covered two areas of research in the broad field of vocabulary acquisition. These two areas may at first sight appear to be relatively unconnected. In fact, however, they are both linked in that they share a common defect: their concern with the peripheral aspects of vocabulary acquisition rather than the central ones. In the case of research into the uses of frequency counts, we have already seen how the management of learning, rather than an understanding of how learning takes place and what it involves, is the principal driving force behind the investigations reported. Basically, the learner's load is lightened for him, by working out beforehand which words are likely to be of use to him, and which ones are not worth the trouble of learning. What happens to the words that are learned is not in question. With mnemonics, too, the emphasis is placed squarely on the management of the learning process, the main theoretical questions asked being ones concerned with the effectiveness of different forms of presentation.

Both these approaches, then, are concerned with what is basically the periphery of acquiring new vocabulary. Yet it must be obvious that these peripheral aspects, important though they may be, leave unanswered a large number of questions which are of considerable relevance to our understanding of how vocabulary is acquired. Learning new words is not an instantaneous process – if it were, and if presentation were the only critical variable involved, then words would not be forgotten and need to be relearned. As it is, however, it seems that words are absorbed slowly over time, and that only gradually do they become fully integrated into the learner's personal stock of words, when he can use them with the same sort of fluency that characterises the words he uses in his native language. Some work that is relevant to this rather more difficult question is discussed in the sections that follow.

There does exist a reasonably large body of experimental work which has attempted to investigate how bilingual speakers store words in their mental dictionaries. These studies may not appear to be of direct relevance to language teaching and language learning, but in fact their relevance is often greater than appears at first sight. Their importance lies in the fact that they provide us with some clues about what the end product of learning a foreign language ought to consist of, and what sort of behaviour can be expected of a fluent bilingual. Information of this kind should, in theory at least, enable us to compare the behaviour of non-fluent bilinguals – i.e. language learners – with that of fluent bilinguals, and so to make inferences about the way a developing vocabulary in a second language grows. Basically, this work provides us with a model, albeit a sketchy one, against which to assess the more limited abilities of less fluent learners.

Most of the work to be described in the next sections is not ostensibly concerned with foreign-language learners; the subjects used in these experiments are usually 'balanced bilinguals' – i.e. speakers who are judged to be equally fluent in both their languages. The main purpose of this research has been to compare two types of bilinguals – compound and co-ordinate – a distinction first drawn by Ervin and Osgood (1954). Ervin and Osgood argued that the way in which a language was acquired might be expected to produce different types of structuring in the bilingual's mental dictionary. Compound bilinguals, those who have acquired their two languages together in a single environment, usually in infancy, might be expected to have a single set of meanings tagged by two sets of labels, one for each language. In contrast, Ervin and Osgood argued that co-ordinate bilinguals, who learned their two languages in largely separate environments, might develop what are effectively two separate lexicons, one for each language, which function independently of each other.

Again, this work may not seem to be directly relevant to second-language acquisition, but the relevance is there, none the less. Lambert has argued that certain types of teaching method may be more likely to produce behaviour characteristics of one type of bilingual, rather than the other. Direct Method teaching, for instance, which tries to eliminate reference to the mother tongue, might be more likely to produce learners with the characteristics of co-ordinate bilinguals. Experimental evidence to support this claim is not available, however, and a rather different claim has been put forward by Riegel (1968). Riegel argues that this dichotomy is a false one, and that there is actually a natural development from a sort of compound system to one which is closer in kind to the classical co-ordinate model, irrespective of the language acquisition background.

The second reason why this work is of some relevance to second-language acquisition is that many of the 'balanced bilinguals' used as subjects in these experiments are actually far from equally fluent in their two languages. In fact, the criteria used to decide on an acceptable level of ability in the second language are often ill defined and crude, and in practice the term 'bilingual' can mean anything from fully and equally fluent in both languages, to someone who has only barely begun to acquire his second language, and could not be considered equally fluent by any stretch of the imagination. The unsatisfactory nature of the tests used to measure second-language fluency (often only self-ratings, or impressionistic judgements made by the experimenter) is a major flaw in this literature. It does mean, however, that a number of these studies are actually directly concerned with ordinary language learners.

The work to be considered in the next sections falls into two parts: (*a*) experiments concerned with the general question of whether the bilingual's lexicons are separate or interdependent, and (*b*) experiments concerned with the semantic relationships that exist between words in the bilingual's lexicons. A third area – the ability of the bilingual to handle words in each of his two languages in very demanding situations such as tachistoscopic recognition tasks, or dichotic listening tasks, and so forth – will not be considered here, due to lack of space. Interested readers are referred to Albert and Obler (1979), an excellent book with a superb bibliography (though cf. Green & Newman, 1980, for a critical review). This work suggests that there may be major differences between stronger and weaker languages, and provides some evidence for the claim that second-language words may be processed less effectively by certain parts of the brain. In particular, a number of studies suggest that there are hemispheric asymmetries for different languages (cf. Walters & Zatorre, 1978, for Spanish; Hamers & Lambert, 1977, for French; Kershner & Jeng, 1972, for Chinese; and Orbach, 1953, for Hebrew). This type of research is becoming increasingly sophisticated and influential and looks like becoming one of the major growth areas in psycholinguistics in the immediate future.

E. Memory experiments

The work to be reviewed in this section consists of a number of experimental studies which have all attempted to test the claim that bilinguals have two separate, independently functioning lexicons, rather than a single fully integrated one.

For reasons which are not wholly clear, this claim seems to have been most often investigated by the use of memory tasks, and in particular by the use of tasks where interference from one language to another is observed. This is obviously a fairly crude tool, and the results found in these experiments are correspondingly limited. The general line of argument is that if the bilingual's two sets of words were stored totally independently, then very little interference would be expected in tasks that require the subject to use both his languages. Where interference is found, this is usually interpreted as supporting the claim that the two languages function interdependently, and are not wholly separated.

The more important studies of this kind are summarised in Table 1. Useful discussions of this work will be found in Albert and Obler (1979) and McCormack (1977). The experimental methods may seem rather obscure, but in general they are techniques which have been widely used in experiments with monolingual subjects, and which produce robust results which are reasonably well understood.

The bulk of the work reported in Table 1 is generally taken as supporting the interdependence position, rather than the independence position: i.e. it seems to support the claim that words in a second language are indeed integrated in some way with words in a first language to form a complex whole lexicon. The logic of this argument is not always as clear as it might be, however, and some of the data argues strongly against this position (e.g. Tulving & Colotla, 1970, who showed that in mixed-language lists of words, recall was much worse than in single-language lists, and that the greater part of this deficit seems to be due to the fact that L1 words are handled less satisfactorily in secondary memory than words from the weaker languages). This finding is at odds with some of the other findings reported, and is not what would have been expected, but there are no obvious faults with this experiment, and it therefore needs to be taken seriously. Some of the other experiments, particularly the ones that use Spanish as one of the languages tested, are rather less satisfactory, and need to be treated with some caution. The subjects in these studies were usually school children brought up speaking Spanish as their mother tongue, but being taught English as the medium of instruction in the American schools. Most of these subjects rated themselves as more fluent in English than in Spanish, and were thus classified as English dominant, but this seems rather implausible, and the use of self-ratings with subjects such as these seems to be an unreliable method of assessment, in view of the obvious pressure that subjects must be under to overrate their competence in English and to underplay their abilities in Spanish.

Generally speaking, the results of these studies show that subjects are aware of the language in which words are presented, and that they use

Table 1. *List learning and recall tasks*

Author	Task	Languages	Brief comments
Lambert, Havelka & Crossby, 1958	(1) Learn English word list (2) Learn French word list or learn nonsense word list (3) Recall English word list	French/English	For compound bilinguals task (2*a*) facilitated (3) but for co-ordinates (2*a*)+(2*b*) were equally disruptive
Ervin, 1961	(1) Name pictures in English or Italian (2) Practice with It. (3) Recall items from (1)	Italian/English	For compound bilinguals (dominant in It.), objects named fastest in It. were easy to recall. Objects named fastest in Eng. recalled equally well in either language.
Kolers, 1965	Recall of lists coded by colour and language	French/English	Mixing colours reduces number of words remembered, but mixing languages has no effect.
Kolers, 1968	Recall of mixed lg word lists with some repeated items	French/English	Interlingual and intralingual repetitions both increased probability of recall
Lambert, Ignatow & Krauthamer, 1968	Recall of lists, mixed lg or monolingual, semantically categorised or not	French/English Russian/English	Greater recall in stronger lg. No effect of mixed lists, but when categories and lgs conflicted, large numbers of translation errors found
Nott & Lambert, 1968	Recall of mixed lg lists containing semantically related items or not	French/English	Categories crossing lgs produced worse recall
Tulving & Colotla, 1970	Recall of mixed lg lists	French/English	No difference in primary memory, but large differences in secondary memory, with most proficient lg being most impaired on multilingual lists
Kintsch, 1970	Words presented in list with repetitions; Ss required to judge whether each word was new or repeated	German/English	More accurate performance in the dominant language. Ss. found it hard to treat translations as new words

Goggin & Wickens, 1971	Release from proactive interference (1) Learn short list (2) Learn similar short list (3) Learn another similar short list (4) Learn another similar short list or list with new characteristics, in this case lg of list is chief characteristic considered	Spanish/English	Language shift produces a marked improvement in recall for balanced bilinguals, but smaller improvement with greater dominance
Saegert, Kazarian & Young, 1973	Part–whole transfer (learn a short list, then a longer list that includes all items from first in different order)	Spanish/English Arabic/English	Learning part list in dominant language and whole list in non-dominant language produces negative transfer. Positive transfer found in opposite condition
Champagnol, 1973	Recall of mixed language lists semantically categorised	French/English	Better recall in French: worse recall in mixed lists. Usual category effects
Lopez & Young, 1974	Learn list A Learn list B Recall list B	Spanish/English	When list B contained items translated from list A recall was better, though more so when B was in English
Lopez, Hicks & Young, 1974	(a) Learn list of Eng. pairs (b) Learn new list where items or language are changed	Spanish/English	Translation errors frequent where language change was made
Liepmann & Saegert, 1974	Repeated learning of lists of words drawn from either a monolingual pool or a bilingual pool	Arabic/English	Performance deteriorates more in bilingual condition

language as a classifying label more successfully than they use other more arbitrary coding features such as colour, though this last finding is hardly surprising in view of the artificiality and unfamiliarity of the colour coding task (cf. McCormack, 1976). More interesting is the finding that it is much harder to remember the language of presentation when languages and semantic categories are confused, and the finding that subjects have some difficulty in recognising words in a list as new ones when they have previously been presented in translation form. These results show clearly that when some kind of cognitive operation other than simple recall of the phonetic form is called for, it does become extremely difficult to keep two languages apart. In this sense, forms in one language clearly evoke the corresponding related forms in the other language, a finding which would be very difficult to explain if the independent lexicons claim were true.

F. Semantic tests

The work reported in the previous section is rather unsatisfactory in that it all treats the bilingual's lexicon as though it consisted of one or two undifferentiated wholes about which it was possible to make sweeping generalisations. There is, of course, no reason to assume that all the words in a lexicon should behave in the same way as each other, and just as words are differentiated in the lexicons of monolingual speakers in terms of frequency, length, and other similar objective characteristics, it is quite likely that similar features may produce subsets of words in the bilingual's mental lexicon which also have quite different behavioural properties. Perhaps, then, it is inappropriate to ask whether the bilingual's two word stores are integrated or independent as wholes, and it might make much more sense to assume that some words will be integrated while others will not, and thus to shift the focus of attention to individual words and relatively small semantic fields.

Some work of this kind has been carried out, and a good example of what can be done is to be found in a number of studies using the Stroop test with bilingual subjects (Stroop, 1935). In this technique, subjects are given lists of words to read which have been printed in different colours. Typically three sets of words are used: (*a*) a set of neutral words or colour patches; (*b*) a set of colour words congruent with the printed colours, e.g. *red* printed in red, *green* printed in green, etc.; (*c*) a set of colour words that are incongruent with the printed colours, e.g. *red* printed in blue, *green* printed in red, and so forth. The subjects' task is to ignore the actual printed words, and to state the colour that the word is printed in. Thus, given *red* printed in green ink, the correct response is 'green' and not 'red'. Task (*c*) proves to be extremely difficult in practice, since the colour words interfere with the naming of the printed colours. It is relatively easy to introduce a bilingual variation on this theme, by producing further sets of words that contain the names of colours in the subject's second language. Again the cards are either congruent of incongruent with respect to the colours of the print. Thus (*d*) *rouge* written in red, *bleu* written in blue is congruent in French, while (*e*) *vert* written in blue, or *rouge* written in green, would be incongruent. Subjects can then be asked to call out the names of colours either in their first or their second language, and this introduces an additional layer of interference.

A number of languages have been studied using this technique: Dalrymple-Alford and Budayr, 1967 (English and Arabic); Dalrymple-Alford, 1968 (English and Arabic); Preston and Lambert, 1969 (English, French, Hungarian and German); Dyer, 1971 (English, Greek, Italian, French, German and Spanish); Albert and Obler, 1979 (English and Hebrew); and Evans and Townsendson, 1979 (English and Welsh). Hamers and Lambert (1972), who use an auditory version of the Stroop test in English and French, are also worth mentioning here. What this work shows, without exception, is that interlingual conditions do show strong evidence of interference, though less than would be expected in the case of monolingual subjects. Dyer showed that the level of interference was in part related to the phonetic shape of the words. Thus, for an English speaker, for example, when asked to name a word printed in red ink, the Spanish word *azul* would be much less disruptive than the French *bleu* because of the similarity between this latter and the English *blue*. Other things being equal, however, the amount of interference caused by the foreign-language words appears to depend on the level of proficiency of the subject, though this correspondence has been measured only in very gross terms. Again, the logic of these data is that they support the idea that the bilingual's two lexicons are integrated into a single whole. However, if the bilingual's colour words in the second language were totally integrated with his L1 colour words, then one would expect to find Stroop interference equally great in either language. In as much as the weaker language produces less interference, this suggests that words in the second language are not fully integrated at the semantic level, or at least that they are not treated with the fluency that is usually accorded to first-language words. A similar argument based on data using semantic differentials in two languages is to be found in Jakobovits and Lambert, 1961, and Lambert and Jakobovits, 1960.

One of the most accessible and most easily understood methods of studying the structure of semantic relationships in the bilingual's lexicon is the use of word associations. In its simplest form, this technique involves the presentation of a number of single words to the subjects participating, and they are then instructed to reply with the first word that each of the stimulus words makes them think of. The bulk of responses produced in situations of this sort are noteworthy principally for their banality, at least as long as unemotive common words are used. Far from being original, most people's responses are characteristically shared with a large proportion of the rest of the population of normal adult native speakers (cf. Pollio, 1966; Deese, 1965; Postman & Keppel, 1970). In English, for example, over 70 per cent of people produce WHITE in response to BLACK, WOMAN in response to MAN, BUTTER in response to BREAD, and so on. This phenomenon, known as associational stereotypy, is found in all languages that have been investigated, though the absolute levels of stereotypy vary from one culture to another. English has particularly high levels of stereotypy compared to other languages. French, German, Italian and Polish are all significantly less stereotyped than English is (cf. Rosenzweig, 1961; Szalay & Deese, 1978; Vikis-Freibergs & Freibergs, 1976; Kurcz, 1966).

In addition to being very similar to the responses produced by other members of a similar population of subjects, responses to common words generally fall into one of two major classes. *Paradigmatic* responses are responses that belong to the same major form class as the stimulus word. Thus CAT, BONE, TAIL, COLLIE would all be classed as paradigmatic responses to the stimulus DOG. *Syntagmatic* responses are responses that typically combine with the stimulus words to form a phrase or syntactic whole. Thus BITES, BARKS, FIERCE, STUPID and HOT would all be syntagmatic responses if produced in response to DOG. Normal adult native speakers tend to produce many more paradigmatic responses than syntagmatic ones, at least as long as the stimulus words are fairly common words. Infrequent words, such as ABDICATE or INITIATIVE are more likely to produce syntagmatic response forms such as KING or TAKE (Stoltz & Tiffany, 1972). A good account of these typical responses is to be found in Clarke (1970), who also provides a good basic bibliography.

These normal response patterns are not preserved in abnormal native speakers (de Wolfe, 1971) nor are they found in children. This latter group tends to produce response patterns that differ markedly from those of adults in that they contain a large number of syntagmatic associations in place of the more normal paradigmatic ones. Children also tend to produce lots of *clang associations*, i.e. responses that are phonetically related to the stimulus word, but fail to have any clear semantic connection with it. Typical examples of clang associations would be FIGHT, TIGHT, WHILE or WIDE produced in response to WHITE (Ervin, 1961; Entwhistle, 1966; McNeill, 1963; Entwhistle, Forsyth & Muss, 1964).

114

Table 2 below summarises the main studies of word association behaviour in which foreign-language learners and bilinguals were used as subjects. These studies are very disparate in nature, and it therefore is rather difficult to summarise the findings briefly, or even to compare one study directly with another, since often the principal questions which the data were collected in order to elucidate do not have much in common. This variation can be seen in the large number of different entries in the columns headed Subjects, Methods and Materials. These differences are explained below.

Explanatory notes on Table 2

(*a*) *Materials used.* There is almost no agreement over what sort of stimulus words to use in studies of word associations. Most of this work has used unstandardised and apparently unmotivated lists of words, some so extremely small in number that one is forced to wonder whether results based on these stimuli can be considered at all generalisable. The standard list of stimuli is the Kent–Rosanoff list, first used by Kent and Rosanoff (1910) in their study of the word associations produced by mental patients. This list has the advantage that it has been very widely used in a large variety of studies, and there thus exist well documented sets of response norms for these 100 words, covering different dates of collection, geographical locations, and types of subjects providing the responses. This word list has also been translated into a number of languages other than English (Rosenzweig, 1961, for French, Italian and German; Haworth, 1979, for Spanish) and this makes it possible to compare the responses of native English-speaking learners of these languages with responses that would be expected of a normal native-speaker population. The principal disadvantage of using the Kent–Rosanoff list is that a large proportion of the words that make it up consist of high-frequency words which produce highly stereotyped response patterns which do not vary greatly from one language to another. This means that only a small subset of the list is of any real interest where the main purpose of the study is to make cross-language comparisons.

(*b*) *Method.* The standard word association method has already been described. A number of variations on this basic theme will be found in table 2, however. The chief of these is the continuous association method, in which a single word is presented as a stimulus, but instead of providing only a single word as response, subjects are required to produce a continuous stream of responses for a given length of time (usually in the region of one minute). These responses are then pooled and counted as in the standard method. This technique produces patterns of responses that closely resemble those produced with the

115

Table 2. *Principal studies of word associations in a second language*

Author	Method	Languages	Subjects	Materials	Main object of enquiry
Lambert, 1956	Continuous assocs., 45 sec	English and French	N = 42; native speakers + students	16 words in each lg	Compares responses produced by groups at different levels of proficiency in terms of stereotypy and quantity
Kolers, 1963	Single responses	German, Spanish, Thai and English	N = 38; 10 Germans, 14 Spanish, 14 Thai learning English	55 nouns in 5 different categories from Jenkins and Palermo norms	Compares interlingual responses with intralingual ones, esp. frequency of translations
Lambert & Moore, 1966	Single responses	English and French	136 English speakers, 206 French speakers, 88 bilinguals	Kent–Rosanoff list	Stereotypy and equivalence of responses
Macnamara, 1967	Continuous assocs. with lg switching, 3 min	Irish and English, Latin and English	72 bilinguals, 30 seminarians	3 words	Linguistic independence (compares switching conditions and how this affects number of responses)
Davis & Wertheimer, 1967	Continuous assocs., 15 sec	English and French	N = 59; university students, postgrads, and native speakers of French	8 English words, 8 French words, 8 ambiguous	Relationship between no. of responses and level of competence
Riegel, Ramsey & Riegel, 1967	Restricted assocs.	English and Spanish	N = 48; 24 American, 24 Spanish	35 Common nouns from Kent–Rosanoff list	Stereotypy levels and overlap of responses in 2 languages
Lambert & Rawlings, 1969	Core concepts	English and French	20 bilingual students	60 French and 60 English words	Ability of different types of bilingual to recover stimulus word, given a list of associates

Study	Task	Languages	Subjects	Stimuli	Analysis
Dalrymple-Alford & Aamiry, 1970	Single responses	English and Arabic	English/Arabic bilinguals	12 words from Jenkins and Palermo norms and Arabic equivalents	Stability of responses
Ruke-Dravina, 1971	Continuous assocs., 5 min	Swedish and Latvian	$N = 40$; 13 Swedish, 16 Latvian speakers, 11 young bilinguals	4 words in Swedish and Latvian	Total number of different responses and qualitative differences between groups
Taylor, 1971	Continuous assocs. with lg switching	English and French	30 undergrads learning French	18 English and 18 French words	Compares the effects of different switching rates
Bol & Carpay 1972	Single responses	German			
Champagnol 1974	Continuous assocs., 1 min	French and English	60 French children learning English	40 common nouns + translations	Compares inter- and intra-lingual responses and relates frequency of response to probability of recall in a subsequent memory task
Riegel & Zivian, 1972	Restricted assocs.	English and German	24 undergrads	40 nouns of high, mid + low frequency	Compares inter- and intra-lingual responses
Politzer, 1978	Single responses	French and English	203 1st yr. high school	20 French words, 20 English words	Frequency of syntagmatic + paradigmatic responses
Meara, 1979	Single responses	English and French	76 5th yr. high school	100 words, Kent–Rosanoff list	Differences between learner responses + native speaker norms
Randall, 1980	Continuous assocs., 30 sec.	English	26 EFL students, various backgrounds	Half Kent–Rosanoff list	Changes over time and relationship to lg proficiency

standard method using single responses. The continuous association method has the practical advantage that it is viable with a relatively small number of subjects, however. Deese (1965) claims that a minimum of 50 subjects is necessary to produce stable norms for English using the standard method, and there is some evidence that other languages may require even larger numbers of subjects than this. With the continuous association method, however, stable response patterns can be found with as few as 15 subjects.

(c) *Interlingual associations.* These are associations made in a language that is not the same as the one in which the stimulus word was presented.

(d) *Restricted associations.* This term describes a technique principally used by Riegel and his associates. It consists of the basic elicitation technique for single responses, but with limitations imposed on the type of response allowed. Thus, for example, subjects might be instructed to produce a response that could describe the stimulus, or one that was a superordinate of it.

(e) *Language switching.* This variation is used only in conjunction with the continuous association method. Subjects are required at specified intervals to stop producing associations in one language, and to change to their other one.

Despite these important differences in method, it is possible to draw some general conclusions from these studies of word association behaviour in bilinguals and foreign-language learners. Firstly, on measure of fluency, such as number of responses, speed of responses and so forth, bilingual speakers are less adept in their weaker language than in their stronger one. Secondly, responses in a weaker language tend to be strikingly *less* stereotyped than responses in a stronger language. This finding is odd, in view of the fact that learners must have smaller vocabularies than native speakers, and this would lead one to expect that the range of possible responses would be correspondingly more restricted and less variable. The general inference from these two points is that words in a second language are less well organised and less easily accessible than those in the mental lexicon of a native speaker. However, there is some evidence that these differences diminish with increasing proficiency in the second language, and this suggests that given the right sort of coaxing, words from the second language do end up by becoming fully integrated into the learner's personal lexicon.

Thirdly, clang associates (i.e. responses which are principally phonetically motivated, rather than semantically motivated) account for a large proportion of the responses produced by less advanced students, suggesting that, at certain stages of learning at least, the formal phonetic properties of foreign-language words may be more salient than their semantic forms (cf. also a similar claim made by Henning, 1973, on the strength of a series of recall experiments). Finally, despite claims to the contrary (e.g. Randall, 1980), there is no clear evidence to support the view that learners are like children in that they produce a higher proportion of syntagmatic responses than would be expected in a comparable group of native speakers. Politzer's paper (1978) is the only one to offer clear evidence to support this claim, but this data is of limited value, in that his subjects were absolute beginners and his stimulus list contains some unsatisfactory items. My own experience with the syntagmatic/paradigmatic distinction leads me to believe that it is largely unworkable in practice, as there are no clear criteria for deciding which category any individual response belongs to. Even if unambiguous decisions can be made in a large number of cases, there always seems to be a significant number of responses that cannot be classified with any degree of certainty, and this suggests that claims about a syntagmatic/paradigmatic difference in foreign-language learners need to be treated with caution.

In general, these conclusions are suggestive and interesting as far as they go, but at the same time they are rather unsatisfying. What seems to be missing from this research is any overall strategy which would enable us to follow through these differences between native speakers and learners to the point where we would be in a position to make important and relevant claims about the storing of second-language vocabulary. In addition, it is a pity that this work has concentrated on the study of group responses, rather than the individual subjects who make up these groups. This sort of approach inevitably ignores information of a personal kind and fails to comment on what might be important individual differences.

G. General conclusions

Three principal points seem to emerge from this review. In the first place, a very large proportion of the work on vocabulary acquisition has been concerned with vocabulary teaching, rather than with vocabulary learning, and though this work is not without interest, it does not throw much light on how words are learned. In the second place, the more psychologically oriented work is also rather limited in scope, in that it has used a rather narrow range of investigative techniques, and looked principally at questions concerning the learner's entire second-language vocabularly, which it has treated as a single undifferentiated whole. I have argued here that this view is probably oversimplified, and that it is quite likely that major differences could be found for words of different types within an individual learner. Thirdly, the most comprehensive work in this field is the relatively large number of studies that have looked at word associations in foreign-language learners. However, even this work is unsystematic, and fails to show any signs of a coherent and co-ordinated research strategy. This work also suffers from the drawback that it is concerned principally with groups of learners in an area where large individual differences might be expected.

Clearly, then, the study of vocabulary acquisition is an area where the sort of research work that has been carried out is far from satisfactory, and where a large number of questions still remain to be answered. Levenston (1979) concluded his discussion of some problems in vocabulary research with a list of questions and suggestions for further research. All these questions are worth pondering, but they might be usefully supplemented by some additional questions which have a slightly different emphasis. (*a*) Are there any systematic differences between well known and recently acquired words in a second language? (*b*) Do newly acquired words in a second language pass through any identifiable stages of acquisition? (*c*) Is it the case that L2 words ever produce behaviour that is indistinguishable from what would be expected with L1 words? (*d*) Are there any clear thresholds which it is necessary for an L2 word to cross before it can be considered to be properly acquired, and if so, what types of activity lead to these thresholds being crossed? (*e*) How is it that L2 words which are often learned as paired associates of their L1 translations eventually come to operate in a way that is relatively independent of their translation? (*f*) Is the acquisition of new words affected by such considerations as the morphological structure of L2 words, or their phonetic structure? (*g*) Are the lexical errors of learners (e.g. malapropisms) systematically different from those of native speakers?

Our current understanding of vocabulary acquisition has almost nothing to say on any of these points, and there is no doubt that work along these lines could be the beginnings of a very useful research programme. *October 1980*

References

Albert, M. & Obler, L. K. (1979). *The bilingual brain: neuro-psychological and neurolinguistic aspects of bilingualism.* New York: Academic Press.
Arkwright, T. & Vian, A. (1974). Les processus d'association chez les bilingues. *Working Papers in Bilingualism,* **2**, 57–67.
Atkinson, R. C. (1975). Mnemotechnics in second-language learning. *American Psychologist,* **30**, 821–8.
Atkinson, R. C. & Raugh, M. (1975). An application of the mnemonic keyword method to the acquisition of Russian vocabulary. *Journal of Experimental Psychology: Human Learning and Memory,* **1**, 2, 126–33.
Barnard, H. (1971). *Advanced English vocabulary. Workbook I.* Rowley, Mass.: Newbury House.

Barter, A. R. (1970). *Learning languages: the comparative method.* Newton Abbot: David & Charles.

Becker, D. (1977). The etymological dictionary as a teaching device. *Unterrichtspraxis,* **10,** 1, 70–7.

Birmingham University Russian Language and Literature Department (1976). *Russian social sciences word count.* Birmingham: Birmingham University.

Blum, S. & Levenston, E. A. (1979). Lexical simplification in second-language acquisition. *Studies in Second Language Acquisition,* **2,** 2, 43–63.

Bol, E. & Carpay, J. (1972). Der Semantisierung prozess in Fremdsprachen unterricht: Lernpsychologische Experimente und methodische Folgerungen. *Praxis des neusprachlichen Unterrichts,* **19,** 2, 119–33.

Bongers, H. (1947). *The history and principles of vocabulary control, as it affects the teaching of foreign languages in general and of English in particular.* The Netherlands: Woerden.

Brown, D. F. (1974). Advanced vocabulary teaching: the problem of collocation. *RELC Journal,* **5,** 2.

Burnard, L., Hockey, S. & Marriott, I. (1979). *Oxford Concordance Project.* Oxford: Oxford University Computing Services.

Butler, D., Ott, C. & Blake, R. (1973). Cognitive scaffolding in the learning of foreign-language vocabulary. Paper given at the Association of Educational Communications and Technology. Las Vegas.

Champagnol, R. (1973). Organisation sémantique et linguistique dans le rappel libre bilingue. *Année Psychologique,* **73,** 115–34.

Champagnol, R. (1974). Association verbale, structuration et rappel libre bilingues. *Psychologie Française,* **19,** 83–100.

Clark, H. H. (1970). Word associations and linguistic theory. In J. Lyons (ed.), *New horizons in linguistics.* Harmondsworth, Mddx.: Pelican.

Crothers, E. & Suppes, P. (1967). *Experiments in second-language learning.* New York: Academic Press.

Culhane, P. T. (1977). Lexis in applied linguistics: word frequency in preparation and presentation of Russian reading texts. *Russian Language Journal,* **31,** 109, 25–33.

Dagut, M. B. (1977). Incongruities in lexical gridding – an application of contrastive semantic analysis to language teaching. *IRAL,* **15,** 3, 221–7.

Dale, E., O'Rourke, J. & Bamman, H. (1971). *Techniques of teaching vocabulary.* Field Educational Publications.

Dale, E. & Razik, T. (1963). *Bibliography of vocabulary research.* Ohio: Ohio State University.

Dalrymple-Alford, E. (1968). Interlingual interference in a colour-naming task. *Psychonomic Science,* **10,** 215–16.

Dalrymple-Alford, E. & Aamiry, A. (1970). Word associations of bilinguals. *Psychonomic Science,* **21,** 319–20.

Dalrymple-Alford, E. & Budayr, B. (1966). Examination of some aspects of the Stroop colour-word test. *Perceptual and Motor Skills,* **23,** 1211–14.

Davis, B. J. & Wertheimer, M. (1967). Some determinants of associations to French and English words. *Journal of Verbal Learning and Verbal Behavior,* **6,** 574–81.

Deese, J. (1965). *The structure of association in language and thought.* Baltimore: Johns Hopkins University Press.

de Wolfe, A. S. (1971). Cognitive structure and pathology in the associations of process and reactive schizophrenics. *Journal of Abnormal Psychology,* **78,** 148–53.

Desrochers, A. (1980). Effects of an imagery mnemonic on acquisition and retention of French article–noun pairs. Ph.D., University of Western Ontario.

Dyer, F. N. (1971). Colour naming interference in monolinguals and bilinguals. *Journal of Verbal Learning and Verbal Behavior*, **10**, 297–302.

Ek, J. A. van (1977). *The Threshold Level for modern language learning in schools.* London: Longman.

Entwhistle, D. (1966). *Word associations of young children.* Baltimore: Johns Hopkins University Press.

Entwhistle, D., Forsyth, D. & Muss, R. (1964). The syntagmatic-paradigmatic shift in children's word associations. *Journal of Verbal Learning and Verbal Behavior*, **3**, 19–29.

Ervin, S. (1961). Learning and recall in bilinguals. *American Journal of Psychology*, **74**, 446–51.

Ervin, S. (1961). Changes with age in the verbal determinants of word association. *American Journal of Psychology*, **74**, 361–72.

Ervin, S. & Osgood, C. (1954). Second-language learning and bilingualism. In C. E. Osgood & T. A. Sebeok (eds.), *Psycholinguistics.* Bloomington, Indiana: Indiana University Press.

Evans, I. & Townsendson, J. (1979). Another view on the bilingual Stroop test. *Polyglot*, **1**, 2, E13–G5.

Galisson, R. (1970). *Vers un apprentissage systématisé du vocabulaire.* Paris: Hachette.

Galisson, R. (1979). *Lexicologie et enseignement des langues.* Paris: Hachette.

Genesee, F., Hamers, J., Lambert, W. E., Mononen, L., Seitz, M. & Starck, R. (1978). Language processing in bilinguals. *Brain and Language*, **5**, 1–12.

Goggin, J. G. & Wickens, D. D. (1971). Proactive interference and language change in short term memory. *Journal of Verbal Learning and Verbal Behavior*, **10**, 453–8.

Gouin, F. (1880). *L'art d'enseigner et d'étudier les langues.* Paris.

Green, D. & Newman, S. (1980). Review article: *The bilingual brain* by M. Albert and L. K. Obler, 1979. *Polyglot*, **2**, 1, D4–F5.

Groberg, D. (1972). *Mnemonic Japanese.* Salt Lake City: Interac.

Hamers, J. & Lambert, W. (1972). Bilingual interdependencies in auditory perception. *Journal of Verbal Learning and Verbal Behavior*, **11**, 303–10.

Hamers, J. & Lambert, W. (1977). Visual field and cerebral hemisphere preferences in bilinguals. In S. Segalowitz & F. Gruber (eds.), *Language development and neurological theory.* New York: Academic Press.

Hammerly, H. (1975). Teaching of second language vocabulary. Pacific North West Council on Foreign Languages. Proceedings, Vol. **26**, 2, 131–38.

Haworth, S. (1979). Spanish word-association norms for 100 words of the Kent–Rosanoff list. M.A. thesis, Birkbeck College, London.

Henning, G. H. (1973). Remembering foreign-language vocabulary: acoustic and semantic parameters. *Language Learning*, **23**, 2, 185–96.

Hockey, S. & Marriott, I. (1979–80). The Oxford Concordance Project. *Association for Literary and Linguistic Computing Bulletin.* Part I: **7**, 1, 35–43; Part II: **7**, 2, 155–64; Part III: **7**, 3, 268–75; Part IV: **8**, 1, 28–35.

Hoffmann, H. G. (1976). Cabbage at the Cabaret. *Zielsprache Englisch*, **2**, 17.

Holec, H. (1974). *Structures lexicales et enseignement du vocabulaire.* The Hague: Mouton.

Holley, F. M. (1971). The mental lexicon: vocabulary acquisition as a problem of linguistics and human memory. Pacific North West Conference on Foreign Languages. Proceedings, Vol. **22**, 266–76.

Jakobovits, L. & Lambert, W. (1961). Semantic satiation among bilinguals. *Journal of Experimental Psychology*, **62**, 576–82.

Johnson, D. B. (1972). Computer frequency control of vocabulary in language learning reading materials. *Instructional Science*, **1**, 1, 121–31.

Judd, E. L. (1978). Vocabulary teaching and TESOL: a need for reevaluation of existing assumptions. *TESOL Quarterly*, **12**, 1, 71–6.

Juilland, A. & Chang-Rodriguez, E. (1964). *Frequency dictionary of Spanish words*. The Hague: Mouton.

Juilland, A., Brodin, D. & Davidowitch, C. (1970). *Frequency dictionary of French words*. The Hague: Mouton.

Juilland, A. & Traversa, V. (1973). *Frequency dictionary of Italian words*. The Hague: Mouton.

Kent, G. H. & Rosanoff, J. A. (1910). A study of association in insanity. *American Journal of Insanity*, **67**, 37–96 and 317–90.

Kershner, J. & Jeng, A. (1972). Dual functional hemispheric asymmetry in visual perception: effects of ocular dominance and post-exposural processes. *Neuropsychologia*, **10**, 437–45.

Klein, G. S. (1964). Semantic power measured through interference of words with colour naming. *American Journal of Psychology*, **77**, 576–88.

Kintsch, W. (1970). Recognition memory in bilingual subjects. *Journal of Verbal Learning and Verbal Behavior*, **9**, 405–9.

Knop, C. (1971). Mnemonic devices in teaching French. *French Review*, **45**, 337–42.

Kolers, P. A. (1963). Interlingual word associations. *Journal of Verbal Learning and Verbal Behavior*, **2**, 291.

Kolers, P. A. (1965). Bilingualism and bicodalism. *Language and Speech*, **8**, 122–6.

Kolers, P. A. (1968). Bilingualism and information processing. *Scientific American*, **218**, 78–90.

Kucera, H. & Francis, W. N. (1967). *Computational analysis of presentday American English*. Rhode Island: Brown University Press.

Kurcz, I. (1966). Interlanguage comparison of word association responses. *International Journal of Psycholinguistics*, **1**, 151–61.

Lado, R., Baldwin, B. & Lobo, F. (1967). Massive vocabulary expansion in a foreign language beyond the basic course: the effects of stimuli, timing and order of presentation. USOE Bureau of Research. Project 5, 1095.

Lambert, W. (1967). A social psychology of bilingualism. *Journal of Social Issues*, **23**, 91–109.

Lambert, W. (1955). Developmental aspects of second language acquisition. *Journal of Social Psychology*, **43**, 83–104.

Lambert, W., Havelka, J. & Crossby, C. (1958). The influence of language acquisition contexts on bilingualism. *Journal of Abnormal and Social Psychology*, **56**, 239–44.

Lambert, W., Ignatow, M. & Krauthamer, M. (1968). Bilingual organization in free recall. *Journal of Verbal Learning and Verbal Behavior*, **7**, 207–14.

Lambert, W. & Jakobovits, L. (1960). Verbal satiation and changes in the intensity of meaning. *Journal of Experimental Psychology*, **60**, 376–83.

Lambert, W. & Moore, N. (1966). Word association responses: comparisons of American and French monolinguals with Canadian monolinguals and bilinguals. *Journal of Personality and Social Psychology*, **3**, 313–20.

Lambert, W. & Nott, C. R. (1968). Free recall of bilinguals. *Journal of Verbal Learning and Verbal Behavior*, **7**, 1065–71.

Lambert, W. & Rawlings, C. (1969). Bilingual processing of mixed language associative networks. *Journal of Verbal Learning and Verbal Behavior*, **8**, 604–9.

Leopold, W. (1948). Semantic learning in infant language. *Word*, **4**, 173–80.

Levenston, E. A. (1979). Second language acquisition: issues and problems. *Interlanguage Studies Bulletin*, **4**, 2, 147–60.

Levenston, E. A. & Blum, S. (1977). Aspects of lexical simplification in the speech and writing of advanced adult learners. In S. P. Corder & E. Roulet (eds.), *Actes du 5eme Colloque de Linguistique Appliquée de Neuchâtel.* Geneva: Droz.

Liepmann, D. & Saegert, J. (1974). Language tagging in bilingual free recall. *Journal of Experimental Psychology*, **103**, 1137–41.

Linnarud, M. (1979). A performance analysis of Swedish students' English. Symposium report, Hanasaari (cited in Levenston, 1979).

Lopez, M., Hicks, R. & Young, R. (1974). Retroactive inhibition in a bilingual A–B, A–B' paradigm. *Journal of Experimental Psychology*, **103**, 85–90.

Lopez, M. & Young, R. K. (1974). The linguistic interdependence of bilinguals. *Journal of Experimental Psychology*, **102**, 981–3.

Lord, R. (1974). Learning vocabulary. *IRAL*, **12**, 3, 239–47.

Lyne, A. (1975). A word frequency count of French business correspondence. *IRAL*, **13**, 95–110.

Mackey, W. (1965). *Language teaching analysis.* London: Longman.

Macnamara, J. (1967). The linguistic independence of bilinguals. *Journal of Verbal Learning and Verbal Behavior*, **6**, 729–36.

Martin, A. V. (1976). Teaching academic vocabulary to foreign graduate students. *TESOL Quarterly*, **10**, 1, 91–8.

Marton, W. (1977). Foreign language vocabulary learning as problem number one of language teaching at the advanced level. *Interlanguage Studies Bulletin*, **2**, 1.

McCormack, P. D. (1976). Language as an attribute of memory. *Revue Canadienne de Psychologie*, **30**, 4, 238–48.

McCormack, P. D. (1977). Bilingual linguistic memory: the independence/inter-dependence issue revisited. In P. A. Hornby (ed.), *Bilingualism: psychological, social and educational implications.* New York: Academic Press.

McNeill, D. (1963). The origin of association within the same grammatical class. *Journal of Verbal Learning and Verbal Behavior*, **2**, 202–62.

Meara, P. M. (1978). Schizophrenic symptoms in foreign-language learners. *UEA Papers in Linguistics*, **7**, 22–49.

Meara, P. M. (1978). Learners' word associations in French. *Interlanguage Studies Bulletin*, **3**, 2, 192–211.

Meara, P. M. (in prep.). Vocabulary in a second language: an annotated bibliography.

Miron, M. & Pratt, C. C. (1973). *Manual for the development of language frequency counts.* Syracuse University Research Corporation.

Morton, A. Q. (1979). *Literary detection.* London: Bowker.

Neufeld, G. (1973). The bilingual's lexical store. *Working Papers in Bilingualism*, **1**, 35–65.

Orbach, J. (1953). Visual fields as a function of cerebral dominance and reading habits. *Neuropsychologia*, **5**, 127–34.

O'Rourke, J. P. (1974). *Towards a science of vocabulary development.* The Hague: Mouton.

Ott, C. E., Blake, R. S. & Butler, D. C. (1976). Foreign language vocabulary. *IRAL*, **14**, 1, 37–48.

Ott, C. E., Butler, D. C., Blake, R. S. & Ball, J. P. (1973). The effect of interactive-image elaboration on the acquisition of foreign-language vocabulary. *Language Learning*, **23**, 2, 197–206.

Paivio, A. (1978). On exploring visual knowledge. In B. S. Randhawa & W. E. Coffman (eds.), *Visual learning, thinking and communication.* New York: Academic Press.

Paivio, A. & Desrochers, A. (1979). Effects of an imagery mnemonic on L2 recall and comprehension. *Canadian Journal of Psychology*, **33**, 17–28.

Palermo, D. & Jenkins, J. J. (1964). *Word association norms.* University of Minnesota Press.

Philpot, M. (1977). A study of the predictability of learner and native speech. M.A. thesis, Birkbeck College, London.

Pollio, H. (1966). *The structural basis of word association behaviour.* The Hague: Mouton.

Politzer, R. B. (1978). Paradigmatic and syntagmatic associations of first-year French students. In V. Honsa and M. J. Hardman-de-Bautista (eds.), *Papers in linguistics and child language.* The Hague: Mouton.

Postman, L. & Keppel, G. (1970). *Norms of word association.* New York: Academic Press.

Pressley, M. (1977). Children's use of the key word method to learn simple Spanish vocabulary words. *Journal of Educational Psychology,* **69**, 5, 465–72.

Pressley, M. R. (1980). The keyword method and foreign language word acquisition. *Journal of Experimental Psychology : Human Learning and Memory.* In press.

Pressley, M. & Levin, J. R. (1978). Developmental constraints associated with children's use of the keyword method of foreign-language vocabulary learning. *Journal of Experimental Child Psychology,* **78**, 26, 359–72.

Preston, M. & Lambert, W. (1969). Interlingual interference in a bilingual version of the Stroop colour word test. *Journal of Verbal Learning and Verbal Behavior,* **8**, 295–301.

Randall, M. (1980). Word association behaviour in learners of English as a second language. *Polyglot,* **2**, 2, B4–D1.

Raugh, M. (1975). Teaching a large Russian vocabulary by the mnemonic keyword method. Psychology and Education Series Technical Reports, 256.

Raugh, M. R. & Atkinson, R. C. (1974). A mnemonic method for the acquisition of a second-language vocabulary. Psychology and Education Series Technical Reports, 224.

Raugh, M. R. & Atkinson, R. C. (1975). A mnemonic method for learning second-language vocabulary. *Journal of Educational Psychology,* **67**, 1–16.

Richards, J. C. (1976). The role of vocabulary teaching. *TESOL Quarterly,* **10**, 77–89.

Ridout, R. (1976). The use of word puzzles in teaching English. *Revue des Langues Vivantes,* **42**, 3, 313–17.

Riegel, K. F. (1968). Some theoretical considerations of bilingual development. *Psychological Bulletin,* **70**, 6, 647–70.

Riegel, K., Ramsey, R. & Riegel, R. (1967). A comparison of the first and second languages of American and Spanish students. *Journal of Verbal Learning and Verbal Behavior,* **6**, 536–44.

Riegel, K. & Zivian, I. W. M. (1972). A study of inter- and intra-lingual associations in English and German. *Language Learning,* **22**, 151–63.

Rosenzweig, M. R. (1961). Comparisons among word associations in English, French, German and Italian. *American Journal of Psychology,* **74**, 347–60.

Rüke-Dravina, V. (1971). Word associations in monolingual and multilingual individuals. *Linguistics,* **74**, 66–85.

Saegert, J. S., Kazarian, S. & Young, R. K. (1973). Part/whole transfer with bilinguals. *American Journal of Psychology,* **86**, 537–46.

Salt, M. J. (1976). Vocabulary acquisition with the help of photographic transparencies. *ELT Journal,* **30**, 4, 320–6.

Segalowitz, N. & Lambert, W. (1969). Semantic generalization in bilinguals. *Journal of Verbal Learning and Verbal Behavior,* **8**, 559–66.

Setzler, H. H. & Clark, R. E. (1976). Research briefing: recent research on mnemonic techniques for learning foreign-language vocabulary. *Educational Technology,* **16**, 8, 43–4.

Singer, J. G. (1977). Enjoying vocabulary learning in junior high: the keyword method. *Canadian Modern Language Review*, **34**, 80–7.

Stoltz, W. & Tiffany, J. (1972). The production of childlike word associations by adults to unfamiliar adjectives. *Journal of Verbal Learning and Verbal Behavior*, 11.

Stroop, J. R. (1935). Studies in serial verbal reactions. *Journal of Experimental Psychology*, **18**, 643–61.

Syracuse University Research Corporation (1973). *The counting of words: a review of the history, techniques and theory of word counts*. Springfield, Va.: National Technical Information Service.

Szalay, L. B. & Deese, J. (1978). *Subjective meaning and culture*. Lawrence Erlbaum Associates.

Taylor, M. (1974). Speculations on bilingualism and the cognitive networks. *Working Papers in Bilingualism*, **2**, 68–124.

Thorndike, E. L. & Lorge, I. (1944). *The teacher's word book of 30,000 words*. Columbia University: Teachers' College.

Tulving, E. & Colotla, V. A. (1970). Free recall of trilingual lists. *Cognitive Psychology*, **1**, 86–98.

Twaddell, W. F. (1973). Vocabulary expansion in the TESOL classroom. *TESOL Quarterly*, **7**, 61–78.

Twomey, E. (1979). A bibliography of research carried out in the field of vocabulary acquisition in a second language. M.A. thesis, Birkbeck College, London.

Vikis-Freibergs, V. & Freibergs, I. (1976). Free association norms in French and English: interlinguistic and intralinguistic comparisons. *Canadian Journal of Psychology*, **30**, 123–33.

Walters, J. & Zatorre, R. (1978). Latency differences for word recognition in bilinguals. *Brain and Language*, **6**, 158–67.

Webber, J. (1977). An investigation into the effect of degree of competence in a language on the type–token ratio. M.A. thesis, Birkbeck College, London.

West, M. (1936). *A general service list of English words*. London: Longman (revised to 1953).

Wilkins, D. A. (1972). *Linguistics in language teaching*. London: Edward Arnold.

Wicklow, C. R. (1974). Review of Barnard (1971). *Language Learning*, **24**, 167–70.

Yoshida, M. (1978). The acquisition of English vocabulary by a Japanese-speaking child. In E. Hatch (ed.), *Second language acquisition: a book of readings*. Rowley, Mass.: Newbury House.

LANGUAGE TESTING

Alan Davies
University of Edinburgh

PART I

0.1   This review article appears in two parts, the first in this issue and the second in the next. In the first we discuss discrete point tests with particular reference to the major textbooks on language testing. Then we go on to a brief discussion of tests of reading comprehension and end with a note on criterion referenced testing. In the second part we discuss integrative tests, giving special consideration to cloze tests and dictation tests, followed by a discussion of tests of spoken and written production. Part 2 ends with a consideration of the testing of communicative competence. A full bibliography is given for both parts at the end of Part 2.

0.2   Reviews of the literature of language testing (apart from those in the books discussed below) are given in Carroll (1963), Brière (1969) and Birkmaier (1973) and reviews of language tests in print in Buros (1972, 1975). Useful bibliographies appear in Savard (1969, 1977), Plaister (1972), Fehse and Praeger (1973), Riley (1973), CAL (1975), Rodriguez-Mungia *et al.* (1972), Garcia-Zamor and Birdsong (1977) and Perren (1977). The annotations in the last two are particularly useful and, since the first deals with the testing of English as a second language and the second with foreign-language testing, helpfully complementary.

1. Discrete point tests

1.1   In 1977 Rebecca Valette brought out the second edition of her *Modern language testing* (Valette, 1977), ten years after the first edition. The second edition represents a considerable revision and expansion of the original book. The difference between the two editions is a good indication of the change in language testing in the decade from the mid '60s to the mid '70s. That change was a major one and it reflects the clash of ideas in other parts of the language field (Davies, 1977*a*). Views on language testing, as on language teaching, in the late '50s and early '60s were behaviourist, or, more happily, structuralist. Robert Lado's book *Language testing* (Lado, 1961, 1964) is the main testing exemplar of the structuralist view of language and of language learning.

127

Valette's 1967 edition can be regarded as a latter-day Lado, a Lado for the 1970s.

Between 1967 and 1977 Valette's view of language testing changes; what form this change takes we shall see in a moment. The causes for the change are not of central concern to us; they have, no doubt, to do with the greater interest in language in context and with social interaction. They have to do with the apparent inadequacy of microlinguistics on its own as an explanation of language behaviour. Hence the various attempts recently to bring more of semantics into grammar and to push out the boundaries of grammar incorporating speech acts, presuppositions and 'knowledge of the world'. It is as though the centre of interest in linguistics has moved from microlinguistics to macrolinguistics. As far as language testing is concerned we can characterise the difference between Valette (1967) and Valette (1977) as a move from linguistics to sociolinguistics, from structuralism to functionalism, from taxonomy and breaking down into skills, into discrete parts, to integration and building up into wholes. Of course the two editions have a great deal, perhaps most of their content, in common. Let us look at them in turn.

Valette (1967) is called *Modern language testing: a handbook*. In the preface the author writes: 'In the past 20 years a number of new methods of teaching languages have appeared. These methods have been based largely on the results of research in learning theory and linguistics... The foreign-language teacher now has available to him an abundance of texts and other instructional materials that suggest the sequential development of the four fundamental skills of listening, speaking, reading and writing... This handbook introduces the teacher to a diversity of testing techniques based on modern measurement theory... The terminology of traditional grammar has been used in most instances instead of the precise vocabulary of the linguists so that even teachers without formal training in linguistics will find the handbook convenient and useful.' The book contains two parts. Part 1 has four chapters: Testing – its role in the classroom; Preparing the test; Giving the test; Evaluating classroom test results. Part 2 has five chapters: The listening test; The speaking test; The reading test; The writing test; Culture and literature. Finally there is an appendix on commercial language tests (prognostic, progress, achievement and proficiency tests). There is a brief bibliography with four references. The book contains 200 pages.

Valette (1977) is still called *Modern language testing* but the subtitle *a handbook* has disappeared. In the preface to the second edition Valette writes: 'When *Modern language testing* appeared ten years ago, its aim was to introduce teachers to a diversity of testing techniques based on the teaching and testing theories of the mid-1960s. This revised and expanded edition represents a natural extension of that basic objective. . . . Several changes characterise the new edition. . . it reflects contemporary concerns in measurement and evaluation...(it) reflects contemporary changes in teaching aims. The growing interest in language as a means of interpersonal communication has led to the development of a variety of tests of communicative competences. Chapters 5 through 8 of Part 2 all end with sections devoted to the evaluation of listening, speaking, reading and writing as communication skills. Chapter 9 describes a broad range of techniques for measuring students' progress in the area of culture. The testing of literature is the topic of a new Chapter 10. Finally, Chapters 11 and 12 touch lightly on new developments in testing and the role of evaluation in bilingual programs. The bibliography and appendix have ...been expanded and brought up to date.' The second edition contains three parts. Part 1 is very like Part 1 of the first edition. It is in Parts 2 and 3 that the major differences lie.

Part 2 has the same chapter headings as in the first edition. But the contents of each chapter are quite different. Here are the contents of 'The listening test' (Chapter 5 in both editions) tabled side by side to illustrate that difference:

Chapter 5, 1st edition	*Chapter 5, 2nd edition*
'The listening test'	'The listening test'
1. General considerations	1. General considerations
2. Listening tests for FLES and beginning classes	2. The sound system
3. Discrimination of sounds	3. Understanding vocabulary
4. Intonation tests	4. Understanding structures
5. Stress and accent tests	5. Listening comprehension: communication
6. Retention tests	6. Listening comprehension: retention
7. Listening comprehension: vocabulary	7. Listening comprehension under adverse conditions
8. Listening comprehension: syntax and grammar	
9. Listening comprehension: different types of speech	

The two versions are related. But there are important differences which reflect two sorts of change. First, there is the decline of interest in the early beginning, FLES (Foreign Languages in the Elementary School), and, second, there is a move from a concentration on sound, the production of speech, the phonology, to meaning and communication. In a way, these two differences are really one difference, in that the interest in beginning language learning as a special kind of acquisition (separate from intermediate and advanced learning and needing a special treatment) could only be maintained by acceptance of the view presented in the first edition, that language is learnt by a successive progression through the skills, from sounds to meaning. This view is no longer orthodox. Meaning in language teaching (and therefore in language testing) must come in from the beginning. Valette (1977) does not, of course, abandon all taxonomy: she still has sections on 'The sound system', 'Vocabulary' and 'Structures', but the acceptance of meaning and of communication as what really matters is obvious. (Even the addition of 'Understanding' to both 'Vocabulary' and 'Structures' underlines this.) At the end of Part 2 Valette has changed a single chapter on 'Culture and literature' (Valette, 1967) into two chapters. Again there is an assumption of a move away from an analytical view of language to a wholistic or global view of language use.

Part 3 is new. It contains two chapters, Chapter 11, 'Directions in modern language testing' and Chapter 12, 'Testing in bilingual and English as a second language programs'. In both of them Valette pushes out the bounds of modern-language achievement and proficiency testing to take in language aptitude, affective goals and special kinds of language learning, such as those of the bilingual or the child in an American English as a second language programme. Like the first edition, the second contains an appendix on 'Commercial language tests', and a selected bibliography, this time containing 21 entries. The book as a whole has 349 pages, nearly twice as many as Valette (1967).

1.2   Valette (1977) gives several pages in her Chapter 11 to a summary of Spolsky (1975), a keynote address at the Fourth AILA Congress in Stuttgart in 1975. Spolsky's address was called 'Language testing: art or science'. In essentials his argument is the one presented so far in this article and exemplified in the development between Valette (1967) and Valette (1977). Spolsky identifies three stages in the development of language testing in this century: the pre-scientific, the psychometric–structuralist and the psycholinguistic–sociolinguistic. At the pre-scientific stage, tests took no account of validity and reliability; they were largely of the translation, composition and sentence completion type. Valette comments, interestingly, '(My) first edition...was written to help teachers...move from this "pre-scientific" method...to the more objective evaluation techniques of the "psychometric–structuralist" trend.'

Spolsky's name for his second stage, the psychometric–structuralist, is well taken. As well as becoming more objective (in order to increase reliability), there were attempts to achieve validity by relating the tests of this stage directly to a coherent view of language. Hence Valette can say that structural linguistics was used as a basis for contrastive analysis in order to 'identify the problems faced by the second language learner; these problems...are patterns and units that have no counterpart in the native language or a different distributional pattern. The resulting language tests were "discrete point" tests, of which the best examples are the standardised language tests developed and administered

by the Educational Testing Service; the CEEB Achievement Tests, the MLA
Cooperative Tests, the Graduate Record Tests, and the Test of English as
a Foreign Language (TOEFL).' Lado (1961, 1964) was both the herald and
the spokesman of this view of language testing.

At the third of Spolsky's stages, the psycholinguistic–sociolinguistic, the
emphasis is on the integrative or global test which attempts to assess proficiency
(both in production and in comprehension) of the total communicative effect
of a message. It is interesting that in her discussion of the three stages, Valette
gives examples (in terms of published tests) only for the second stage. It is
easy to understand that there were no published standardised tests produced
at Stage 1, the stage of subjective adhocery. It is less clear why there are none
at the third stage. It may, of course, be that it is still too soon. But, as we
shall see, there may be a more fundamental reason for this lack of exemplification
of the psycholinguistic–sociolinguistic stage, a reason which has to do with the
lack of rigour at the third stage, a lack much in contrast to the rigour of the
second stage and perhaps caused by a reaction against that rigour.

1.3   In testing as in teaching there is a tension between the analytical on the
one hand and the integrative on the other. It is likely that 'progress' in language
teaching consists of a swing from the predominance of one emphasis to a
predominance of the other. Thus Spolsky's (1975) story of the movement from
Stage 2 (analytical) to Stage 3 (integrative) takes up no more than the decade
of Valette's two editions. Further, his Stage 1 (traditional) could well be
regarded as a form of Stage 3, i.e. as a kind of integrative or global view in
which whole or real tasks of the kind of communication demanded are
presented to the students, e.g. translation, composition. Arguing that these
are not integrative or wholistic is beside the point, since these activities have
always been regarded by some teachers as what language teaching is for, the
purposes and goals of learning. It is the view of this article that the most
satisfactory view of language testing, and the most useful kinds of language
tests, are a combination of these two views, the analytical and the integrative.
It is probable in any case that no test can be analytical or integrative alone,
that on the one hand all language 'bits' can be (and may need to be)
contextualised; and on the other, that all language texts and discourse can be
comprehended more effectively by a parts analysis. The two poles of analysis
and integration are similar to (and may be closely related to) the concepts of
reliability and validity. Test reliability is increased by adding to the stock of
discrete items in a test: the smaller the bits and the more of these there
are, the higher the potential reliability. Validity, however, is increased by making
the test truer to life, in this case more like language in use. We can extend
the distinction between analysis and integration to a series of similar and related
distinctions, thus:

analytical	integrative
discrete point	wholistic
norm referenced	criterion referenced
reception	production
linguistic competence	communicative competence
summative	formative
form	function
usage	use
idealisation	raw data
deep structure	surface structure

and we can add:

reliability	validity

Compared with this major dichotomy the distinctions among test names, such as aptitude, achievement, attainment, proficiency, diagnostic, are of minor importance, since they have to do not with the nature of language nor with the view of learning but with a particular test use (Davies, 1977a). Similarly, distinctions as to skill, such as oral, written, listening, reading, are of less primary importance since they are again concerned with a mode of language or of learning transmission. The argument is frequently heard these days that 'reading' or 'listening' comprehension are a unitary form of comprehension and that their separation is at a surface level (Sticht, 1973; Brown, 1977).

1.4   Lado (1961, 1964) we have called the spokesman of the structural testing school and therefore of analytical, discrete point tests. His view is summed up by the famous phrase, that 'testing control of the problems is testing control of the language'. Lado's book was followed by a series of books very much in the same tradition: Valette (1967), Harris (1968), Davies (1968), Clark (1972), Heaton (1975). Even Allen and Davies (1977) has to be regarded as part of this prevailing orthodoxy, that language is a linguistic phenomenon and that in order to test it, it must be broken down into its linguistic components. The metaphor of the machine and its parts is rarely absent in discussions of structuralism in relation to language. Lado, though, more than anyone, is held to be responsible for mindlessness in language testing, for testing forms in isolation. Now it seems to us that Lado has two defences, the first that language must be tested in the way in which it is taught; and in the early '60s teaching orthodoxy was in favour of language components. His second defence is that he tests lots of other things as well as minimal language contrasts. Hence his chapters on 'Testing the integrated skills' (auditory comprehension, reading comprehension, speaking, writing, translation, overall control, cross-cultural understanding, and the higher values). If analytical testing consists solely of language contrasts in isolation both from other language and from context, a set of language contrasts all at the same level being summed in order to construct a homogeneous test, then there is more to Lado than analytical tests, since his culture, literature, comprehension tasks, while themselves offering points of contrast on critical points of difficulty, all subsume within themselves control over a whole range of forms which are, in miniature, integrative. For this reason a rigid separation of integrative and analytical is just not possible.

By 'discrete point' is meant two things (Aitken, 1976): first, analysis of the language on some taxonomic basis, thus phonology, grammar, semantics or vocabulary, and then subdividing, e.g. phonology into phonemes, stress, intonation, rhythm. In other words, the analysis is in the terms of structural linguistics. The discreteness of items is a quality of their being categorised within a taxonomic system which is set up so as to contain discrete items. The second meaning of discrete point follows: since the linguistic analysis consists of linguistic items which do not overlap with one another, then the task presented to the students is to distinguish between one discrete item and another, which differ from one another by only one feature. Here are some typical discrete point items:

1. I want (a) going (b) go (c) to go (d) to going home now.

2. I saw a nasty..........between two cars this morning.

   (a) happening   (b) danger   (c) damage   (d) incident

Not all discrete point items appear thus nakedly. Many also appear under the labels of Reading, Writing, etc. The relevant question here is whether integrative testing has to do with the language task given to the student (e.g. the text for reading or the communicative problem to be solved orally) or with the method of decision by the tester as to whether the student has succeeded or not. The pure discrete point item has no task other than itself; it is most obviously seen as, e.g., phoneme discrimination. As we pass along the continuum through Lado's integrated skills, the tasks become more complex (a text for reading and then a translation) until we come to the currently popular cloze and dictation (see Part 2). But even in these highly complex tasks, in which no distinction is being made for the student between skills and/or language levels, the tester still has a decision to make as to success or failure. This decision is essentially a discrete point decision. Once again then, we argue that the distinction made between discrete point and integrative testing is not a real or an absolute one.

The textbooks on language testing (Lado, 1961, 1964; Valette, 1967; Harris, 1969; Clark, 1972; Heaton, 1975) have largely kept a decent balance between

133

discrete point and integrative ideas, the latter being dealt with under a variety of names (e.g. general comprehension, communication, cross-cultural understanding). It is perhaps the case that books in an academic discipline tend to be conservative and cherishing of the tradition, while the new thinking, the creative ideas and the results of new research are placed in articles and papers. As we might expect, then, it is in the books that we find most discussions of discrete point testing and in the articles new ideas about integrative testing. In the same way the standardised tests, e.g. TOEFL (ETS, 1964 . . .), CELT (Harris & Palmer, 1970) are made up of what are essentially discrete point items while admitting the occasional integrative newcomer. Research, on the other hand, has been less interested in the reliability of discrete point items and has tended to concentrate on integrative items. Again, this is understandable since research is concerned with experiments in validity while standardised tests, like textbooks, must take care above all of reliability. Research can afford to be less immediately responsible, and this comes through in the articles which report that research.

1.5   The textbooks (in contrast with the articles, among which we include the published collections of articles) owe much to Lado (1961, 1964). Indeed Heaton (1975) points out how difficult it is to write on language testing 'without being aware of a debt to Robert Lado's *Language testing*'. Lado leads his followers in a firmly structuralist view of language testing; his 'theory of language testing assumes that language is a system of habits in communication' (Lado, 1964, p. 27). He advocates objective multiple-choice items of the skills-levels taxonomy consisting of discrete point items, and based on contrastive analysis between the target language and the mother tongue. Problems in language learning are shown up by contrastive analysis and 'testing control of the problems is testing control of the language'. Since this view cannot mean that all possible points of contrast show up learning problems, which would be both trite and vacuous, it must be the case that Lado is advocating a contrastive analysis as the basis for drawing up an inventory of test items. Further, it would seem from what he says about testing that this inventory will contain only linguistic contrasts. (It is, after all, presumably possible for an integrative test of communicative competence to be based on a contrastive analysis of communication problems.) His followers are more ready to accept his structuralism than his insistence on contrastive analysis (e.g. Upshur, 1962). Heaton (1975) does not even mention contrastive analysis. What we see develop in the '60s and early '70s is a rejection of contrastive analysis and a turning away from analytical structuralism towards integrative communication tests. However, when we look at what Lado actually does, as opposed to what he says he does, we find that some of his test proposals are more integrative than not. Once again we must make the point that no test can be wholly analytical or wholly integrative. Lado is well aware that 'one must use a range or combination of both skills versus the elements of language, and of objective versus subjective methods of test construction, depending on the purposes and conditions of the test' (Lado, 1964, p. 27).

Valette (1967) and Clark (1972) accept Lado's framework and extend and develop it for the testing of achievement in modern European languages, especially French and German. Harris (1969) and Heaton (1975) do the same for achievement in English. The Harris and Heaton books are complementary. Harris provides the reader with a general but adequate introduction to English language testing. Heaton offers teachers a practical, comprehensive guide for the actual writing of test items. There are not very important differing emphases. Heaton spends more time on the actual construction of the test, Harris more on computing and analysing test results. In each of his chapters Harris proceeds as follows: what the test should measure; how to determine test content; item types; advice on item writing. Harris is more interesting on the first two of these sections, Heaton is more useful on the last two. According to Harris, structure tests for foreign students will have as their purpose the testing of control of the basic grammatical patterns of the spoken language. Native speakers would expect to have perfect scores. As far as the content of the two books is concerned, both contain (though in different order) the following major components: introduction to language testing; writing items; constructing and analysing the test. The kinds of items discussed are of the psychometric–structuralist school: grammar, vocabulary, listening comprehension, oral production, reading comprehension, writing. (Notice once again the inclusion of both integrative and discrete point testing in a structuralist framework.)

1.6   Davies (1968) and Allen and Davies (1977) stand apart both from the single author books and from the collections (see below), in that they attempt to bring language testing under the umbrella of applied linguistics, within a general theory. The full title of Davies (1968) is *Language testing symposium: a psycholinguistic approach*. It soon became clear that the subtitle was a mistake, as more than one reviewer pointed out. In spite of its close relation to psychology through the psychometric connection, and in spite of the chapter by J. B. Carroll on the psychology of language testing, it would have made more sense to claim language testing as an applied linguistic rather than a psycholinguistic activity. This is what Allen and Davies (1977) do. The title of this book is *Testing and experimental methods, Edinburgh Course in Applied Linguistics*, Vol. 4. This time there has been no public disclaimer that language testing is not properly part of applied linguistics, perhaps because the field of applied linguistics seems not as well charted as that of psycholinguistics. At the same time it remains clear to one editor of Allen & Davies (1977) that language testing remains stubbornly apart from the main applied linguistic concerns, in a way that pedagogical grammar, syllabus design, applied sociolinguistics and interlanguage studies do not (perhaps because measurement is necessarily an externally applied procedure); and that the attempt to bring language testing into applied linguistics was only as successful as the attempt in the same volume to link testing and experimentation as twin aspects of the same endeavour, two sides of research in applied linguistics.

Several important and influential collections have taken the discussion on from the consolidating, textbook work of the books we have been discussing towards what Spolsky has called the psycholinguistic–sociolinguistic view. Still in the '60s, Upshur and Fata (1968) edited a set of conference papers with the general title *Problems in foreign language testing* which included such 'advanced' notions as the testing of culturally different groups, global proficiency, aural cloze technique, and integrated testing. Oller (Oller & Richards, 1973) examines discrete point tests and tests of integrative skills and comes down in favour of the latter, though he does mention the advantages of the former as well. But he finds discrete point tests artificial and reflecting an inadequate model of the language they purport to test. Jones and Spolsky (1975) contains no paper on any of the discrete skills. The main thrust of the Jones and Spolsky collection (of papers given at a conference on language proficiency) is towards integrative testing and we will take up some of its detail in Part 2. But it is relevant here that several of the published discussions contain direct discrete point/integrative confrontations (to be expected, no doubt, since both Lado and Oller were participating) and that Davies's paper ('Two tests of speeded reading') in Jones and Spolsky (1975) suggests theoretical reasons for the move from discrete point to integrative tests. Palmer and Spolsky (1975) continues the development away from discrete point tests and shows an interesting sensitivity to the importance of cultural factors in influencing the nature of test items and their evaluation. At the same time, we observe here and in Jones and Spolsky (1975) that there is an attempt to make the scoring procedures of integrative type tests (e.g. oral production) more rigorous. As we have already suggested and will do again, the effect of this may well be to turn what starts off as an integrative test into what is effectively a discrete point one; that in fact one approach cannot properly exist in isolation from the other.

1.7   Use of the discrete point test item has continued into the '70s. The length of the following (short) list is an indication of the continuing value of the discrete point approach to research: Rivers, 1968; Burstall, 1969; Rowe, 1969; Paquette & Tollinger, 1969; Brings, 1970; Famiglietti, 1971; Pinel, 1971; Truchot, 1971; Zierer, 1971; Bubenikova, 1971–2; Stoldt, 1973; Denham, 1974; Donnerstag, 1974; Di Cristo, 1975; Green, 1975; Ilyin & Best, 1976.

1.8   As we have pointed out above, Valette's list of standardised tests has no entry for the psycholinguistic–sociolinguistic stage of test development. It may be that standardised tests belong only to the previous psychometric–structuralist stage, i.e. that there is something illogical about the construction of a standardised test to represent the psycholinguistic–sociolinguistic stage. Our view is not that it is illogical but that it is very difficult to construct a fully integrative standardised test; indeed it may not be possible to provide a fully communicative competence test of an integrative design, which is scorable. (But see Trim, 1975; Savignon, 1972; Morrow, 1977, and Part 2 of this article.)

The tests mentioned by Valette (1977) are: the CEEB Achievement Tests (ETS, no date); the MLA Cooperative Tests (ETS, 1963); the Graduate Record Tests (ETS, no date); the TOEFL (ETS, 1964...), and the CELT (Harris & Palmer, 1970). An earlier one in the same mould (the Michigan) was prepared by Upshur and John (1961). It is intesting that there are so few English tests – no doubt this has something to do with the differing roles of English and other languages in the USA, the fact that on the whole one level of English has been required, that of proficiency for higher education, and by adults, whereas several levels are required among children as well as adults, for modern languages. The MLA has constructed and marketed tests only for the five major European languages: French, German, Italian, Spanish and Russian. The MLA Coop. Tests (ETS, 1963) and the CEEB Tests (ETS, no date) are good workmanlike tests for secondary-school language learning, deriving from a structuralist view of language. Thus the Coop. tests contain four parts – listening, speaking, reading and writing. Under 'listening' the following types of items are used: discrete statements or questions, questions about a recorded conversation, appropriate rejoinders for a telephone conversation. Under 'writing' the following types are used: fill-in-the-blanks, transformations of sentences, dehydrated sentences and directed composition. 'Reading' has fill-in-the-blanks, substitution of words or phrases and questions on short reading passages. 'Speaking' involves repetition of recorded sentences, reading aloud, answering questions about pictures and free oral description of a picture. The formats, in other words, contain a variety of discrete point items and integrative items (e.g. 'free oral description'), with the stress on the former.

In addition to these American tests we must mention two British tests of proficiency, the English Proficiency Test Battery (Davies, 1964) and the English Language Battery (ELBA) (Ingram, 1964), both deriving from a structuralist view of language. Both also contain integrative elements, Davies through modified cloze and a test of reading speed and Ingram through listening comprehension. Davies, in the latest version of the test (Davies, 1977 b), has moved from the extreme analytical position of earlier versions by substituting an overall listening comprehension sub-test (containing, for example, questions and answers and simulated note-taking of a lecture) for the earlier phoneme discrimination and stress and intonation tasks.

The language aptitude tests by Carroll & Sapon (1959) and Pimsleur (1966) belong here again by virtue of their construct of language aptitude which in both cases is a structuralist–behaviourist one. The pioneering work of Carroll & Sapon was followed up by Pimsleur, who showed that language aptitude tests could be designed for secondary-school children, and by Davies (1972) whose results indicated that the best predictor of success in learning a foreign language is success in previous language learning. Some further work is reported in the literature but no marked advance has been made on the work of Carroll & Sapon. Recent work includes: Chastain (1969); Kobersky (1969); Culhane (1970); Asher (1972); Kollarik (1972); Carroll (1973); Novak (1973); Partington (1974); Harding (1974–5); Green (1974–5); Robinson (1975); Berry & Moore (1975); Nizegorodcew (1975). No doubt the opening up of school language learning to many more children (and the parallel cut-back in language learning in the armed forces) has contributed to the lessening of interest in language aptitude. Indeed, Robinson's (1975) finding is that language aptitude is non-significant in her Australian experiment, and that educators should be committed to the principle of equal opportunity for all children as language learners. It does, however, seem a pity that more theoretical interest in language aptitude has not continued, since success in language learning remains of paramount interest. It is of both theoretical and practical interest to investigate how far success is determined by social and contextual factors, which in recent years has been a fashionable view, and how far it remains, at least in part, a special ability. Work on motivation (Gardner & Lambert, 1969, 1972; Jakobovits, 1970) has continued but motivation as an explanation becomes increasingly unsatisfactory. Oller, Hudson and Liu (1977) do, however, take up the question of the relation between language attitude and attained proficiency in English as a second language, and state that according to their results there is tentative support for the intuitive feelings of language teachers, namely that the most successful language learner is the 'outgoing, friendly and talkative student'. Brière et al. (1973), Burt, Dulay and Hernandez (1975) and Rudd (1971) take up questions relating to the special cultural interests and linguistic behaviours which published tests have tried to cater for; Garcia-Zamor and Birdsong (1977) provide a comprehensive list of available tests in this area.

It is noticeable that standardised language tests are being increasingly used for evaluation and experimental purposes. Scoon and Blanchard (1970), Heil and Aleamoni (1974), and Irvine and Oller (1974), among others, have worked with the TOEFL; Moller (1975) with the EPTB, and Ingram (1973) with the ELBA. Ibe (1975) has reported on interesting comparative work with two standardised tests.

2. Reading

It is not intended to report fully on work on reading and reading tests in this article, most of which is concerned with the acquisition of reading in the mother tongue. However, it is of interest to report on some of the work on reading in a second language, with special reference to the testing of reading. The standard textbooks (Lado, 1961, 1964; Valette, 1967; Harris, 1969; Clark, 1972; Heaton, 1975) all have sections on the testing of reading. It is interesting that Clark in 1972 makes use of a thorough-going discrete point framework. His section on the testing of reading starts with character recognition and proceeds through the testing of vocabulary and the testing of grammar to tests of general reading comprehension. Heaton (1975) proceeds in much the same way, but he does give some useful hints on testing the comprehension of reading texts, and goes on to a short discussion of cloze tests. Davies and Widdowson (1975) provide advice on ways of formulating different types of test question, which are not just large discrete point items. But so far there has been no satisfactory discussion of testing which makes use of research and developments in discourse analysis. Such discussion is urgently needed. Motta *et al.* (1974) look at different methods for testing reading comprehension. Henning compared seven commonly employed techniques for testing reading comprehension in terms of predictive validity, difficulty and discrimination and found that multiple-choice sentence selection (and synonym–antonym selection for intermediate comprehension) proved to be the most valid predictor of the criterion. Engineer (1978) has looked at the effect of length of text of reading comprehension (defining a long text as over 1,000 words) and concludes that discrimination improves considerably after about 600 words of running text, that at that point reading comprehension tests become very good predictors of overall proficiency in English as a second language. Shearer (1975) has reported on a restandardisation of the Burt–Vernon and Schonnell Graded Word Reading Tests. In view of the renewed interest in vocabulary in second-language teaching, it would be useful to have a similar test constructed for a second-language population. Most reading discussions in the recent past, however, have been on cloze testing and we leave that over until Part 2, where we discuss integrative testing.

3. Criterion and norm referenced tests

In terms of the dichotomies presented earlier in this article, norm referenced tests belong with discrete point, analytical, structuralist, etc., while criterion referenced tests belong with integrative, global, communicative competence, etc. This is, of course, a travesty of the real situation but it does seem arguable that *tests* (in the sense of the definition that a test is a procedure which establishes a rank order) do require discrete point items. The question then arises (a question for Part 2) whether tests of communicative competence can contain, as we have suggested above, discrete point items.

Interest in criterion referenced tests has come in part from a greater interest in the whole question of curriculum development and partly from a distaste for the ranking function of tests. Ideally, criterion referenced tests have the following characteristics: they test externally defined objectives, they test on a syllabus or content rather than on a rank order, they are useful diagnostically, and they test all relevant behaviour, not just samples of it (Bormuth, 1970). Naturally, there are difficulties in using criterion referenced tests for language: there is no finite inventory of learning points or items; there are very many behavioural objectives; there are variable (or no) external criteria of success, fluency, intelligibility, etc.; there is no obvious way of establishing adequate knowledge, of saying how much of a language is enough. As Cronbach has reminded us, 'setting a cutting score requires a value judgement'.

Carter (1968), Valette and Disick (1972), Savignon (1972) and Valette (1977) describe the role of criterion referencing in language testing. Valette and Disick propose a model based on two claims: one, that criterion referencing gives a relevant and non-subjectively defined learning programme, and two, that it can be used to provide an individualised instruction programme. (It is useful here to link criterion referencing with the attempt at item and objective specification of programmed instruction in the early '60s.) In order to specify student learning objectives, Valette and Disick suggest an interrelationship of two performance objectives, formal and expressive, and two taxonomies, the subject-matter and the affective. It is, however, difficult to see how criterion referenced tests can be constructed in a completely separate way from norm referenced tests, i.e. without the usual canons of item discreteness and discrimination.

There is another way of looking at the two kinds of test. Most teachers are concerned with very small (and often quite homogeneous) samples. What they require is a criterion referenced use of a norm referenced test, i.e. a test that does not discriminate greatly among their students but which does establish an adequate dichotomy (or cut-off) between knowledge and no knowledge. If we accept this point of view then criterion referenced tests are essentially special uses with small samples of norm referenced tests. For every criterion referenced test there must be a population for whom the test could be norm referenced. As Blatchford (1971) points out, criterion referenced tests are suitable for diagnostic testing, and Ewen and Gipps (1973) have also pointed to their usefulness in separating two populations. But our conclusion must be that criterion referencing is more properly regarded as suitable for an exercise (a task that all the population can do, as opposed to a test – norm referenced – which they cannot), or as a means of deciding on where to draw a cut-off, establishing how much of language learning is enough, i.e. what is adequate proficiency. Neither use is new. Criterion referencing is a valuable and salutary way of looking at existing tests and reminding us that in a given situation we are always concerned with determining how much is enough. More optimistically, Birkmaier (1973) reviews what she describes as 'innovative work . . . in the field of criterion referenced testing', and suggests that more attention to mastery learning and to formative (as opposed to summative) evaluation 'could eliminate the attrition rate in foreign languages'. She includes within her discussion of criterion referencing, kinesics, culture and 'real' communities. Pimsleur (1975) has also argued for greater use of criterion referenced tests. From our point of view, a criterion referenced test is a use of a norm referenced test; but the argument is often presented as though criterion referencing were in itself a method of test construction. It is not. *July 1978*

PART II

4. Integrative tests

Three separate arguments are used to support the general non-discrete approach to language testing. The first is that language is not a set of unrelated bits, that it forms a whole and that the bits must be integrated and tested in combination with one another. The second is that language learning is purposeful, that the purpose is always communicative and that what must be tested is communicative ability and not formal knowledge. The third is that discrete point language tests are too general to be of value and that what are required are specific tests. This last argument relates to the unit credit system idea (Trim, 1973) and to the special purpose approach in language teaching – certainly these developments have aroused more demand for specific tests. But it would be possible to devise specific tests of discrete point items related to levels and to selections from a structural syllabus. The integrative and the specific arguments are neutral as to type of test and the persuasive argument for change has been the communicative one. However, as we have noted above in Part 1 and will see again below, it makes sense to see integrative and discrete point items as forming a continuum; in the same way it makes sense to see general and specific tests as one continuum and communicative and linguistic tests as another. Indeed it may well be that these three arguments and three continua are in fact one argument and one continuum and that what they reflect is a focusing of attention and not a difference of scale.

Oller (1976) puts forward a very strong claim on behalf of integrative tests. 'It is my opinion that so-called integrative tests are better than discrete point tests for precisely this reason' (p. 161) (that) 'the redundancy (or grammatical organisation) of verbal materials is a key factor accounting for a large portion of the variance in verbal experiments' (and it therefore follows that) 'language tests should invoke the examinee's capacity to utilize such organisational constraints' (p. 160). Oller includes among integrative tests 'cloze, dictation, translation, essay, oral interview' (p. 156). Oller's claim here is expressed in the terms of his own speculations about a grammar of expectancy (Oller, 1972), his term for the notion that prediction is the central element in language performance and that a test which captures that prediction is likely to be more valid than one that does not. Oller's argument, then, is about validity, that integrative tests are more valid than discrete point tests. We shall look below at some of the evidence for this claim (which has been widely made) but it is important to remind ourselves that discrete point tests are themselves typically intended for use in combination in test batteries, e.g. TOEFL (1964); ELBA (Ingram, 1964), EPTB (Davies, 1964). It was always recognised that the sum of the whole was greater than any one of the parts. A test battery gives a total score (in which certain parts may be weighted) and on one meaning of integrative this total score provides an integrated description of the testee's language ability. The other meaning of integrative, the view that Oller, for example, takes, is a *Gestalt*-type view which uses a performance-type task to assess performance. Further, it is Oller's claim that integrative tests such as cloze, dictation, etc., are not only more valid in themselves (performance tasks testing performance ability) but also that they contain greater validity than test batteries in relation to appropriate criteria.

4.1 *Cloze*

Cloze procedure was introduced by Taylor (1953) as a device for measuring readability of texts. Taylor himself (1956) proposed its use as a test of reading comprehension. Carroll (1959) suggested the possibility of using cloze as a reading comprehension measure for foreign-language learners. More recently, Anderson (1971) has used cloze as a criterion reference test in an attempt to determine the readability of materials for an English as a Second Language class, and Jongsma (1971) has claimed that cloze is a valid test of reading comprehension for non-native speakers. Since the mid 1960s there has been an increasingly wide use of cloze for a variety of purposes. It has been used to test readability, reading comprehension, listening comprehension and general English proficiency. It has also been used in diagnostic and criterion reference tests and as a teaching device.

The remarkable speed with which cloze has come to play so large a role in the testing of reading comprehension is an indication of its acceptance as an integrative test of reading comprehension. The claims for cloze as an at-a-stroke measure of overall English proficiency (Oller, 1972) indicate the desire to find a single integrative measure. (Such a desire may, of course, be vain.) Cloze has been used to a limited extent with languages other than English (references in Riley, 1973 and Douglas, 1978). Bibliographies and reviews are found in Rankin, 1974; Robinson, 1972; Anderson, 1976; Riley, 1973; Alderson, 1978.

Major issues in the literature on cloze are: choice of text, seen or unseen text, deletion rate and type of deletion, scoring procedure, reliability and validity. We shall consider each of these briefly.

4.1.1 Choice of text: this is governed by exactly the same constraints and meets the same problems as item selection. There is first an assessment in terms of content validity (Is the passage about the right level? etc.) and then a suspension of judgement until there are results to analyse. Exactly the same judgement and the same luck enter into item writing. Of course it is more difficult to change a text, if it proves to be the wrong one, than an item, and it is understandable therefore that judges are employed to select appropriate texts and that readability measures are used for selection (Moyle, 1973).

4.1.2 Seen or unseen texts: Oller (1972) quotes Jongsma (1971): 'It is known that if a student is familiar with the text of a cloze passage he will perform significantly better, and in proportion to his familiarity with the passage.' But Oller concludes that there is no need to separate out such passages. Hafner (1964) suggests that differences between means of passages which had been 'taught' previously and those which had been read previously was not significant and that familiar and unfamiliar passages correlated highly with each other.

4.1.3 Deletion rate and type of deletion: the most commonly used deletion rate is every fifth word. It is assumed that the rates are equivalent though there has been little research. Oller (1972) found that deletions between every fifth and every twelfth word keep results stable. Alderson (1978) claims that deletion rates do differ, even between five and twelve, and that the reason for the difference has nothing to do with the amount of context provided. Rather, it reflects the change of text with the change of deletion rates, given that the text adds and subtracts words each time the rate is changed. Various modified types of deletion have been proposed. All such modifications are in fact stages along the continuum from productive to receptive testing, multiple choice being at the receptive end. No doubt it is convenient for a test of reading comprehension with gaps to have multiple choice alternatives at each gap, but such a test is not cloze. Indeed the same criticism has been made of rational or modified cloze (also called selective or structural) as opposed to the orthodox random cloze. In the random type of cloze test every nth word is deleted; in the rational type deletions are categorial, namely every noun (or every nth noun). Jongsma (1971) maintained that an nth rate deletion would correlate more highly with comprehension measures than would rational deletion. Given the present state of knowledge, a fifth rate deletion seems preferable, as Taylor (1953) suggested, on the grounds of economy. Alderson (1978) argues for more work on rational deletion which does admit of linguistic hypotheses.

4.1.4 Scoring procedure: there are two main recognised procedures, (a) the verbatim or exact word replacement, and (b) acceptable alternative word replacement – any contextually acceptable word is counted as correct. It is worth noting that there are several kinds of acceptable word replacement, e.g. grammatically acceptable, semantically acceptable, or both together, and so on. Comparisons have shown that different scoring methods are about equal in discrimination (Anderson, 1972), an acceptable alternative word mean score always being higher than the verbatim word mean. One important reason for the characteristically high correlation between verbatim and acceptable mean is that the verbatim is always included within the acceptable, so that the correlation includes a large component of self correlation. Darnell (1970) has worked on the cloze entropy scoring method, a variant of the acceptable alternative word replacement in which the criterion of word replacement is determined by the population under test.

4.1.5 Reliability and validity: the exact word replacement is practical and efficient (Taylor, 1953; Potter, 1968), other methods providing less inter-marker reliability. Claims have been made recently for greater validity for the acceptable word method of scoring. Oller (1972) found that M2 (exact word plus any contextually acceptable word) was better than M1 (exact word only) for validating correlations. Although the item discrimination for all passages is slightly better with M1 than M2, the item reliability is better with M2. Oller thus advocates the suitability of M2 scoring with EFL students. Haskell (1973), on the other hand, tried with EFL students the exact method against that of scoring for synonyms and scoring for appropriate words, and discovered that for measuring EFL proficiency verbatim methods were best. Irvine, Atai and Oller (1974) seem to agree with Haskell. Correlation studies of cloze tend to be contradictory, though as Oller (1972) points out, cloze does tend to correlate highly with standardised language proficiency tests. Darnell (1968) and Mason (1972) find low correlation with external criteria. Alderson (1978) concludes that cloze is a potentially interesting measure of language proficiency for non-native speakers.

In spite of the great vogue that cloze has enjoyed recently, a number of doubts have been expressed, largely concerned with the validity of cloze. MacGinitie (1971) has suggested that no true understanding of the text is needed and that cloze is less a measure of comprehension than a measure of redundancy. Rankin (1974) echoes this doubt and suggests that cloze is a better measure of readability than of reading comprehension. Alderson (1978), after a remarkably thorough review of the literature, concludes that the evidence tends to support Carroll's claim (Carroll & Freedle, 1972) that cloze depends largely on local redundancy. From a factor analysis Alderson (1978) concludes that cloze is more associated with core proficiency than with a dictation factor, and further that dictation is less associated with the more integrative parts of a proficiency test than with discrete point tests of grammar, vocabulary or sound recognition. He concludes that what cloze and dictation have in common is a measurement of formal linguistic skills. Cloze must be treated with caution. Evidence is contradictory about the result of different scoring procedures and the relationship with other measures.

4.2 *Dictation*

Views on dictation have changed radically from that of Lado (1961): 'On critical inspection it appears to measure very little of language' and Harris (1969): 'As a testing device dictation must be regarded as generally both uneconomical and imprecise.' Rivers (1968) is in agreement: 'It cannot be considered a valid test of listening comprehension alone' and is probably best used only as a teaching exercise. Valette (1967) was of the view that 'foreign language specialists... are not in agreement of the effectiveness of the dictation as an examination for more advanced students. It is evident that the art of taking dictation is a specialised skill.' She goes on to say that more research is needed. But in Valette (1977), she feels able to say that dictation is a precise measure of the student's listening comprehension. It is Oller who, both alone and with colleagues, in a series of articles, has brought dictation back into popularity as a testing device. He sees it as a global test of overall proficiency (Oller, 1971; Oller & Streiff, 1975; Oller & Conrad, 1971; Oller, 1972; Irvine, Atai & Oller, 1974). In the last mentioned study the authors looked at cloze, dictation and TOEFL. They concluded that TOEFL provides little information other than that provided by cloze, dictation and a listening sub-test. Dictation is closely related to various measures of ability in English as a Foreign Language, one of which is the cloze. Why this should be so is less clear. In his 1971 article, Oller presents an explanation for dictation as a valid testing technique. He suggests that a dynamic process of analysis by synthesis is involved. He claims that the listener's mechanism which operates in dictation is a grammar of expectancy (Oller & Streiff, 1975). Since cloze is also tapping the grammar of expectancy, this leads to the high correlations found between dictation and cloze. It does seem that some of Lado's objections must be refuted. The fact that dictation does not test anything very precise is to Oller a virtue, in that he is looking for integrative tests. The findings on dictation, Alderson (1978) points out, are contradictory. The only consistent finding is the high correlation with reading tests and with cloze. Alderson himself claims as a result of his research

145

(1978) that dictation measures lower order skills rather than the higher order skills of inference and the like measured in comprehension tests. Further work on dictation is needed, especially on scoring procedures. Fountain (1974) has described an interesting experiment in which only key words were scored. This is a promising development. Dictation, like cloze, still needs to be treated cautiously. Some interesting work has been done on reduced redundancy tests using masking noise (Johansson, 1973), but very few studies have been reported.

5. Spoken and written production tests

Productive tests are at the extreme end of the discrete point–integrative continuum. The interesting work on spoken production tests is in the devising of frameworks and analytical grids to make scoring reliable. All such frameworks have the effect of making productive tests less integrative and more discrete point by providing some method of scoring. Much less work has been done on testing writing. In the CILT bibliography (Perren, 1977) only five items listed of the 132 articles appear to relate to writing and the main concern in these is in the controlled composition which is a kind of framework. Doble (1974) suggests that pupils might be less inhibited by a more controlled exercise than the free composition such as the structured essay. Gipps and Ewen (1974) discuss the use of a t-unit for scoring purposes. Sako (1969) examines the use of objective items for testing writing skills. It is interesting that in her discussion (Valette, 1977) of 'Writing for communication', the most integrative type of test, the free composition, suffers from two drawbacks: the scoring is time-consuming and the grades tend to lack objectivity. She suggests ways of improving composition tests through careful preparation, pre-planned scoring and appropriate selection of composition topics. The ways of improving scoring are indeed the provision of rating scales, one example of which is to provide sub-part scores for organisation, clarity of expression and breadth of vocabulary – in other words that is how the integrative test is brought back somewhat towards a discrete point position.

Testing spoken production: there has been little follow up to McCallien (Davies, 1968) to provide a discrete point type of oral proficiency test, though Beardsmore and Renkin (1971) do indicate some progress along these lines. Most work is on testing overall fluency, i.e. at the integrative end of the continuum. As Bachman (1973) points out, recent research has focused on global techniques, and Beardsmore (1971) reports some work on combining discrete point and integrative methods in a test of oral fluency. Robinson (1971 a, b) argues in favour of participating tests, which presumably means integrative tests of oral fluency, and Roy (1969) has done some interesting work on measuring the rate of output as a factor in oral proficiency. Seward (1973) reports that an indirect method of testing oral fluency is possible. Townson (1973) supports this view. Valette (1977) is concerned with speaking for communication and presents a number of frameworks for scoring. She points out that a framework of some kind is essential: 'Although a free expression test allows the students to demonstrate their linguistic creativity, one cannot simply put the student before a tape recorder or in front of a class and say "speak". A testing framework that will facilitate student talk must be established (Valette, 1977, p. 152). One of the frameworks she mentions is in connection with an item type on picture writing. In such a test, points are given as follows: one point for each sentence in which the intent of the picture would be correctly conveyed to a native speaker, one point for each correct response that sounds fluent and natural. Of course there are problems with such a scoring system since we have to agree on whether the intent of the picture is correctly conveyed to a native speaker, and so on. Another scale that she provides is that of Jakobovits and Gordon (1974). This is a scale for free expression tests in which the emphasis is on transactional competence rather than on correctness of pronunciation and syntax. There are eight items, each one going from zero to ten, for example accuracy of information from very poor to fully accurate, fluency of speech from very hesitant to ordinary fluency, complexity of transactional performance from straight to skilful restatement. She also includes Bartz' scale (Bartz, 1974) and the Schulz communicative competence scale (Schulz, 1977), which includes Fluency, Comprehensibility, Amount and Quality of Communication. The Comprehensibility Scale has six levels, e.g. (1) no comprehension, (2) the examiner comprehended small bits and pieces, isolated words, (3) the examiner comprehended some word clusters. As will be obvious, there are problems in applying these methods but they are in each case an attempt to introduce some objectivity and there is good examiner moderating beforehand.

The Schulz scale provides a useful link with the whole question of the testing of communicative competence. Beardsmore (1972) suggests that 'oral fluency is understood to imply a communicative competence requiring an ability to formulate accurate and appropriate utterances of more than one sentence in length'. However it is not necessarily the case that a test of oral production tests communicative competence, because an oral production test may be concerned with idealised and not authentic language. Published tests of oral production include the John test (1976), the Bilingual Syntax Measure (Burt *et al.*, 1975) and Ilyin Oral Interview (Ilyin, 1976). The problems of oral testing remain very much those discussed by Perren (1967, 1968).

6. Testing the communicative skills

Three arguments are put forward for the teaching of communicative competence. The general argument is that linguistic competence is not enough in itself, in the sense that the structural rules have been learned and the learner can't put them to use. Communicative competence is also needed. This seems a correct view, though we might ask what are the rules that have been learned – they must represent a narrow view of language. The specific argument is that there is now less opportunity for communicative competence to be acquired and practised in situations where the status of English, for example, has changed from a second to a foreign language, or because English for general purposes has become English for special purposes. In neither case is there opportunity to put the language into use. So what is needed is emphasis on language use. Again this is a correct view. The heretical argument goes as follows: since language is not communication (a correct statement) and since it is communication that is needed, then it is communication rather than language that needs to be taught. We notice this heresy in the testing and examining situation because of the inadequate level of proficiency accepted by the tester/examiner, but in reality it is a teaching problem and a teaching heresy.

6.1 It has always been common practice to include among the goals and objectives, and therefore among the assessments, some form of global testing which attempts to activate the elements, to put into situational operation the command over discrete language forms, i.e. the competence. Such assessments have been the essay and the interview. Such global tests can be both receptive and productive. Harris (1969, p. 84) provides a typical framework for a global test which happens to be of the oral production variety. Even in the heyday of structural syllabuses it was normal to make use of what amounted to integrative tests. The attraction of the new or renewed techniques which we have discussed (e.g. cloze and dictation), the reasons for their popularity, have been that they (1) make the global aspects of structural syllabuses more reliable (the major and constant doubt about the more traditional integrative tests such as the essay and the interview), and (2) represent a move of some kind towards a communicative type of test. We can discern five patterns of relationship between integrative and discrete point (DP) test items in terms of the stimulus, the task, the item and the scoring method, thus:

	Stimulus	Task	Item	Scoring	Example
1.	DP	DP	DP	DP	Phoneme discrimination
2.	Integ.	DP	DP	DP	Reading comprehension
3.	Integ.	Integ.	DP	DP	Cloze-verbatim
4.	Integ.	Integ	Integ.	DP	Cloze-acceptable
5.	Integ.	Integ.	Integ.	Integ.	Essay

All frameworks in tests are attempts to provide a method of scoring, i.e. they (normally) increase reliability by the use of discrete point test items and thus decrease validity by not using integrative-type items. This relationship can also be represented in a 2 by 2 table in which the parameters are integrative–discrete point and linguistic–communicative competence. The relation between the two parameters is made by the twin features of reliability and validity.

	DP	*Integ.*
Linguistic	– V	– V
Competence	+ R	– R
Communicative	+ V	+ V
Competence	+ R	– R

As the table shows, it is possible for both R(eliability) and V(alidity) to be present and not present. As the table also shows, the most desirable test (having + V + R) is a DP test of Communicative Competence; the least desirable (– V – R) an Integ. test of linguistic competence. We may surmise that the most useful tests are probably those that make a compromise, i.e. tests that make up on Reliability by testing linguistic competence through discrete point items, and make up on Validity by testing communicative competence through integrative items.

6.2 A description of a typical communicative competence test is given by Valette (1977): 'When students are being evaluated on their ability to communicate orally, the main emphasis focuses on the transmission of a message or series of messages. The essential consideration is whether the students are able to make themselves understood. The accent on the meaning of the message rather than on its grammaticality, characterises speaking tests of this type. The student is instructed about what to say. The choice of words and structures, however, is not specified and is left up to the student.'

6.3 Testing of communicative competence is still largely programmatic. Examples of test items employing visual and verbal cues have been noted by Valette (1977). Various rating scales for testing written or spoken production have been put forward (e.g. Jakobovits & Gordon, 1974). The Foreign Service Institute Rating Procedure (see Wilds, in Jones & Spolsky, 1975) has been widely used – indeed it was already in use before mention of testing communicative competence. It is interesting that the first parameter of the Schulz communicative competence scale is the whole of the FSI Rating Procedure. The four parameters of the Schulz scale are: fluency, comprehensibility, amount of communication and quality of communication. Schulz (1977) set out to 'inquire into the effect of testing in foreign-language learning. The main question to be investigated was: do tests of communicative proficiency when administered in lieu of currently prevailing discrete point item tests further the student's spontaneous communicative ability?' Schulz applied a series of communicative tests to one experimental group and a series of discrete point tests to another. Both groups received the same 'modified audiolingual teaching' over ten weeks. A combined communicative and discrete point test was given as a post-test. All significant findings were in favour of the discrete point group, but Schulz found that there was a trend (non-significant) 'showing that testing procedures in general can effect achievement on tests'. Schulz concluded that 'if the major goal of instruction is correct language use, it seems safe to conclude that discrete point testing methods are superior. If communicative ability (meaning above grammar) is the major aim of instruction, simulated communicative tests tend to increase this kind of achievement'. Schulz gives as examples of the communication testing procedures used: 'summaries in English of information heard or read in French, drawing pictures or following directions on a map according to instructions given in French; and asking and answering questions, giving oral or written summaries, describing and reporting'. The major study of communicative testing (of learners of French) so far reported is that of Savignon (1972), who concludes after an elaborate and careful study that valid communication tests can be designed and made reliable. Savignon made use of four major kinds of assessment, each with two or more scales. The assessments were: a discussion, an interview, a reporting session, and a description. McDonough (1977) and Rea (1978) comment helpfully on the problems of testing communication and give examples of techniques they have employed.

6.4   One of the most instructive and helpful considerations of communicative testing is that by Morrow (1977). Morrow points out that 'the use of language in a communicative situation has a number of features which are not measured in conventional language tests'. Example features are: communication is interaction based, it is unpredictable, it has context, it is purposive, the language is authentic, and the language is behaviour-based. Morrow argues that communicative testing can employ either discrete point items or integrative items. Examples of discrete point items would be manipulative ones (e.g. a multiple choice judgement about the situation of a given stimulus), or productive (e.g. a request to produce appropriate linguistic behaviour from an array of choices in a given situation). Examples of integrative items would be: answering questions freely, asking questions freely, participating in an interaction, providing a narrative. Morrow points to the well-known validity –reliability tension (which we have referred to) in all language testing; he describes an interaction participation test in which the testee's part in a dialogue is blank: 'he therefore has to find fillers for the blanks in his dialogue. The blanks may . . . be of varying lengths ranging from single words to complete utterances. It should be noted, though, that the smaller the blank, the more the test becomes one of grammatical rather than communicative competence' (pp. 41–2). Morrow's very informative report ends with an outline of some of the investigations which should be carried out into the validity and feasibility of the specific techniques presented earlier.

6.5 Recent investigation into language tests of specific purposes (Carroll, B. J., 1978) is of interest here. Such an approach provides us with a paradox, namely that the desire to provide for variety through delineating the specific purposes may lead to the strait-jacket of exact specification. Such tests as B. J. Carroll suggests, remain at the programmatic level and it remains to be seen how different they will be. This, after all, is the real issue over the testing of communicative competence. Is the teaching (and therefore the testing) of communicative competence intended to be a syllabus issue or a method issue? Often it seems really to be about strategy rather than about basic content. If it is about strategy, then the case for replacing linguistic tests by communicative ones disappears and communicative tests (and teaching) appear as another version of linguistic tests. If there is a real difference then we may query whether non-native-speaking language teachers can use a communicative syllabus if they cannot in fact turn a structural syllabus to communicative ends. What remains a convincing argument in favour of linguistic competence tests (both discrete point and integrative) is that grammar is at the core of language learning: hence, perhaps, the Schulz finding quoted above. Grammar is far more powerful in terms of generalisability than any other language feature. Therefore grammar may still be the most salient feature to teach, and to test. Upshur (1976) raises interesting doubts about Oller's claims for integrative tests.

6.6 All tests require structure, a framework of some kind to preserve reliability. It looks as though the contribution of the communicative competence drive will be to provide a little more validity in the shape of examples of language use. Tests will continue to use a combination of discrete point and integrative items and there will be a serious attempt to make the language provided in these items more realistic.

Rea (1978), quoting Jakobovits (Savignon, 1972), points to the need to bring testing procedures into step with teaching goals. From a teaching point of view this is wholly correct. But the argument of this review article has been that there is a testing point of view to put alongside the teaching one, and that in this case the testing view can act as a corrective to over-eager assumptions about teaching syllabuses. We raise the question: is communicative testing feasible?

The typical extension of structuralist language frameworks (e.g. Lado, 1961) could accommodate the testing of the communicative skills through, for example, context. Naturalism is a vulgar error; all education needs some measure of idealisation, and the search for authenticity in language teaching is chimerical. The linguist, the language teacher and the tester are all concerned with generalising from a language sample to the whole of the language. Language is not divorced from communication and cannot be taught or tested separately. Testing (like teaching) the communicative skills is a way of making sure that there are tests of context as well as of grammar; testing (and teaching) the communicative skills is not doing something parallel to or different from testing (and teaching) the linguistic skills – what it does is to make sure that they are complete.

The arguments presented in this and the previous article owe much to discussions with friends and students in Edinburgh (Department of Linguistics, Edinburgh University) and Montreal (TESL Centre, Concordia University) and especially to J. C. Alderson and A. D. Moller. The shortcomings of the discussion and opinions are entirely mine.   *October 1978*

Addendum, December 1981

The three years that have passed since the above survey was written have seen considerable development of work on language testing. There has been an expansion on the side of test construction: tests of English for specific purposes (ELTS, 1980), communicative language tests (RSA, 1981; Harding *et al*, 1980); there have been more frequent research meetings and seminars devoted to language testing issues under the auspices of such organisations as the British Association of Applied Linguistics, Teachers of English to Speakers of Other Languages, and the *Interuniversiteit Sprachtestgruppe*; a growth in the number of publications concerned with language testing (e.g. Oller, 1979; Cohen, 1980, Carroll, B. J., 1980; Alderson & Hughes, 1981) and most recently a new *Newsletter* concerned with language testing research (Hughes & Porter, 1981).

Most noticeable has been the increasing emphasis on research in language testing and on the reporting of that research (e.g. Oller, forthcoming; Vollmer, 1981 and forthcoming; Palmer & Bachman, 1981). The central research topics reported include communicative language tests (Canale & Swain, 1979), the testing of languages for specific purposes (Carroll, B. J., 1980) and, perhaps most important, the unitary competence hypothesis, where, among others, Oller (1979 and forthcoming) and Vollmer (1981) have engaged in a continuing debate on the structure of language proficiency. It is to this issue that Palmer and Bachman (1981) and their associates have also addressed themselves in their continuing multi-method–multi-trait research programme.

What seems to have happened in these last three years is that language testing has come of age and is now regarded as providing a methodology that is of value throughout applied linguistics and perhaps in core linguistics too. Here we see parallels to developments in sociolinguistics and in interlanguage (or second-language acquisition studies). In both cases the construction of a methodology (Labovian analysis for sociolinguistics and implicational scaling for interlanguage) has led to a growth in research. In both cases also there has been some feedback to core linguistics. Indeed Labov has called his kind of sociolinguistics 'secular linguistics' and increasingly interlanguage research seems more concerned with linguistic theory than with applied linguistics or with language teaching. In the same way, language-testing methodology has been seized on as a valuable tool for use in theoretical research about language. Certainly that is the view that Oller has taken, that language testing is a way of investigating language, of doing linguistics. In all the cases mentioned, applied linguistics seems to be proving methodologies for furthering knowledge of core linguistics. This is admirable. Language testing is now better known and more widely appreciated and what we have in fact been seeing is greater acceptance of the role of construct validity such that the approach of, for example, John Carroll to aptitude testing, which furthered our understanding of language, has now been extended to proficiency testing.

But this emphasis has its dangers. Of course we need to think more about testing—as about everything else. It would, however, be unsatisfactory if the effect of the greater prominence now given to language testing research was to divorce research from development, to separate language testing research from the necessary and continuing development of language tests. That rift has emerged in interlanguage studies, with the result that interlanguage research seems to have less and less to do with language teaching. Research in language testing has now established itself in a central position in applied linguistics where it can properly work to further our understanding of language and language learning. It must also continue to do what Lado called for at the conclusion of the book that still has useful things to say (Lado, 1961) '... precise knowledge of the task and precise testing of the amount learned under clearly defined conditions can bring language teaching out of the confusion of thoughtless or interested opinionism into the more productive realm of scientific investigation' (p. 389). Language testing has a very useful role to play within applied linguistics: it must not overreach itself. [References follow main References section.]

References

Aitken, K. G. (1977). Using close procedure as an overall language proficiency test. *TESOL Quarterly*, **11**, 1, 59–67.

Alderson, J. C. (1978). A study of the cloze procedure with native and non-native speakers of English. University of Edinburgh, Ph.D. thesis.

Allen, J. P. B. & Davies, A. (eds.) (1977). Testing and experimental methods. *Edinburgh Course in Applied Linguistics*, vol. 4. London: O.U.P.

Anderson, J. (1971). A technique for measuring reading comprehension and readability. *English Language Teaching*, **25**, 2, 178–82.

Anderson, J. (1972). The application of cloze procedure to English learned as a foreign language in Papua and New Guinea. *English Language Teaching*, **27**, 1, 66–72.

Anderson, J. (1976). *Psycholinguistic experiments in foreign language testing*. University of Queensland Press.

Asher, J. J. (1972). *Differential prediction of student success in intensive language training*. Final Report, Defence Language Institute. Monterey, California.

Bachman, Lyle F. (1973). Testing oral production. *Bulletin of the English Language Center*, **3**, 1, 41–58.

Bartz, W. H. (1974). A study of the relationship of certain learner factors with the ability to communicate in a second language (German) for the development of measures of communicative competence. Ohio State University, Ph.D. thesis.

Beardsmore, H. B. (1974). Testing oral fluency. *IRAL*, **12**, 4, 317–26.

Beardsmore, H. B. & Renkin, A. (1971). A test of spoken English. *IRAL*, **19**, 1, 1–11.

Berry, Susan & Moore, B. (1975). *Testing for language aptitude*. Behavioural Sciences Research Division, Civil Service Division, Whitehall, London.

Birkmaier, Emma (1973). Research on teaching foreign languages. In R. M. W. Travers (ed.), *Second handbook of research on teaching*. Chicago: Rand, McNally & Co.

Blatchford, C. H. (1971). A theoretical contribution to ESL diagnostic test construction. *TESOL Quarterly*, **5**, 3, 209–15.

Bormuth, J. R. (1970). *On the theory of achievement test items.* Chicago and London: University of Chicago Press.

Brière. E. J. (1969). Current trends in language testing. *TESOL Quarterly,* **3**, 4, 333–40.

Brière, E. J. *et al.* (1973). Test of Proficiency in English as a second language (TOPESL). Bureau of Indian Affairs, Washington, D.C.

Brings, F. (1970). Zur Konstruktion eines informellen Sprachleistungstests. *Praxis des neusprachlichen Unterrichts,* **17,** 4.

Brown, Gillian (1977). *Listening to spoken English.* London: Longman.

Bubenikova, Libuse (1971/2). Formy jazykovych testu. *Cizi jazyky ve skole,* **15,** 5, **15,** 6 and **15,** 7.

Buros, O. K. (ed.) (1972). *Seventh mental measurements yearbook,* vol. 1. New York: Gryphon Press.

Buros, O. K. (ed.) (1975): *Foreign language tests and reviews.* New York: Gryphon Press.

Burstall, Clare (1969). The main stages in the development of language tests. In H. H. Stern (ed.), *Languages and the young school child.* London: O.U.P.

Burt, M. K., Dulay, H. C. & Hernandez, Ch. E. (1975). *Bilingual syntax measure.* New York: The Psychological Corporation.

Carroll, B. J. (1978). *An English language testing service: specifications.* London: British Council.

Carroll, J. B. (1959). *An investigation of cloze items in the measurement of achievement in foreign languages.* Cambridge, Mass.: Harvard University Laboratory for Research in Instruction. 138 pp.

Carroll, J. B. (1963). Research on teaching foreign languages. In N. L. Gage (ed.), *Handbook of research on teaching.* Chicago: Rand, McNally & Co.

Carroll, J. B. (1973). Implications of aptitude test research and psycholinguistic theory for foreign-language teaching. *Linguistics,* **112,** 5–15.

Carroll, J. B. & Freedle, R. O. (1972). *Language comprehension and the acquisition of knowledge.* New York: Winston & Sons Inc.

Carroll, J. B. & Sapon, S. M. (1959). *The Modern Language Aptitude Test.* New York & London: Harcourt Brace Jovanovich, for The Psychological Corporation, N.Y.

Cartier, F. A. (1968). Criterion-referenced testing of language skills. *TESOL Quarterly,* **2,** 1, 27–32.

CEEB (no date). *College Board Achievement Tests.* Princeton, N.J.: Educational Testing Service.

Chastain, K. (1969). Prediction of success in audio-lingual and cognitive classes. *Language Learning,* **19,** 1/2, 27–39.

Clark, J. L. D. (1972). *Foreign language testing: theory and practice.* Philadelphia, Pa.: Center for Curriculum Development.

Culhane, P.T. (1970). Occasional paper No. 7, pp. 1–24. University of Essex Language Centre.

Darnell, D. K. (1970). Clozentropy: a procedure for testing English language proficiency of foreign students. *Speech Monographs,* **37,** 1, 36–46.

Davies, A. (1964). *English Proficiency Test Battery,* Version A. London: British Council.

Davies, A. (ed.) (1968). *Language testing symposium.* London: O.U.P.

Davies, A. (1971). Language aptitude in the first year of the U.K. secondary school. *RELC Journal,* **2,** 1, 4–19.

Davies, A. (1977*a*). Introduction. In J. P. B. Allen & A. Davies (eds.) *op. cit.*

Davies, A. (1977*b*). *English Proficiency Test Battery,* Version D. London: British Council.

Davies, A. & Widdowson, H. G. (1975). Reading and writing. In *Edinburgh Course in Applied Linguistics,* vol. 3. London: O.U.P.

Denham, Patricia A. (1974). Design and three-item paradigms. *English Language Teaching Journal*, **28**, 2, 138–45.

Di Cristo, A. (1975). Présentation d'un test de niveau destiné à évaluer la prononciation des anglophones. *Revue de Phonétique Appliquée*, **33**, 4, 9–35.

Doble, G. (1974). How free should the composition be? *Modern Languages*, **55**, 1, 6–11.

Donnerstag, J. (1974). Differenzierung im Englischunterricht auf der Grundlage lernziel orientierter Tests. *Der fremdsprachliche Unterricht*, **8**, 3, 19–29.

Douglas, D. (1978). Gain in reading proficiency in English as a Foreign Language measured by three cloze scoring methods. *Journal of Research in Reading*, **1**, 1, 67–73.

Engineer, W. (1977). Proficiency in reading English as a second language. University of Edinburgh, unpublished PhD thesis.

Ewen, Elizabeth & Gipps, Caroline (1973). Tests of English for immigrant children. *Multiracial School*, **2**, 2, 22–4.

Famiglietti, M. (1971). Sperimentazione sulle prove grammaticati di construzione giudata. *Rassegna Italiana di Linguistica Applicata*, **3**, 1, 29–53.

Fehse, K. D. & Praeger, W. (1973). *Bibliographie zum Testen in der Schule: Schwerpunkt: Fremdsprachenunterricht.* Freiburg i. Br.: Becksmann.

Foreign Service Institute: Rating Procedure: see Claudia P. Wilds, 'The oral interview test', in R..L. Jones & B. Spolsky (eds.), q.v.

Fountain, R. (1974). *A case for the dictation test in the selection of foreign students for English medium study in New Zealand.* Edinburgh University, Department of Linguistics.

Garcia-Zamor, Marie & Birdsong, D. (1977). *Testing in English as a Second Language: annotated bibliography.* Washington, D.C.: TESOL; and Center for Applied Linguistics.

Gardner, R. C. & Lambert, W. E. (1969). Motivational variables in second language acquisition. *Canadian Journal of Psychology*, **13**, 266–72.

Gipps, Caroline & Ewen, Elizabeth (1974). Scoring written work in English as a second language: the use of the T-unit. *Educational Research*, **16**, 2, 121–5.

Graduate Record Tests (no date). Princeton, N.J.: Educational Testing Service.

Green, P. S. (1974/5). Aptitude testing – an ongoing experiment. *Audio-Visual Language Journal*, **12**, 3, 205–10.

Hafner, L. E. (1964). Relationships of various measures to the cloze. *Thirteenth Yearbook of the National Reading Conference*, 135–45.

Harding, Ann (1974/5). Transfer at 13 and the assessment of aptitude for modern languages. *Audio-Visual Language Journal*, **12**, 3, 201–3. ERIC EJ111176.

Harris, D. P. (1969). *Testing English as a second language.* New York: McGraw-Hill.

Harris, D. P. & Palmer, L. A. (1970). *Comprehensive English language test for speakers of English as a second language.* New York: McGraw-Hill.

Haskell, J. F. (1973). Refining the cloze testing and scoring procedures for use with ESL students. Columbia University, Ed.D. thesis.

Heaton, J. B. (1975). *Writing English language tests.* London: Longman.

Heil, D. K. & Aleamoni, L. M. (1974). Assessment of the proficiency in the use and understanding of English by foreign students as measured by the TOEFL. (ERIC ED 093 948).

Ibe, M. D. (1975). A comparison of cloze and multiple choice tests for measuring the English reading comprehension of southeast Asian teachers of English. *RELC Journal*, **6**, 2.

Ilyin, Donna (1976). *Ilyin Oral Interview.* Rowley, Mass.: Newbury House.

Ilyin, Donna & Best, J. (1976). *English language structure tests.* Rowley, Mass.: Newbury House.

Ingram, E. (1964). *English Language Battery* (ELBA). University of Edinburgh, Department of Linguistics.

155

Ingram, E. (1973). English standards for foreign students. *University of Edinburgh Bulletin*, **9**, 12, 4–5.
Irvine, P., Atai, P. & Oller, J. W. (1974). Cloze, dictation and the Test of English as a Foreign Language. *Language Learning*, **24**, 2, 245–52.
Jakobovits, L. A. (1972). Introduction. In Sandra J. Savignon, *op. cit.*
Jakobovits, L. A. & Gordon, Barbara (1974). *The context of foreign language teaching.* Rowley, Mass.: Newbury House.
Johansson, S. (1973). An evaluation of the noise test: a method for testing overall second language proficiency by perception under masking noise. *IRAL*, **11**, 2, 107–33
John Test, the (1976). Language Innovations Inc., 200 West 72nd St. 67A New York 10023.
Jones, R. L. & Spolsky, B. (eds.) (1975). *Testing language proficiency.* Washington, D.C.: Centre for Applied Linguistics.
Jongsma, E. (1971). *The cloze procedure as a teaching technique.* Bloomington, Ind.: Indiana University. Also available from the International Reading Association, Newark, Del.
Kobersky, Eva (1969). Testing recognition and production with oral stimuli. *Contact*, **12**, 22–4.
Kollarik, T. (1972/3). Niektoré poznatky so zist' ovaním sposobilosti učit' sa cudziè jazyky. *Cizi' jazyky ve skole*, **16**, 5, 206–11.
Lado, R. (1961, 1964). *Language testing: the construction and use of foreign language tests.* London: Longman.
McDonough, S. H. (1977). Testing communicative competence in English as a foreign language with science and social science students. Paper given at BAAL annual meeting, Sept. 1977.
MacGinitie, W. H. (1971). Comments on Professor Coleman's paper. In E. Z. Rothkopf and P. E. Johnson (eds.), *Verbal learning research and the technology of written instruction.* Columbia University: Teachers' College Press, pp. 205–15.
Mason, V. (1972). Report on cloze tests administered to Thai students. *Bulletin of the English Language Centre*, **2**, 1, 31–9.
Modern Language Association of America (1963). *Cooperative foreign language tests.* Princeton, N.J.: Educational Testing Service.
Moller, A. (1975). Validity in proficiency testing. *ELT Documents*, **3**, 5–18.
Morrow, Keith (1977). *Techniques of evaluation for a notional syllabus.* London: Royal Society of Arts.
Motta, Janice et al. (1974). *Reading evaluation for adult non-English students.* Fall River, Mass.: Bristol Community College (ERIC ED 098 513).
Moyle, D. (1971). Readability: the use of cloze procedure. In *U.K. Reading Association Proceedings.* London: Ward Lock.
Nizogorodcew, Anna (1975). Przydatnosc tzw testu prognostycznego jako metody pomiaru zdolnosci do uczenia sie jezyka obcego u mlodziezny licealnej. *Jezyki obce w szkole*, **19**, 5, 299–303.
Novak, Z. (1973/4). K vyvoji testu predikce vykonu u uceni se cizim jazykům. *Cizi jazyky ve skole*, **17**, 1, 66–74.
Oller, J. W. (1971). Dictation as a device for testing foreign-language proficiency. *English Language Teaching*, **25**, 3, 254–9.
Oller, J. W. (1972). Cloze tests of second language proficiency and what they measure. *Language Learning*, **23**, 1, 105–18.
Oller, J. W. (1976). A program for language testing research. In H. D. Brown (ed.), *Papers in second language acquisition. Language Learning*, Special issue no. 4, 141–66.
Oller, J. W. & Conrad, Christine A. (1972). The cloze technique and ESL proficiency. *Language Learning*, **21**, 2, 183–95.

Oller, J. W. & Ina, N. (1971). A cloze test of English prepositions. *TESOL Quarterly,* **5,** 4, 315–26.

Oller, J. W. & Richards, J. C. (1973). *Focus on the learner: pragmatic perspectives for the language teacher.* Rowley, Mass.: Newbury House.

Oller, J. W. & Streiff, Virginia (1975). Dictation: a test of grammar-based expectancies. *English Language Teaching Journal,* **30,** 1, 25–36.

Palmer, L. & Spolsky, B. (eds.) (1975). *Papers on language testing, 1967–1974.* Washington D.C.: TESOL.

Paquette, A. & Tollinger, Suzanne (1968). *Handbook on foreign language testing: French, German, Italian, Russian, Spanish.* New York: Modern Language Association of America.

Partington, J. A. (1974). An experiment in aptitude testing in two British schools. *Modern Languages,* **55,** 3, 123–6.

Perren, G. E. (1967). Testing ability in English as a second language. *English Language Teaching,* **21,** 1, 129–36; **21,** 2, 99–106; **21,** 3, 197–202.

Perren, G. E. (1968). Testing spoken language: some unsolved problems. In A. Davies (ed.), *op. cit.*

Perren, G. E. (ed.) (1977). *Foreign language testing: specialised bibliography.* Centre for Information on Language Teaching and Research. 2nd ed. 1981.

Pimsleur, P. (1966). *Language Aptitude Battery.* New York: Harcourt Brace & World Inc.

Pimsleur, P. (1975). Criterion versus norm-referenced testing. ERIC ED112681.

Pinel, Nicole (1971). Test d'évaluation de niveau oral pour les jeunes débitants en français. *Français dans le Monde,* **79,** 14–19.

Plaister, T. (1972). *Language testing: a selected bibliography.* Honolulu, Ha.: University of Hawaii.

Potter, T. C. (1968). *A taxonomy of cloze research.* Technical Report No. 1. Inglewood, Calif.: Southwest Regional Laboratory for Educational Research and Development.

Rankin, E. F. (1974). The cloze procedure revisited. In P. L. Nacle (ed.), *Interaction: research and practice for college-adult reading.* 23rd Yearbook of the National Reading Conference, 1–8.

Rea, Pauline M. (1978). Assessing language as communication. *MALS Journal,* New series, No. 3. University of Birmingham: Department of English.

Riley, Pamela M. (1973). *The cloze procedure: a selected annotated bibliography.* Lae, New Guinea: PNG University of Technology.

Rivers, W. M. (1968). *Teaching foreign-language skills.* London and Chicago: University of Chicago Press. 2nd ed. 1981.

Robinson, Gail L. (1975). Linguistic ability: some myths and some evidence. Sydney: New South Wales Department of Education, Australian Centre for Research in Measurement and Evaluation. ERIC ED 126689 FL 007727.

Robinson, P. (1971 *a*). Oral Expression Tests (1). *English Language Teaching,* 25, 2, 151–5.

Robinson, P. (1971 *b*). Oral Expression Tests (2). *English Language Teaching,* 25, 3, 260–6.

Robinson, R. D. (1972). *An introduction to the cloze procedure: an annotated bibliography.* Delaware: International Reading Association.

Rodriguez-Mungia *et al.* (1972). *List of testing materials in English as a second language and Spanish.* Boston, Mass.: Bureau of Transitional Bilingual Education. ED 084 917.

Rowe, H. M. (1969). Language testing at universities. *Babel* (Melbourne), **5,** 2, 14–17.

Roy, R. (1969). Rate of output – a factor of oral proficiency. *Canadian Modern Language Review,* **26,** 1, 14–22.

Rudd, Elizabeth (1971). Language tests for immigrant children. *Multiracial School,* **1,** 1, 26–9.

Sako, S. (1969). Writing proficiency and achievement tests. *TESOL Quarterly*, **3**, 3, 237–49.

Savard, J. G. (1969, 1977). *Analytical bibliography of language tests*. Québec: Presse de l'Université Laval.

Savignon, Sandra J. (1972). *Communicative competence: an experiment in foreign language teaching*. Philadelphia, Pa.: Center for Curriculum Development.

Schoelles, I. S. (1971). Cloze as a predictor of reading group placement. Paper presented at the meeting of the International Reading Association. Atlantic City, N.J.

Schulz, Renate A. (1977). Discrete-point versus simulated communication testing in foreign languages. *Modern Language Journal*, **61**, 3, 91–101.

Scoon, Annabelle R. & Blanchard, J. D. (1970). The relation of the test of English as a second language to measures of intelligence, achievement and adjustment in a sample of American Indian students. Paper given at TESOL. ERIC ED 039 530.

Seward, B. H. (1973). Measuring oral production in EFL. *English Language Teaching Journal*, **28**, 1, 76–80.

Shearer, E. (1975). A restandardisation of the Burt–Vernon and Schonell Graded Word Reading Tests. *Educational Research*, **18**, 1, 67–73.

Stoldt, P. H. (1973). Kontrolle mündlicher Sprachfertigkeiten in Unterricht und Prüfung. *Praxis*, **20**, 1, 33–42.

Stubbs, J. B. & Tucker, G. R. (1974). The cloze test as a measure of English proficiency. *Modern Language Journal*, **58**, 5/6, 239–41.

Taylor, W. C. (1953). Cloze procedure: a new tool for measuring readability. *Journalism Quarterly*, **30**, 415–33.

Taylor, W. L. (1956). Recent developments in the use of the cloze procedure. *Journalism Quarterly*, **33**, 42–9.

Templeton, H. R. (1973). Cloze procedure in aural proficiency tests for foreign students studying in English. University of Manchester, M.Ed. thesis.

TOEFL (1964 and annually). *Test of English as a foreign language*. Princeton, N.J.: Educational Testing Service.

Townson, M. (1973). Testing oral skills at university level. *English Language Teaching*, **27**, 2, 199–205.

Trim, J. L. M. (1973). Draft outline of a European unit/credit system for modern language learning by adults. Strasbourg: Council of Europe. Republished in J. L. M. Trim *et al.*, *Systems development in adult language learning*. Oxford: Pergamon Press, 1980.

Truchot, C. (1971). Les tests de langue: réévaluation critique. *Langues Modernes*, **65**, 2, 103–12.

Upshur, J. A. (1961). *Michigan Test of English Language Proficiency*. Ann Arbor, Mich.: University of Michigan English Language Institute.

Upshur, J. A. (1962). Language proficiency testing and the contrastive analysis dilemma. *Language Learning*, **12**, 123–8.

Upshur, J. A. (1967). *English language tests and prediction of academic success*. Selected conference papers of the Association of Teachers of English as a Second Language, National Association for Foreign Student Affairs.

Upshur, J. A. (1976). Discussion of a 'Program for Language Testing Research'. In H. D. Brown (ed.), *Papers in second language acquisition. Language Learning*, Special issue, no. 4, 167–74.

Upshur, J. A. & Fata, Julia (1968). Problems in foreign language testing. *Language Learning*, special issue No. 3.

Valette, Rebecca M. (1967). *Modern language testing – a handbook*. New York: Harcourt, Brace & World.

Valette, Rebecca M. (1977). *Modern language testing* (2nd ed.) New York: Harcourt Brace Jovanovich.

Valette, Rebecca M. & Disick, Renée S. (1972). *Modern language performance objectives and individualization.* New York: Harcourt Brace Jovanovich.
Zierer, E. (1971). The test of aural perception in foreign language teaching from the standpoint of information theory. *IRAL* 9, 2, 125–30.

Addendum references

Alderson, J. C. & Hughes, A. (eds.) (1981). Issues in language testing. *EIT Documents,* **111.**
Canale, M. & Swain, M. (1980). Theoretical bases of communicative approaches to second language teaching and testing. *Applied Linguistics* 1, 1–47.
Carroll, B. J. (1980). *Testing communicative performance.* Oxford: Pergamon Press.
Cohen, A. D. (1980). *Testing language ability in the classroom.* Rowley, Mass.: Newbury House.
ELTS *English Language Testing Service* (1980). A test produced by the EITS Management Committee of the British Council and the Cambridge University Examinations Syndicate, Cambridge.
Harding, A., Page, B. & Rowell, S. (1980). *Graded objectives in modern languages.* London: Centre for Information on Language Teaching and Research (CILT).
Hughes, A. & Porter, D. (eds.) (1981). *Language testing newsletter.* Produced on behalf of the British Association of Applied Linguistics; Dept. of Linguistic Science, University of Reading, England, first issue December, 1981.
Hughes, A. & Porter, D. (eds.) forthcoming. *Proceedings of BAAL Seminar on Language Testing.* University of Reading, December 1981. New York: Academic Press.
Oller, J. W. (1979). *Language tests at school.* London: Longman.
Oller, J. W. (ed.) forthcoming. *Issues in language testing research.* Rowley, Mass.: Newbury House.
Palmer, A. S. & Bachman, L. F. (1981). Basic concerns in test validation. In Alderson & Hughes (eds.), 1981.
R.S.A. (1981). *Examinations in the Communicative Use of English as a Foreign Language.* London: Royal Society of Arts.
Vollmer, H. J. (1981). Why are we interested in general language proficiency? In Alderson & Hughes (eds.), 1981.
Vollmer, H. J. (forthcoming). The structure of foreign language competence. In Hughes & Porter (eds.).